FIGHTING WORDS

THE MEDIA, THE RED SOX AND THE ALL-ENCOMPASSING PASSION FOR BASEBALL IN BOSTON

Jerry Beach

ROUNDER BOOKS

Copyright © 2009 Jerry Beach
Published by Rounder Books

an imprint
Rounder Records Corp.
One Rounder Way
Burlington, MA 01803

ISBN-13: 978-1-57940-121-4
ISBN-10: 1-57940-121-X

by Jerry Beach

Fighting Words
The Media, the Red Sox and the All-Encompassing Passion for Baseball in Boston
1. Boston Red Sox (baseball team). 2.Media I T.
First edition

Library of Congress Control Number: 2008942407
796.357

Design and composition by Jane Tenenbaum
Cover design by Rachael Sullivan

In memory of my wonderful mother Maureen,

who died shortly before this book was published.

Mom was never all that into baseball, but did an

impressive impersonation of a Red Sox fan

by unconditionally believing in and never giving up

on me—even when I surely exasperated her.

I hope I gave her, at some point, her October 27, 2004.

Contents

Foreword, vii
Introduction, xi
Cast of Characters, xiii

Chapter 1: **The Writers and The Sox:
A Complicated Relationship, 1**

Chapter 2: **Nomar, Pedro, Ted, and Yaz, 28**

Chapter 3: **Lou Gorman and Dan Duquette:
Different Approaches—Same Result?, 49**

Chapter 4: **The Boston Media:
The Ultimate Insiders, 71**

Chapter 5: **"Gehrig38" and the
Bridge Between the Mainstream
and Alternative Media, 90**

Chapter 6: **New Ownership,
Familiar Suspicions, 111**

Chapter 7: **From "The Hawk"
to "Cowboy Up", 133**

Chapter 8: **Managing the Media, 151**

Chapter 9: **The Evolution of Theo Epstein, 175**

Chapter 10: **Challenges Old and New
in the Post-"Curse" Era, 194**

Acknowledgments, 223
Bibliography, 229

Foreword

by Kevin Millar

Players have to understand that the media has a job to do, but we have concerns, too. In a major market like Boston, you may have six or seven guys writing for one paper. With maybe four papers covering us, now, all of a sudden, you've got 25, 30 writers trying to cover the same stories, a win or a loss.

And there has to be a story. You've got a job to do. There's only so many ways to write up a game. So they start writing different situations—whether a guy is struggling, whether a guy's doing well, whether a player's hitting .150, or a player's hitting .450. It goes both ways. I'm probably fortunate, not getting my feelings hurt as much as some players do, maybe luckier in being able to take the pressures of a big market and not having a thin skin.

As players, we notice the way the media conduct themselves in the clubhouse. Is there a story, have you got a job to do, or who you're trying to interview. Rarely does the media member come in, do a story, and then depart. They'll do their story but then linger because they don't want to miss another story. There have been many times we're hanging out, watching the football game and the media member will be there watching the football game, hanging out. If your job is to talk to player A or player B, why not just get the player A or player B story and then head up to the press box and start writing your piece? But you've got to wait for the manager, you've got to wait for the starting pitcher, you've got to wait for the catcher . . . it's like a domino effect. I think that's the most frustrating thing for the players.

Sure, you guys have got a job to do. Do it and leave. We start thinking, "What's that guy doing? What's that guy doing? He hasn't really talked to anyone. He's kind of hanging out." Sometimes we don't know what story you're seeking. From our side, from the players' side, we want you guys to do your story and then leave, not do your story and then hang out and watch the football game or ESPN with us. I think that's where the struggle becomes between the player and the media. When we don't know your assignment or what your boss is telling you to do, we'll just see a guy watch TV for an hour straight and we don't realize you might be doing something, maybe waiting for somebody to arrive.

What's it like playing for a team in a smaller market? You miss the passion. Boston's a big market and the Red Sox have a big national television organization in NESN. A lot of good things come from that. There's a broad fan base—and there's the passion, the depth of the love for the Red Sox. You miss that as a player if you go to another team. Then you really see the difference. There's no other scene like Sox Nation. There really isn't. I don't think the Yankees, the Cubs . . . there's no other team coast to coast—that has a scene like Red Sox Nation.

Back to the question of the way the players and the media relate, I have to say—even for someone like myself—there are times you don't feel like talking. You don't feel like doing anything. You just feel like playing baseball today. You don't feel like answering any questions. We're human beings, too. Despite the magnified salaries and the magnified fame or popularity—we're still human. There are situations where your kids might be sick or you might have been up all night, a time when you just want to say, "OK, I want to hang out at my locker today." You don't get that opportunity at times. It's always, "Do you have a second, do you have a second, do you have a second, do you have a second, do you have a second?" And a second turns into another minute. Then the next guy comes up to you. That's the other side, the players' side. Sometimes we just want to hang out, but there's always a radio interview, there's always a TV interview. That's part of our job, too. We understand that. But sometimes it just becomes too much.

There's good on both sides and bad on both sides. There's bad players and bad writers. One bad writer shouldn't stereotype all the writers as bad. And one bad player shouldn't stereotype all players. You get a dickhead writer who just doesn't like athletes or is jealous or envious and he attacks. Flip side, you get a dickhead player who gives a bad name to all of us.

Everybody's got a job at the end of the day. Everybody's got a job: You guys and the players. We just have to try to do the best we can, and try and appreciate the needs of each other.

Introduction

The coverage of the Boston Red Sox has resulted in some of the most comprehensive, informed, and passionate beat writing in any sport—as well as some of the most memorable stories ever penned. *The Best American Sports Writing of the Century* anthology featured two stories about Ted Williams—only one other baseball player, Babe Ruth, was the subject of two pieces—as well as more than a half-dozen Boston-based writers listed among the "Notable Sports Writers of the Century" in the appendix.

The Red Sox beat is one of the elite jobs in sports writing. Baseball writers cannot imagine a better place to prove their abilities than Boston, where coverage of the Red Sox dwarfs the Patriots, Celtics, and Bruins no matter how well those teams perform. Most of the writers who cover the Sox hail from New England and grew up rooting for the Red Sox, which infuses the coverage with an additional layer of provincial knowledge.

Red Sox fans have a never-ending thirst for news and hold players and writers alike to an improbably high standard. The demand for information about the Sox doubly benefits some writers, who have been able in recent years to supplement their incomes and raise their profiles with radio and television appearances that are not as plentiful in other cities. Other cities may have a sports talk show on local radio; Boston may have two or three competing sports talk radio programs at one time and specialized Red Sox TV programs on multiple stations.

But that passion for and excellence at the job has come with a heavy price for writers and the Red Sox alike. Though most beat writers are non-confrontational, the sheer volume of reporters covering the team frays the nerves of even the most patient players and has made it difficult for executives to be as candid as they might like.

For generations, players have used the tale of Ted Williams as proof of the Boston media's sensationalistic nature, even though Williams' rancorous relationship with the press was mutually combative. In recent years, the press' poor relations with superstars such as Jim Rice, Roger Clemens, Nomar Garciaparra, and Carl Everett have further fueled players' suspicions of the media.

Many of the traveling beat writers come to realize their dream job is a Faustian endeavor. Covering the Red Sox is a year-long grind with little to no down time. It has strained and broken up marriages and sent many a writer scurrying to smaller and less stressful beats.

The explosion of the Internet has provided opportunities for writers and fans unimaginable even a decade ago. Online coverage is the future of the industry, but transitioning into the 24-hour news cycle has been challenging for writers, who must balance the demand for immediacy with the traditional ethics and approach of news-gathering.

And writers must adapt in an era in which newspaper staffs and news holes are leaner than ever and the competition—much of which is generated by the consumer—immense and immeasurable. The Internet contains limitless information—most of it free—as well as endless opportunities to discuss the most minute details of Red Sox games and personalities. It also allows fans to scrutinize those chronicling the club and create their own coverage of the Sox and the media. This fan-generated coverage has forced the traditional media to follow in the footsteps of the alternative media as beat writers now double as bloggers at most newspapers and websites.

This is their story—the writers, the Red Sox players and executives, and the fans—who have combined to create one of the most fascinating dynamics in American sports.

Cast of Characters

This book was written over a four-year period, during which numerous people I interviewed and refer to have changed jobs—multiple times, in some cases. In the interest of minimizing confusion as well as the removing need to mention each person's movement the first time I refer to him/her in a chapter, here is an alphabetical list of writers and personalities who have switched positions during the course of the research for this book.

Writer/Personality	Then	Now
Ron Borges	*Boston Globe*/WEEI.com	*Boston Herald*
Rob Bradford	*Lowell Sun*/*Eagle-Tribune*/ *Herald*	WEEI.com
Howard Bryant	*Herald*/*Washington Post*	ESPN.com
Gordon Edes	*Boston Globe*	Yahoo! Sports
Michael Felger	*Boston Herald*/ESPN Radio	WEEI/WEEI.com
Michael Gee	*Boston Herald*	Freelance
Glenn Geffner	VP/PR Red Sox	Broadcaster/ Marlins
David Heuschkel	*Hartford Courant*	SI.com/freelance
Jeff Horrigan	*Boston Herald*	Freelance
Jackie MacMullan	*Boston Globe*	ESPN
Tony Massarotti	*Boston Herald*	*Boston Globe*
Peter May	*Boston Globe*	Yahoo! Sports
Sean McAdam	*Providence Journal*	*Boston Herald*
Chris Snow	*Boston Globe*	VP/Minnesota Wild
Charles Steinberg	Exec. VP/Red Sox	CMO/Dodgers

Chapter 1
The Writers and The Sox: A Complicated Relationship

Bob Hohler arrived on the Red Sox beat in the summer of 2000 after two memorable decades in hard news. As a news columnist/writer for the *Concord Monitor* in New Hampshire in the mid-1980s, he chronicled the journey of local teacher Christa McAuliffe, who was the first civilian to participate in a NASA space flight, and the subsequent *Challenger* tragedy.

After moving to the *Boston Globe*, Hohler covered breaking national news for the *Globe* before he became the newspaper's correspondent in Washington, where he followed the Monica Lewinsky scandal and Bill Clinton's impeachment.

And nothing at all prepared Hohler for what awaited him as the Red Sox beat writer over the next four-and-a-half seasons. "Absolutely the most intense experience that I've had," Hohler says.

There's no underestimating the importance of covering the White House and covering the issues and events that shape America. But the Red Sox were covered by the media and treated by fans as if they were the most important thing in the world long before the era of mass media saturation.

The Boston Americans (it was 1908 before they became the Red Sox) won the 1903 pennant and played in the first World Series. Interest in the Series was so high that all the city's papers each added a sports section—even the *Transcript*, a financial paper.

"The series made newspaper publishers smile," wrote Glenn Stout and Richard A. Johnson in *Red Sox Century*. "They'd learned that baseball sold papers."

A Red Sox pennant pursuit overshadowed the deaths of at least two Popes. The passing of Pope Leo XIII in July 1903 contended for coverage with the Americans on the front pages of Boston's newspapers. And

1

when Pope John Paul I died in 1978, a WBCN radio broadcaster teased the morning news with "Pope Dies, Sox Still Alive."

When the Red Sox won the World Series in 1918, the game story appeared above the fold in the *Globe*, ahead of three stories about World War I—including one about the torpedoing of a United States naval ship. The contentious summer of 1967 featured race riots, Vietnam War protests, and the burgeoning counter-culture movement, but from mid-summer on, the Red Sox were regularly featured on the front page of the local newspapers.

When Theo Epstein resigned as general manager of the Red Sox on October 31, 2005, his twin brother Paul marveled at how it overshadowed everything else in the news. "Pretty crazy, how excessive the coverage was," Paul Epstein says. "I read the letters to the editor: 'Why is Osama Bin Laden below the fold?' And it's true. Why does Boston care so much about Theo leaving? It's kind of troubling."

"Listen: We're not curing cancer," says Blue Jays general manager J.P. Ricciardi, a native of Worcester. "I'll never forget this as long as I live: I was watching a press conference on TV [and someone] had just found some development [and was] getting closer to a cure for a certain kind of cancer. So they said 'We're going to have a press conference.' The guy comes out, there's like 10 people in the audience asking questions. And then I'm sitting there thinking 'If this is the Red Sox making a trade, there would be 800 guys in the audience.'

"I don't think it paints us too well, you know?"

If world wars, terrorists, and disease could not knock the Red Sox off the front page, then what hope did the New England Patriots have—even as they won three Super Bowls in a four-year span from 2001 through 2004 and twice broke the NFL record for longest regular season winning streak?

On Sept, 19, 2004, the Patriots, who had just won their 17th straight game, shared the dominant front page photo in the *Boston Globe* with the wild card-leading Red Sox, who had just lost their second in a row to the Yankees to all but fall out of contention in the AL East. The headline inside the box—17 IN A ROW . . . TWO IN A ROW—made it seem as if the Sox' losing streak and Patriots' winning streak were equally significant feats.

"The Patriots definitely should get more attention," Theo Epstein said in 2004. "But it's not a meritocracy."

Actually, it was for the better part of 40 years, during which the Patriots underperformed—on and off the field—and failed to overcome the day-to-day drama and generational bond created by the Red Sox.

While the weekly NFL game crashed ashore with great fanfare but receded quietly, allowing fans—and writers—to fully digest it before embarking on the next contest, baseball was, as the *Boston Globe*'s Tony Massarotti told author Bill Nowlin in *Fenway Lives*, the soap opera of sports.

Three- and four-game series allowed fans to invest in every Red Sox opponent. And each game was a communal experience in which fans could participate—and commiserate—by listening to the radio, watching television, or by logging on to message boards.

"I'm 41 years old and I don't have stories from my childhood of sitting on my grandfather's lap in the summertime listening to the Patriots," says Trish Saintelus, the moderator of "The Remy Report"'s chat room. "I have great memories of sitting with my grandfather [who was] 80 years old, listening to the Red Sox on a hot summer night. And it's part of my childhood. It's part of what I grew up with. I think it just has a different place in our heart than football. You live and die with these guys 160 games a year. You're with them from early April, you hope, right up through late October. It's part of your childhood, going to ballgames.

"You don't get that from football. It's very, very different. Baseball is accessible."

For the writers as well as the fans. Baseball writers see the players they cover for several hours per day nearly every day from February through October. While NFL teams typically open their locker rooms for 45 to 60 minutes three or four days a week, a baseball locker room is open every game three-and-a-half hours before first pitch.

The time is not as ample as it may appear, though. For a night home game, Terry Francona typically holds his pregame press conference at

4 p.m., which gives reporters half an hour to gauge the mood of the locker room and begin working on pregame notebooks and features. Francona's meeting lasts anywhere from 15 to 30 minutes, which gives writers only a few minutes afterward to follow up on any leads unearthed during the manager's session.

The Red Sox, like all teams, close the locker room once players go out for batting practice, which lasts just over an hour. The locker room is open after batting practice, but upon returning from the field, most players immediately disappear into an off-limits area of the clubhouse to eat, relax, and prepare for the game.

Those who remain often—purposely or not—give off an unapproachable air. Some relax at their locker by reading, going through mail, chatting on the phone and/or with a teammate. Others move to the couch area, where they watch television, play cards, or nap.

Invariably, the reporter who walks into the locker room after batting practice feels awkward standing and waiting for a player to appear out of the back room or pull himself away from the couch area. So while the media is allowed to remain in the locker room, the clubhouse is usually empty of non-uniformed personnel long before it officially closes.

As a result of the compressed time frame, Red Sox beat writers often live by a routine and display a preparatory focus which rivals that of the players they cover. Some are pictures of nervous energy, shifting their weight from one foot to the other and frequently changing the topic of conversation as their eyes dart around the clubhouse.

Some walk around the clubhouse with a faraway look in their eyes, as if they are plotting the evening. And others stand in the middle of the clubhouse, calmly surveying the scene.

"You might be on your 18th straight day of working, so on that day, it might be tough to have your game face on at 4 o'clock, three hours before the first pitch," former *Hartford Courant* beat writer David Heuschkel says. "But my mind is always working when it comes to that stuff. I'm always thinking. A lot of times I'm thinking 'OK, I've got to come up with something for my notebook.' So yeah, I'm enterprising as I'm standing there."

Such pregame behavior and rituals are not unique to Boston. But the competition in the area stokes a reporter's aggressiveness and his sense of paranoia and inspires him to leave no stone or angle unturned.

"You have to worry about the competition—if the *Globe* got it or where is the *Globe* guy or the *Herald* guy or the *Courant* guy, they must be doing something," Associated Press reporter Howard Ulman says. "You kind of worry about that, too. That makes you kind of increase your workload a bit, your stress load, because on top of this—covering a team that's important—you've got to worry about what the other guy's doing."

"You've got to play defense," Heuschkel says.

After the locker room closes, writers go upstairs to the press box and work on their notebooks and early edition stories, most of which have to be filed by the first pitch or shortly thereafter. The *Globe* writer often has to find time for an appearance on the NESN pregame show (the *Globe*'s parent company, The New York Times Company, has a 17 percent stake in the Red Sox, who share ownership of New England Sports Network with the NHL's Boston Bruins), while other writers are often asked to appear on radio shows both inside and outside of Boston.

By the seventh inning, most writers have begun to write a running gamer that will be ready to be sent as soon as the final out is made, but a late comeback by either team will render those stories irrelevant and force an emergency, last-second re-write. After the game, reporters file downstairs to the interview room, where Francona and the starting pitcher meet the press along with any other notable contributor, before heading into the clubhouse for postgame reaction and analysis. Writers then head back to the press box—quiet except for the sound of fingers clicking keyboards—and file their final stories.

By the end of the season, the beat writer has written several hundred stories, many of which were never read by a vast majority of the audience because they appeared in early editions distributed to far-off suburbs. "It's September 25 and I did a search yesterday," former *Boston Globe* beat writer Chris Snow said as he ate breakfast at Camden Yards during the penultimate weekend of the 2005 regular season. "Four hundred fifty, 500 stories. So you're looking at 550 for the year. That's a lot."

While Red Sox writers are quick to point out that they enjoy the voluminous challenges that come with the Sox beat, they admit to occasionally and longingly wondering what it would be like to cover a team in a smaller market—especially late in the season, when writers who cover an also-ran usually file only a short story that combines a "game" with a "notebook."

"I dream about covering the San Diego Padres," Heuschkel said during spring training in 2005. "I picture myself showing up at 5:30 in the afternoon for a 7 o'clock game, going to the batting cage and chatting with [former manager Bruce] Bochy about what's going on. Going upstairs, writing my notebook, and then watching a game. That's just not possible in Boston."

Not with the two city newspapers being joined by a vast suburban and out-of-state presence at Fenway. There are usually close to 20 newspapers—from points as far west as Springfield, as far north as Portland, Maine, and as far south as Woonsocket, Rhode Island—represented daily, plus wire services, websites, and various other non-daily publications.

"New England has a number of really high quality newspapers," Boston Herald beat writer Sean McAdam says. "I just read something recently that there are more newspapers available per one thousand residents throughout New England than any other region in the country.

"The Red Sox are not really Massachusetts' team, but New England's team. And that's reflected in the huge number of papers that staff them on a daily basis, both home and away. I think people, for the most part, look at New England as a cool place to live and it does have a tradition of good newspapers. And the appetite for sports and baseball, in particular, is unrivaled. So there's a good atmosphere to work."

It's also a taxing one. During the season, the beat writer is at the park a minimum of 10 hours a day. Most writers arrive at least half an hour before the locker room opens in order to read the competition online and prepare for the game.

The baseball beat involves more games, more travel, more work, more manpower, and more deadline pressure than any other beat—not to mention more missed birthdays, anniversaries, and family time.

"The thing you get scared about is you get used to it—I don't want to get used to it," WEEI.com writer/editor Rob Bradford says. "I don't want my kids to get used to it. I don't want my wife to get used to it. It's one of those things where I don't think about it. I just deal with what's in front of me, because if I think about how could I possibly keep doing this for the next eight to 10 years [and] what's your family life going to be—there's no way I can think of that."

Hohler says covering the Red Sox reminded him of covering the final month of a presidential election—except it lasts seven months and features four deadlines per night. Theoretically, the baseball beat lasts from the beginning of spring training in mid-February until the end of the regular season in late September or the playoffs in mid-to-late October.

But in reality, the modern baseball beat is never-ending nationwide and especially all-consuming in Boston. Major League Baseball's off-season schedule is staggered so that there's no down time. Free agency begins within 24 hours of the final out of the World Series. The general manager meetings and the Rookie of the Year, Cy Young, and Most Valuable Player awards are presented in early-to-mid November.

Player movement most often occurs in early December at the winter meetings. Arbitration-eligible players swap numbers with their team in January and hearings, if necessary, take place in mid-to-late February, by which time spring training has begun.

Of course, this does not account for common yet unpredictable events such as the firing and hiring of a manager and other executives as well as the blockbuster trades that unfold with no regard to the calendar. So Red Sox beat writers spent their 2003 Thanksgiving tracking the club's negotiations with Arizona ace Curt Schilling and most of December detailing the Sox' attempts to trade the second-highest paid player in baseball, Manny Ramirez, to Texas in exchange for the highest-paid player, Alex Rodriguez.

The *Globe* and *Herald* had at least one Red Sox story in the paper every day from the start of spring training in 2003 until Christmas Day.

"When I started on this beat, I thought it was, at the time, an eight-month beat," Heuschkel says. "Now it's a 12-month beat. If there were 14 months in a year, then it would be a 14-month beat. It's crazy."

The frenetic and seemingly never-ending schedule lends itself to burnout: Former beat writers often say they would rather look for a new job than return to a baseball beat.

"They have no break whatsoever," CBS4 television reporter Dan Roche says. "And I think it does wear them out, and I think it's hard and it's gotten harder because there's so many more media outlets—Internet, TV, radio, there's so many more people covering the team that I think it's harder and harder to get a scoop or to stand out as a beat writer. And I give those guys all the credit in the world."

Hohler left the Sox beat following the 2005 season to write long-form sports features. "I wanted to go somewhere in the desert and get de-programmed," Hohler said in December 2005. "I wanted to get my life back."

The players, meanwhile, often felt as if they wanted to get their life back—from the reporters who, they felt, received too much access and spent too much time lounging around the locker room.

"The best part about my [locker] right now," Mike Timlin said during a series against the Yankees in September 2004, "is that I have this row of lockers here to block the view of you guys standing there watching TV."

The concept of ballplayers bothered by the presence of the press is not unique to Boston. To most players league wide, reporters in the clubhouse were a necessary annoyance—typically treated with some measure of politeness but never made to feel welcome. As longtime New York baseball writers Bob Klapisch and John Harper wrote in *The Worst Team Money Could Buy*, a book about the 1992 New York Mets: "You're on opposition turf—there's no avoiding the antagonistic nature of the job—and the majority of the players don't want you there—it's as simple as that."

In reality, the writer rarely spends more than two hours in the locker room per day and doesn't have much time to channel surf. The differing perceptions of the writer's job underscored the lack of commonality between players and the media and the difficulty in establishing a mutual trust.

"Unfortunately, there's a line drawn between the media and the athletes," Timlin says. "There's a lot of assumptions made on our side, there's a lot of assumptions made on their side."

The gulf between the two sides is as much a result of the social and economic changes writers and players have undergone over the last two generations as it is the naturally inquisitive nature of a reporter's job.

In the early days of the 20th century, it was not uncommon for writers and players to befriend one another and spend time hunting, fishing, and vacationing with each other after the season. For several decades, Red Sox beat writers traveled with the team. Sharing quarters for much of the year did not remove the possibility of confrontation—writers were unhappy in 1946, when owner Tom Yawkey held separate parties for the Sox and the writers after the Sox won the American League pennant—but it allowed the writers to bond with the players.

"They were on planes with us, they were on buses with us, they played cards with us, they drank beer with us," former Red Sox player and manager Butch Hobson says. "So it seemed to be a little different atmosphere than it was later on."

The potential conflict of interest was removed in the 1980s, when the Red Sox and other professional sports teams stopped allowing writers to travel on charter planes. And the difference in travel accommodations—players are airborne on a luxurious chartered plane within two hours of the final out while reporters rely on early-morning wake-up calls to make jam-packed commercial jets that may or may not arrive on time—is symbolic of the widening economic gap that makes camaraderie between the sides difficult to attain.

Writers and players were generally of the same financial means as late as the 1960s, when the average big leaguer's salary was less than

$20,000. Players often took on second jobs to make ends meet during the winter and lived in working-class neighborhoods.

But free agency and expansion helped drive the average player salary to more than $55,000 in the 1970s. In 2007, it was more than $2.8 million while the minimum salary in 2008 was $390,000. A journalist's average salary today, meanwhile, is around $43,000.

So the ballpark was almost always the only place for players and writers to interact. In Boston, the largest press corps in baseball attempting to squeeze into one of the smallest home clubhouses had created an annoyance for players for decades.

According to the book *What's the Matter with the Red Sox?*, former Indians pitcher and broadcaster Herb Score said in the early 1970s that there were more writers covering the Red Sox than players on the Red Sox: "I don't see how a Red Sox ballplayer can ever say anything before or after games without some writer hearing him."

New ownership made multiple efforts to lessen the traffic in the home clubhouse. In 2002, the manager's postgame press conference was moved to an interview room behind the locker room. In 2005, the Red Sox added a larger interview room adjacent to the team weight room in between the first and second floor. The Sox manager, starting pitcher, and other players with a pivotal role in the game were brought into the room, which meant writers on deadline could conceivably get postgame quotes without heading into the clubhouse.

And by 2004, a spacious dining room for the players—complete with hot food prepared by an onsite chef—was built in a private area of the locker room. Such a luxurious setup was a marked improvement over the conditions that greeted pitcher and club elder statesman Tim Wakefield when he joined the club in 1995. Back then, the millionaire players were forced to eat in a picnic-like setting: the postgame spread was laid out in the middle of the clubhouse and players loaded food onto Styrofoam plates and ate at their locker as they attempted to dodge cameramen and reporters.

For all the 21st century improvements made to the clubhouse at Fenway, it still felt tiny and outdated when packed to the brim with reporters and players. Mark Bellhorn, who played for the Cubs from 2001–03, said the biggest media crush he saw at Wrigley occurred in June 2003, when the Yankees' Roger Clemens went for his 300th win in Chicago.

At Fenway, Bellhorn said during the 2004 season, "It's like when Roger was going for 300. Every day."

Some tried to make light of the situation. "You put 100 people in that locker room, people get cranky," Kevin Millar says. "You can't even get dressed when you're rubbing your ass against somebody."

After a game against the Toronto Blue Jays in August 2004, Jason Varitek, his right shoulder and knees wrapped, surveyed the scene and got into a linebacker's stance as he asked the crowd to part.

A few weeks later, Bill Mueller, whose locker was to the immediate right of the clubhouse door, saw Johnny Damon besieged by interviewers a couple lockers down and climbed atop a stool. A reporter handed Mueller his notebook and pen and Mueller stared at Damon, who was talking about the injury that forced him to the bench for the night's game against the Angels, until the centerfielder finally looked up.

"Do you have the ability to play the rest of the week or is this something [that can linger for] tomorrow's game, possibly the rest of this series?" Mueller said with an exaggerated sense of seriousness.

Said Mueller in a separate interview: "If it's a huge locker room, yeah, you probably don't notice it as much. You've got places to mingle. I'm right inside the door and right across from the lineup [card]. I'm swamped, so I get a different perspective."

A few seconds later, the clubhouse door swung open, nearly hitting the reporter speaking to Mueller. "See what I'm saying?" he said with a grin.

Others were less patient. "Irritating," Red Sox reliever Keith Foulke said in 2004. "This is supposed to be a place where you come and relax and get ready for the day. But you come here, it's almost like you're coming to the mall."

And just like mall traffic tends to stress out shoppers, a locker room logjam stresses out some players. Of course, not many shoppers view the mall as a second home. Baseball players, on the other hand, spend as much or more time in the clubhouse than at home during the season.

"Here's the way I look at it," former reliever Curtis Leskanic says. "The clubhouse is supposed to be your sanctuary, right? The kids are crying, I'm gonna go to the ballpark. I forgot to do this for my wife today, she's yelling, [I'll] go to the ballpark and relax and get prepared for a game. To me, when you go to Fenway Park, you can't do that. I try to show up as late as I can because, first of all, it's so small. And then you have 25 guys on the team and then you have 45 guys in the media.

"By the time you get to your locker, from when you walk in, it takes 25 minutes to get to your locker!" Leskanic says with a laugh.

The tight confines and the sea of faces make it difficult for most players to differentiate between the regular writers and those who cover the team less frequently for smaller newspapers and/or non-daily publications.

Alan Embree was lauded by those who covered the Red Sox for his friendly demeanor and cooperative attitude, but even he admitted he could not get to know reporters like he did at previous stops such as San Diego and Cleveland. In San Diego, in particular, Embree says it was easy to socialize with reporters. Such fraternization was impossible in Boston, where Embree and his teammates had a hard time putting a name to a face.

Foulke's relationship with the media grew increasingly strained during his miserable 2005 season, but one reporter he seemed to trust was the *Globe*'s Snow. Yet at the end of the season, after a long conversation at his Fenway Park locker, Foulke asked Snow which paper he worked for.

Outfielder Gabe Kapler joined the Red Sox after stints in Detroit, Texas, and Colorado, where he says players ". . . knew everybody [in the press corps] by name. There was a familiarity there that you don't have here. Basically, there's two competing newspapers [in the other cities], so if you have a conversation with a reporter, you know where it is. Whereas here, it can [appear] anywhere."

Players learned how to walk through the clubhouse and drop something off at their lockers without ever actually breaking stride. With so many people requesting time, many players found themselves brushing off interview requests by promising to talk later. Often, later never came.

"If you make a habit of giving them time whenever they ask for it, you will never work," former Red Sox ace Pedro Martinez says. "You just have to choose the time and the right time for you [to] actually give them time. Because the attention is always going to be there."

"You have such little time and everybody wants an exclusive," Millar said early in the 2006 season, after he signed with the Orioles. "You don't have an hour to sit at your locker. It just doesn't work out that way. You're better off getting it all out of the way and getting on with your day . . . You've got to work out, you've got to get taped, you've got to get treatment yet you only have this 30-minute window to try and cover [everything].

"Very rarely can you just sit at your locker in Boston. Here [in Baltimore], it's been unbelievable. You can sit at your locker and relax. There you can't sit at your locker. You've got to hide."

Writers must strike a delicate balance and respect a player's busy schedule while also make the type of small talk that won't lead to an immediate interview but could lay the foundation for a future encounter.

"I think I have a good relationship with some of the media people here and I enjoy talking to them on an everyday basis, not just talking about the game," former Sox outfielder Trot Nixon says. "Players don't want to talk about the game all the time. They want to talk about other things—just sit there and chit chat."

"I think a big part of it is just basically not always wanting something from them," Bradford says. "That's hard to do, especially when you don't travel and you only see these guys for very, very short amount of time. But it's important to understand that these guys have lives, and even though they're making all this money, they might be having a bad day and there's a good time to approach them and a bad time to approach them. If J.D. Drew's kid is sick, there's nothing wrong with sincerely asking how his kid is doing."

There are differences in perspective. Ballplayers and managers are trained to worry only about the immediate and to avoid looking back or looking too far ahead. Yet sports reportage is, in many ways, built on putting today's feats into context by examining the past and projecting the future for players and teams alike. Francona, for example, would often grow exasperated with reporters who wanted to ask him about the Yankees when the Sox were still 10 days away from facing their archrivals.

"I've always been driven in the sense of what have you done for me lately?" says Mueller, who ducked out of the clubhouse without comment after he clinched the American League batting title on the final day of the 2003 season and whose unyielding focus unintentionally frustrated reporters assigned to write a feature story about him.

"Think of today and today only. Worry about that first inning. To think about all these other things—those things aren't going to help you. What you need to do is focus on what you can control and how hard you can work and [on] your attitude. That's how I go about my business."

Human nature, too, makes it challenging for writers to gain the confidence of the players. Talking to and opening oneself up to a complete stranger is not something many people are comfortable with, regardless of their profession.

"I don't trust very many people at all," pitcher Josh Beckett says. "It takes a lot for me. I think trust is earned, not given. I've been like that my whole life."

As the catcher and team captain, Jason Varitek spoke to reporters nightly at his locker. But he was reluctant for the relationship to go beyond that. "I don't know if I would call anyone in the Boston media a real friend," Varitek wrote in the foreword to Tony Massarotti's book *Dynasty: The Inside Story of How the Red Sox Became a Baseball Powerhouse.* "I don't let too many reporters get to know me very well."

Wakefield is a previous winner of the "Good Guy Award," given annually by the Boston Baseball Writers Association of America to a player who is cooperative with the media, and as the longest-tenured member of the Red Sox, he has grown especially friendly over the years with longtime beat writers such as the *Globe*'s Massarotti and the *Herald*'s Sean McAdam.

Wakefield was open and revealing during a 30-minute interview for this book, but several months earlier, in his first interaction with the author, he gave one-word answers to the most basic of questions for a magazine article.

"If I don't know [a] person, it takes a little bit for me to warm up to you because I'm not going to volunteer a whole lot of personal information to somebody that I don't really know," Wakefield says. "That goes in my general life skills. I would say I'll answer all kinds of questions about the game and about stuff like that, but some questions are hard to answer when I don't know somebody, because I don't know where they're going with the questions."

Ellis Burks, who was drafted by the Red Sox and played for the club from 1987–1992, was far more comfortable with the media during his second stint with the club in 2004. "My whole theory was the questions that were asked, I answered," Burks says of his philosophy early in his career. "I didn't elaborate any further [or provide] anything extra. It was simple: A and B. You ask, I answered. That's it. Next questions. I realized that things you might say may be taken and twisted in certain ways, so I was very careful of what I said."

Still, as friendly as Burks was during the final year of his career in 2004—when a reporter told him he was having difficulty obtaining a media pass for the American League Championship Series, Burks asked the writer if there was anything he could to do help—he still reached for the author's press pass after their second in-depth conversation in September.

"Now let me see your name so I know who you're writing for," Burks said.

Players were also wary of the power of the pen and the microphone, worried that a mistake by a writer could not or would not be undone.

"That's the problem that we have with a lot of you guys: If you make a mistake, you will walk up and apologize to us," Timlin says. "You will not walk up and say 'Look I wrote this article and this is what I'm gonna print in the paper and it's gonna be in the same spot where my normal article's gonna be, because that's where everybody reads it.' It's going to be in this itty-bitty box way in the back and no one's gonna see it."

Timlin was voicing the general opinion of the masses about media coverage of events: According to a 1997 survey by the Pew Research Center, 67 percent of Americans thought the media was "generally unfair," up from 55 percent in 1985. According to a 1998 *Time*/CNN poll, 73 percent of respondents were "skeptical about the accuracy" while 63 percent said the media was "too negative."

In 2004, during the final season of his rollercoaster seven-year run with the Red Sox, pitcher Derek Lowe marveled at how there were always more people at his postgame press conference when he lost than when he won.

The perception of the news media was further shaken following the occasional lapses into journalistic fraud exemplified by former *New Republic* writer Stephen Glass in 1998 and by former *New York Times* reporter Jayson Blair in 2003. The notion that the media lacked integrity was further fueled when an erroneous report aired on "60 Minutes" in 2004 in which CBS News anchor Dan Rather relied on forged documents during a segment questioning the validity of President George W. Bush's service in the Texas Air National Guard.

Reporters also found that players tended to correlate negative coverage with anything that didn't paint them in the most positive of terms. Bob Hohler joined the beat just as Carl Everett's relationship with teammates and the press was beginning to disintegrate, and he soon learned players were unhappy with him for writing stories he thought were impossible to ignore.

"I realized very quickly that it's a whole different culture, that players don't generally feel the need to be accessible or available and don't generally—especially immediately—treat sportswriters with the respect that I was accustomed to, at least from my days in Washington," Hohler says. "They sort of quickly decided whether you're with them or against them. I couldn't see myself becoming a cheerleader for them, which is what I think they wanted."

Such standards were neither exclusive nor new to Boston. When Ted Williams was booed in Kansas City for failing to run out a grounder in a 1956 game, he said the fact that it was mentioned in the fourth line in the local newspaper—as opposed to the headline treatment it received in Boston—was proof "the Kansas City guy knew his journalism."

Wakefield admits players are protective of one another, even when the criticism aimed at a teammate is reasonable. "We're a family in there, and when something bad is written about one of my teammates—regardless of whether it's warranted or not—I take offense to that a little bit," Wakefield says. "And sometimes it's hard to control that."

"Ninety-nine percent of the players think every city is negative if they're writing negative things about them," says ESPN.com's Howard Bryant, who has worked in Oakland, New York, and Boston. "If you talk to players about how they're perceived or portrayed, I don't think there's any market where they could say 'That's a fair town.'"

Boston's reputation as a tough town with harsh and suffocating writers was rooted in the experiences of Williams, the biggest and most polarizing superstar in Boston history. His words and experiences often formed or reinforced conceptions of the Boston press—even when Williams' incidents were sometimes more urban legend than truth.

"I think Boston kind of got that tag during the Ted Williams time and has always kind of had it," says Leigh Montville, the former *Globe* columnist and the author of *Ted Williams: The Biography of an American Hero*. "The more voices you have, the more dissenting voices or the more opinions—you're always going to have something going on."

The perception of the Boston press as an adversary was fortified when subsequent superstars such as Carl Yastrzemski, Jim Rice, Clemens, Nomar Garciaparra, Martinez, and Manny Ramirez had distant or difficult relations with the press and when former Red Sox mainstays such as Rice, Garciaparra, Clemens, Wade Boggs, and Mo Vaughn were criticized heavily upon their departures.

The vindictiveness of the Boston press towards the city's most combative players could be overstated—most notably in 1947, when it was believed Boston writer Mel Webb cost Williams the American League Most Valuable Player award by either placing him at the bottom of his ballot or leaving him off it out of spite. Williams states as much in his autobiography, *My Turn at Bat*.

But it was later revealed Webb didn't even have a vote and, according to *Red Sox Century*, the three Boston writers who participated were the only ones to cast first-place votes for Williams. He was cost the MVP when a pair of out-of-town voters picked him ninth or tenth.

There are nonetheless players and fans who continue to believe the Boston press ruined Williams' MVP candidacy. "Now that I was there, I'm not at all surprised when the media in Boston voted Ted Williams eighth in the MVP and cost him an MVP," former Red Sox reliever Todd Jones says. "That's a personal vendetta and crap, probably because Ted wouldn't talk to him or didn't give him a quote. [The writers were] 'Like, we're gonna show you. We're gonna cost you an MVP.'"

At times, in fact, it appeared the Boston press went out of its way to avoid confrontation with Williams and cover up some of his misdeeds. Not much was made of his benching for not running out a popup during his rookie season in 1939. In 1955, the press did not publicize his divorce nor criticize Williams several months later, when he refused to attend the Boston baseball writers dinner to accept his Red Sox MVP award.

And while players and fans alike believe Rice's inability to gain enshrinement during his first 14 years on the writer's ballot reflects a bit of retribution for his curtness with reporters, Boston writers say, on and off the record, they do not take Rice's difficult demeanor into account when casting their Hall of Fame ballots. The local papers are filled with columns pitching Rice's candidacy in the weeks leading up to the second Tuesday in January, when the newest inductees are revealed.

The coverage of the Sox features a dynamic unique to Boston: Most of the writers who covered the team were from New England and, if they had not grown up rooting for the Red Sox, were at least quite aware of the team's history of heartbreaking near-misses.

Such appreciation of Red Sox lore led critics to accuse the media of a lack of impartiality. The first rule of sportswriting is "No cheering in the press box." And while the majority of sportswriters simply root for a good story, it was impossible to dismiss, prior to the 2004 world championship, the possibility that the coverage of the Red Sox—as well as the emotionally charged relationship between players and the press—was fueled by the passion a writer once felt as a fan.

"Most players aren't from here," former *Boston Herald* columnist Michael Gee says. "They're amazed writers would be so proprietorial about the franchise. It has also traditionally led to writers expressing the fans' perennial frustration and all-around manic depression more than is professionally seemly."

"I readily admit that I grew up as a fan, but my view of the team changed almost instantly after covering them," McAdam says. "To be able to do your job professionally, you come to regard it as your job and not something you necessarily have a fan's investment in any more.

"But human nature being what it is, you wonder if some of that— the disappointment of having grown up and seen '67, '75, and '86 and what happened to them—if you're sitting there watching them come unglued in the 2003 ALCS, I guess it's hard not to draw upon that disappointment you felt. And that sort of influences your work a little bit."

Legend has it that one New England writer was so overcome with grief after the Sox' shocking loss in Game Six of the 1986 World Series that he could not write. And *Globe* columnist Dan Shaughnessy saw one writer blinking away tears when the Red Sox raised their 2004 World Championship banner on Opening Day 2005.

"I think that, truly, a lot of the writers around here are Red Sox fans, whether they admit it or not," says Gabe Kapler, who believed writers were happier when the Sox won than when they lost—the inverse of what many players believed.

Conversely, some believed the media was less revealing of and inquisitive about the Red Sox precisely because rooting for the team long ago made it difficult for them to view the team with a critical eye. "For a lot of people, this is their destination, where they want to be," author Glenn Stout says. "And they want to be [in Boston] because they grew up as fans of these teams. I think, in general, they tend to take things more personally and less objectively."

The writers of the 1930s and 1940s were willing to overlook poor performances by the team or its players because, in many cases, the Sox had bought the goodwill of the writers by paying for their accommodations and meals on the road. The term "malaria" was used to describe many of the ailments—some of the unseemly variety—suffered by ill ballplayers. An unnamed player once set fire to his hotel room when the cigar he was smoking before he fell asleep fell into a bottle of bourbon. The bottle was pictured in the next day's newspaper, but it was called hair tonic—even though the player was bald.

Longtime Red Sox owner Tom Yawkey was born in Michigan, conducted a lot of business in New York, once considered buying the Yankees, and sometimes spoke of how much he wanted to move out of Fenway Park and, if necessary, Boston. He never maintained anything more than a seasonal residence in Boston, preferring to live most of the year on his farm in South Carolina, yet he did not encounter the same initial or posthumous criticism as another former owner, Harry Frazee.

One of Yawkey's first acts as Red Sox owner was to improve the press box and press bar at Fenway Park and declare that all the food was free. But Frazee was a New Yorker, an unforgivable sin in the arguably more provincial Boston. Frazee's problems were compounded by his wariness with the press, an attitude he'd cultivated from his experiences as a Broadway theatre owner.

And his reticence with the media would prove costly during his stewardship with the Red Sox, especially once Frazee proved too independent for American League founder Ban Johnson. The Babe Ruth trade was often portrayed as a desperate act by a man who was running out of money and needed the cash to fund a Broadway play. However, 1919 was a financially successful year for both of Frazee's businesses: The Red Sox turned a profit and the show "My Lady Friends" was a hit in Boston and elsewhere.

But Johnson's allies in the Boston press—and by extension *The Sporting News*, the national baseball newspaper—continued to foster the perception that Frazee was on the edge of financial disaster. When Frazee died in 1929, *The New York Times* reported he was broke. In fact, his estate was worth $1.3 million. Glenn Stout has advanced the persuasive notion that there was a thread of anti-Semitism running through the harsh treatment of Frazee, despite the little-known fact that he was Episcopalian and not Jewish.

In 1933, Bob Quinn sold the team to Yawkey, who owned the team until his death in 1976—the longest ownership reign by an individual in the history of American professional sports. But Stout said he was disappointed during his research for *Red Sox Century* to find how little the Boston press revealed about Yawkey, who disclosed minimal information about himself, his upbringing, or his family.

"I had a devil of a time finding out anything about Tom Yawkey," Stout says. "Forty-five years Tom Yawkey was in this town and nobody ever did a full explication of who he was and where he came from. In *Red Sox Century*, I did a lot of that [research and it] was a total revelation to people. He'd been here 45 years."

By the time the Red Sox lost to the St. Louis Cardinals in the 1946 World Series, Yawkey had already grown impatient with the press—he sided with Ted Williams in the superstar's media battles—and begun to limit his public appearances. The Red Sox did not return to the World Series for another 21 seasons, during which time Yawkey became a bit of a recluse.

He was captured so infrequently that when the Sox finally became championship contenders again in 1967, most newspapers ran decades-old file photos of Yawkey. When *Herald* beat reporter Tim Horgan walked through the locker room one day during the 1967 season, he didn't even recognize Yawkey passing by him.

It was not revealed until decades after the fact Yawkey was an alcoholic womanizer who owned a bordello and was an absentee father to his only child, Julia Yawkey. And writers proved to be lackadaisical as well in reporting Yawkey's record on race relations.

Until the release of *Red Sox Century* and *Shut Out*—the latter a book by Bryant detailing the history of racial relations within the context of Boston baseball—Yawkey was often portrayed as an innocent, if somewhat inept, bystander in the racist ways of the Red Sox instead of someone who was, at the very least, aware of and complicit in racism.

"When I was a kid growing up in Boston, I was aware that the Red Sox treated people like me and people who looked like me like shit," says Bryant, who was born in 1968. "I was aware that, as a little kid, you wanted to go to a baseball game and those old school ushers would treat you like a pile of dirt. And that was true when I was a little kid, that was true when I went to high school, that was true when I used to come home from college. And [when I] got more into reporting and covering, it was still true."

The Red Sox were the last team to integrate, in 1959, when outfielder Pumpsie Green was promoted to the big leagues midway through the season. Yawkey often said the Sox waited so long to integrate because he trusted his scouts and executives who continually told him they could not find talented African-American players.

But Yawkey and the Sox did little to conceal their contempt for African-Americans. Jackie Robinson—who would eventually break baseball's color barrier in 1947—and two other Negro League superstars (including 1950 NL Rookie of the Year Sam Jethroe, who broke in with the Boston Braves) tried out for the Red Sox at Fenway Park in 1945, but the Sox executives in attendance appeared disinterested. As the trio of players went through the motions on the field, a voice cried out "Get those niggers off the field!" from doorways near the club offices.

Two decades after his ill-fated tryout with the Red Sox, Robinson called Yawkey one of the game's biggest racists. When asked why the Red Sox did not sign any of the Negro Leaguers, player/manager Joe Cronin said it was because he broke his leg. In 1972, Cronin would not appear on stage with Robinson at the latter's final speech, instead eating a hot dog under the bleachers.

In 1959, manager Pinky Higgins said he would never let a "nigger" play for his team and spit tobacco juice at Larry Claflin of the *Boston Record-American* when Claflin asked if Green would be promoted to the big league team. Yawkey, meanwhile, said the team would field a "Negro" once they found one who met their specifications.

The Boston press corps did little to combat the ongoing racism. The *Globe* staffed Robinson's tryout, and their Red Sox beat writer, Clif Keane, was the one who heard the racial slur hurled from the stands. But the *Globe* never ran Keane's story.

When Green was finally promoted to the Red Sox in 1959, the press was overly praiseful of an act that should have occurred at least a decade earlier. The *Traveler* went so far as to write that the Sox could no longer be accused of discriminatory behavior. Longtime beat writer Al Hirshberg wrote in his 1973 book *What's the Matter with the Red Sox?* that the presence of six African-Americans on the 1967 pennant-winning team disproved any theories that Yawkey was racist.

Two generations later, local reporters were still reluctant to tackle or discuss race. In *Shut Out*, Bryant reported that superstar Jim Rice—for years the only African-American player on the Red Sox—told legendary *Globe* writer Peter Gammons in 1979 that the Sox were still giving players passes to an Elks Club in Winter Haven, Florida, that did not accept African-Americans. Gammons met with Red Sox management to discuss the issue but did not write the story because he believed club officials who told him the team was no longer distributing Elks passes.

Six years later, when the *Globe* broke the story of how the Winter Haven Elks didn't allow African-Americans, Red Sox coach Tommy Harper—a former Boston player—told the newspaper the Sox had been condoning racism for 20 years by allowing players to go to the club. Harper was fired by the Red Sox after the season.

Harper said in 2005 he understood, to some degree, why it took so long for a thorough examination of the Sox' history of race relations. To truly discuss the issue takes a great deal of time and investment on the part of the interviewer as well as the interviewee.

"To answer your question would take another hour," Harper says when asked if it's difficult to be an African-American player in Boston. "These kind of questions take a lot of thought. You want to talk about baseball, you can give quick answers. But when you're going to talk about something that's serious, you have to be able to sit down and talk about those kinds of things before you answer, because I don't want to give you some flippant answer."

Bryant is less sympathetic to his media predecessors. "I've always said that for all the high-powered writers that came through the town—for all the ones that went to the *Boston Globe*, to *Sports Illustrated*, to writing books, to all that—how in the world could this story not get told until 2002?" Bryant says. "Because nobody wanted to tell it, and that's not happenstance.

"That's choosing not to write about a story that you don't want to write about, and there's no getting around that. And nobody can convince me otherwise."

Those who did criticize the Red Sox' record on race ran the risk of being ostracized. Stout believes *Boston Record* columnist Dave Egan has been portrayed as Ted Williams' most bitter enemy because he took the club to task for its racism.

"I think he's actually been sort of miscast in history," Stout says. "He was the only guy in Boston that had the balls to say Boston was racist. I think a lot of the way he's been portrayed since was sort of payback [for] speaking out of tune."

John Harrington—the executor of the Yawkey Foundation—and longtime *Globe* columnist Will McDonough continued to defend Yawkey against charges of racism long after the former owner's death. McDonough criticized *Red Sox Century* as inaccurate when it came out in 2000, and nearly a decade earlier, Steve Fainaru's series on race in Boston was criticized by McDonough and powerful *Herald* columnist Mike Barnicle.

"So many members of the press are, heart of heart, also fans," Stout says. "It wasn't until Yawkey was gone and the Red Sox were no longer behaving in an overtly racist manner that it became OK to write about race in this town. And when my book came out, the mere mention of it caused John Harrington and Will McDonough to have conniption fits."

Race wasn't the only issue Stout believed the Boston press was reluctant to tackle. In 1907, Red Sox manager Chick Stahl resigned and said he hadn't eaten or slept in the five days leading up to his announcement. Subsequent press reports indicated he didn't look good during his final weeks on the job, but there was no mention of this while he was still the manager.

Stahl committed suicide shortly after his resignation, but it took more than 80 years before Stout reported he killed himself because he was being blackmailed by a former lover with whom he'd had a child out of wedlock.

More recently, Stout was dismayed by how the local press tackled baseball's steroid issue and the real reasons behind the free agent departure of pitcher Derek Lowe, whose late nights were the stuff of press box whispers and message board postings.

"Go back [to 2002] when [former Sox infielder] Manny Alexander [had] steroids in his car—you don't see that story being brought up with what's going on with BALCO," Stout says. A batboy driving Alexander's car was arrested for previous traffic violations and a subsequent search of the car revealed the steroids in the glove compartment.

"And everybody in town knows why Derek Lowe isn't being re-signed, but you never see that in print. Everybody knows. They'll never write the reasons."

The John Henry ownership group faced far more scrutiny—because, perhaps, they were not from Boston—than the Yawkeys or his successors ever endured. Still, *Providence Journal* columnist Bill Reynolds felt even the biggest of Sox superstars remained a mystery to most Bostonians.

"With the amazing amount of media attention, people like Pedro and Manny—just to name two who have spent a lot of years in Boston—

[there's] very little known about them," Reynolds says. "Some of these guys live here and very, very, very little is known about them. And I think that's a real contradiction somewhere."

Yet Martinez and Ramirez were two players who often chafed at the coverage they received in Boston—an indication that the perception of the Boston media as an overwhelming one could be as much a matter of volume as it is tone.

This was particularly true for the modern player, who was dealing with mediums such as talk radio that were entirely different than print journalism yet often grouped with it. A player who listens to himself getting skewered on the radio might grow angry with the reporters he sees later in the locker room, even though they weren't responsible for what he heard and follow entirely different standards than a talk show host—or caller.

"It's a totally different package—radio and things like that," David Ortiz says. "Sometimes they say whatever they feel like, but they never come down here and see how we try or what our feelings are. That's why I say: One of you guys screw up, all of you guys pay for it, because nobody knows [if] the guy's a media guy."

"I think to a lot of athletes in Boston, there's no difference to them—there's no difference between the guy trying to write a reasoned story in the *Boston Globe* and some guy yelling like a maniac at three in the afternoon on 'EEI," Reynolds says. "There's a big difference, what sports radio as a medium does, and what newspapers do, or at least try to do. But I think they all kind of get lumped together. It creates this kind of 'us against them' [mentality]."

Adding to the potential combativeness was the fact these mediums were often consumed and filtered by people even more sensitive than the player—his friends and family. Such second- and third-party recollections can further inflame tensions between writers and players and jeopardize the relationships a writer has worked to create.

"I was talking to David Wells the other day about this: How often, when a player is upset over what was written, is that player reading that person consistently and have they seen the full body of work and read that story that bothered him first-hand?" Snow said in September 2005. "And he said it's not often. You hear it from a friend second-hand or from a friend. Then it gets to him—interpreted by whoever gave it to him.

"There are so many of us that any work that's done to develop a relationship with a player can kind of fall apart just because there's so many of us. And they have a hard time saying 'OK, he wrote this, this guy didn't write this.' And it's not really their fault. It's just naturally a tough spot for everybody involved. We kind of all do the best we can."

Chapter 2
Nomar, Pedro, Ted, and Yaz

For six consecutive years between 1998 and 2003, Nomar Garciaparra and/or Pedro Martinez appeared on the front cover of the club's yearbook, an appropriate honor for a pair of franchise icons who were touted as potential Hall of Famers even in their late 20s.

The similarities seemed to end there. Garciaparra was a muscular shortstop born and raised in California who was almost painfully shy, suspicious of strangers, and unwilling or unable to open himself up to the media that covered the most chronicled team in professional sports.

Martinez was a native of the Dominican Republic whose vulnerable-looking frame—the website baseball-reference.com lists him at 5-foot-11 and 170 pounds—belied the power and the magic delivered by his right arm. His pitching was as electric as his personality, which filled up the locker room as well as a reporter's notebook.

Yet the two grew to have more in common as their careers progressed. Serious injuries forced each player to confront his baseball mortality. Garciaparra and Martinez were each entering the final year of their contracts in 2004 and questions about their long-term durability had made the once-unthinkable—a divorce from the Sox—a legitimate possibility.

The possibility of Martinez speaking fewer words to the media during a season than Garciaparra was also once unthinkable, but that was reality in 2003—proving, perhaps, that burning out on the media is inevitable for most high-profile Red Sox personalities, some later than sooner.

Martinez' performance during his first three seasons in Boston was more than enough to turn him into the most beloved athlete in Boston and his locker into a daily stop for the beat writers covering the Sox.

Indeed, Martinez may have enjoyed the greatest three-year span ever for a pitcher from 1998 through 2000. He went 60–17 over that period and had a strikeout-to-walk ratio of more than 6:1. His ERA in 1999 (2.07) and 2000 (1.74) was more than three runs lower than the American League average. His performance was all the more impressive considering that Martinez was pitching in the hitter-friendly American League during the heart of the steroid era.

Martinez filled his teammates with a sense of invincibility and awe every five days. When talking about Martinez, Sox catcher Jason Varitek would referentially refer to him as "that man."

Martinez' popularity with writers was aided by his intellect, his remarkably prideful personality, his ability to converse easily in two languages—upon signing with the Dodgers in 1988, Martinez supplemented the English language classes the Dodgers offered by reading books written in English—and his penchant for saying whatever came to mind, often eloquently.

"What do I mean when I say I pitch from my heart?" Martinez told *Esquire* in 1998. "It means something inside me—a feeling I get. It's in my blood, my body. It's not the money . . . it's my pride, my name. My family's name. My reputation. That's worth more than the $75 million they're paying me."

Martinez was so fiercely proud of his name that he was angry with the *New York Post* when it ran a headline calling him the most hated man in New York during the 2004 season. Most players would dismiss such a headline as hyperbole, but Martinez was offended that the newspaper would correlate the pitcher with the man.

"Nobody knows the man," Martinez says. "People know the player."

In 2001, Martinez tired of the talk of a "Curse of the Bambino" and said he might throw at Babe Ruth if he were unearthed and placed into a batter's box. "Wake up the Bambino, I'll drill him in the ass," Martinez told reporters.

Near the end of the 2004 season, after Martinez squandered an eighth-inning lead and suffered a heart-breaking loss to the Yankees—just as he did in Game Seven of the 2003 ALCS—he said he could ". . . just tip my hat and call the Yankees my daddy."

"I wish they would disappear and not come back," Martinez said. "I wanted to bury myself on that mound."

"Pedro's the best quote in any language," former *Boston Herald* beat writer Jeff Horrigan says. "You're talking about a potential Mensa member there. I'd love to see an IQ test with Pedro. It'd be off the charts."

Boston Globe columnist Tony Massarotti remembers everyone—locally and nationally—wanting a piece of Martinez during his first few seasons with the Sox. The Sox would travel to another city and the home team press corps would be waiting in front of Martinez' locker, looking to write a feature on the best and most interesting pitcher in baseball.

Six years later, Curt Schilling would be similarly pursued. But Schilling, already wary of the media after several years in Philadelphia and far more comfortable communicating directly with fans on message boards, would not be as accessible as Martinez, who fulfilled every interview request for a far longer period of time than anyone expected. He even served as a spokesman for Spanish-speaking players who were reluctant to conduct interviews in English—from stars such as Manny Ramirez and Ugueth Urbina to a role player such as pitcher Rolando Arrojo.

"For a superstar to be that accommodating is very unusual, and he became a historic figure," Massarotti says. "Everywhere the team went, everybody wanted to talk to Pedro. I remember him saying one spring that he always felt obligated to help the press and that he had trouble saying no, because he always recognized that the media had a job to do. I always found that fascinating about him."

Massarotti always feared Martinez would eventually grow weary of the attention. "There was definitely a point somewhere along the line where Pedro's feelings towards the media changed, and I think it was inevitable," he says. "I think Pedro was just going this way because he was so accommodating.

"There's no way he could have kept up that pace. It was too hard."

The pace officially became too much for Martinez in April 2003, when he felt as if the comments he made in Toronto during the first week of the season regarding the Sox' decision to pick up his option for 2004 were misinterpreted.

"I said I'm really happy and thankful that the Red Sox chose to pick up my option and [the two sides] kept the doors open for further negotiations," Martinez said during an interview in February 2005. "And somebody took it out of context and wrote it the way they wanted and said 'Well, Pedro, he's not happy with the fact that they picked up his option and he's expecting them to sign him to another extension.' I never said that. I never mentioned that. I never mentioned that I wasn't happy. I always said I was happy and I was very thankful.

"They called me greedy and I didn't like that because it was never in my mind, it was never in my heart. We kept the doors open to further negotiations."

Some inside the Red Sox organization believed Martinez misinterpreted the coverage his quotes received; that he heard about the stories second-hand and formed his opinion without reading the context in which the stories were written. Horrigan says it was one of many times in which Martinez lashed out at the press ". . . before he's really clear on the facts."

However, there seems little doubt Martinez was especially unhappy with the Dan Shaughnessy column which appeared in the April 11 *Boston Globe*, three days after Martinez' comments hit the newspapers.

Shaughnessy, who was not in Toronto when the deal was announced, accused Martinez of spitting on the Sox front office and called his comments ". . . at once ungrateful, combative, greedy, tone-deaf and wildly ill-timed." Shaughnessy noted Martinez will have made $92.5 million from the Sox between 1998 and 2004, a sum which he wrote "no doubt could buy half" of Martinez' native country, the Dominican Republic.

Less than a week later, Martinez told reporters he wasn't going to speak for the rest of the season, a vow of silence he maintained with almost no exception—even in the playoffs, when he was subjected to fines for not appearing at a press conference the day before his scheduled start.

"I just got tired," Martinez told reporters April 18. "I just don't want to talk, I don't feel like it."

ESPN.com writer Howard Bryant believed Martinez took the criticism personally because he was determined to be understood and liked by the paying public. Most ballplayers concede it's impossible for fans to get to truly know them via the newspapers and other media.

But the prideful Martinez was not satisfied with such a concept—in that way, he was no different than Schilling, even if they tried delivering their messages in different ways—and felt wounded by the media he'd gone out of his way to accommodate.

"Pedro wants to be understood, and to be understood, you have to look to the media, because we're the conduit to the public," Bryant says. "Pedro can't really go out and have a conversation with each and every Red Sox fan. They want to do that through us. And I think he would be constantly disappointed every time—every time he thought that he had made progress with the press and then it turns out that he didn't."

After five years in town, he'd hoped the media—and, by extension, the fans—knew him better than to call him greedy or unhappy with the Sox. So Martinez, who once tried to satisfy everybody by granting every interview request, decided the only way to satisfy himself was to remain quiet.

"I don't know the reason, but [the press was] very unfair and I didn't feel like I needed to be treated that way after I had helped so many members of the media and been so helpful to them, because I understood [it] was part of my job to speak to the media," Martinez says. "I understand that that's their job, to make me talk and get some quotes, and I was always there to do that. I can tell you some that I believe were really, really good persons and gentlemen and good reporters as well. I cannot tell you everyone was the same."

Martinez' ebb and flow with the press mimicked that of another Boston icon and baseball immortal—Ted Williams, who went from loquacious to silent more than 40 years earlier. Like Martinez, Williams oozed charisma and inspired thousands of inches of memorable copy, including John Updike's classic piece for *The New Yorker* on Williams' final game, "Hub Fans Bid Kid Adieu."

And like Martinez, Williams initially welcomed the constant attention and requests for his time and shared a mutually fruitful relationship with the media. Williams, wrote Glenn Stout and Richard Johnson in *Red Sox Century*, was ". . . a player whose personality equaled his talent. He had opinions on everything and wasn't yet wary of the printed word."

During Williams' second big league season in 1940, though, *Boston Evening-American* columnist Austen Lake declared Williams had already developed an acid attitude towards everyone, including the press. So began a two-decade sparring match that peaked—or bottomed out—in 1957, when he didn't speak to the press at all.

Williams was a proponent of limiting access to writers, and prompted the Sox to ban the media from the locker room before games and for an hour afterward during the 1950 season. As reporters gathered near the clubhouse, Williams would yell "Not yet, you chowderheads, not yet!" Later, when the postgame cooling-off period was reduced to 15 minutes, Williams would put a chair against the door until the room opened up.

Williams would put a sign in front of his locker reading "No Writers." After Game Six of the 2003 AL Championship Series, police tape surrounded Martinez' locker at Yankee Stadium. The sign hanging from the tape read "BAD MOOD—DO NOT BOTHER."

While Martinez sparred with a handful of writers but complimented many more, Williams acted as if he was livid at the whole group. He once dubbed the Boston press "the world's worst," and longtime Red Sox beat writer Tim Horgan was amazed by how Williams could lace his pronunciation of the word "sportswriters" to make it sound like a four-letter word.

"What do you get when you add water to a sportswriter?" Williams once said. "Instant horseshit."

That was among the tamest of Williams' multi-syllabic descriptions of the press: One such term was "gutless syphilitic fuckin' cocksuckers." He also came up with increasingly outlandish solutions to his problem. When a reporter once managed to find his way to Williams' suite in Boston after a game, Williams bellowed for security to get rid of the writer before he committed homicide. He also once told a New York newspaper that he'd like to do three things: Find uranium, buy a major league club, and bar all writers from the park.

Williams grew so livid with the press in 1956 that he began gazing upward at the press box and spitting as he crossed home plate following home runs. The disdainful feelings were mutual. Leigh Montville wrote in *Ted Williams: The Biography of an American Hero* that the relationship between Williams and the press was as volatile as the one between North Korea and South Korea after the Korean War. "The two sides didn't talk much, and when they did it was in angry outbursts," Montville wrote.

Journalists are trained not to involve themselves in the story, but some writers were so frustrated by Williams that they used the news pages to gain their revenge. He was often dubbed a bad influence on the Red Sox, even though he was respected by teammates and foes alike. When he let go of his bat during a swing in 1958 and hit a woman in the stands, some in the press said he should have been punished more severely for the accident.

Williams' most combative foe was *Boston Record* columnist Dave Egan, who criticized the slugger on April 30, 1952 for setting a poor example for the youth of America—the day Williams, who had already served in World War II, played in his final game before departing to fight in the Korean War.

Author and historian David Halberstam wrote in *Summer of '49* that Egan was ". . . the greatest scoundrel" in an era of American journalistic scoundrels and that his treatment of Williams ". . . was not pleasant to anyone who cares about the American press."

Wrote Howard Kaese near the end of Williams' career: "Someone has to come to the defense of the Boston sportswriters, even if it has to be a sportswriter. On the word of one man—Ted Williams—public opinion generally has classified them with Gen. Nasser, the Chinese Reds and the measles. To be a sportswriter now is to be cousin to the devil. Why? Because Ted Williams says Boston sportswriters are no good."

While Williams came to be idolized by future Sox players who had their own troubles with the press—Jim Rice carried a copy of Williams' autobiography throughout his career—there was evidence that some of his antipathy was exaggerated.

"Ted would answer their questions—sometimes he'd answer it belligerently, but I think deep down he had respect [for the writers]," says Johnny Pesky, the Sox legend who was one of Williams' best friends.

Williams, who once anonymously paid the hospital bills of a beat writer and also took with him to Korea a baseball autographed by Boston writers, enjoyed tweaking the Boston press by feeding stories to a couple of friends in the New York press corps. He also had a fine relationship with the media in Washington and Texas during four seasons as the manager of the Senators/Rangers franchise. And in 1989, he told Shaughnessy in *The Curse of the Bambino* that he ". . . reacted probably a little strongly about" the coverage he received as a player and it wasn't as big a deal as he originally made it out to be.

Martinez never got to speak to Williams about the Boston press. By the time Martinez joined the Sox, Williams was in fading health and making few public appearances. The two occasionally talked pitching, and after Martinez struck out five of the six batters he faced in the 1999 All-Star Game at Fenway Park, Williams told Martinez he was one of the best pitchers he'd ever seen and signed an All-Star Game program for Martinez.

But Martinez' silence in 2003 provided another reminder that he and Williams were, despite their generational gap, kindred souls. At their peak, each was the best at his position in baseball. Both were brilliant beyond the baseball diamond: After his career, Williams became one of the best sport fishermen in the world.

As with Williams, Martinez' shift in media relations philosophies was a reflection of a sensitivity born out of humble beginnings and a superstar's ability to feed off the notion of proving wrong his doubters—real and imagined.

Both men rose out of poverty to become rich beyond their wildest dreams, yet the memories of a poor childhood never abated. Wrote Ed Fitzgerald in *Sport* magazine in 1948: "So many things become clearer to you when you weigh all this information about Ted's background. You can understand, for instance, why he is so eager to make big money. There was never any money around the Williams house and there must have been times when the lack of it was a constant worry."

After he took the loss against the Yankees in Game Two of the 2004 AL Championship Series, Martinez said he liked hearing fans in the Bronx mockingly chant "Who's your daddy" because it proved how far he had come from his poverty-stricken childhood.

"I actually realized that I was somebody important, because I caught the attention of 60,000 people, plus you guys, plus the whole world," Martinez said. "If you reverse the time back 15 years ago, I was sitting under a mango tree without 50 cents to actually pay for a bus. And today, I was the center of attention of the whole city of New York. I thank God for that."

Like Williams, Martinez had a knack for remembering slights, no matter how rare or tepid. Wrote Williams in his autobiography, *My Turn at Bat*: "In a crowd of cheers I could always pick out the solitary boo."

And just like Williams, Martinez could hear the one naysayer in a crowd of 100 adoring fans and remember the one negative paragraph in a sports section full of glowing praise. During the 2004 season, Martinez did not speak to Horrigan because he believed Horrigan was siding with Sox ownership in his ongoing contract standoff.

"He really thought that I had an agenda, [that] I was carrying water for the owners by reporting in spring training his velocity was down so much," Horrigan says. "Which was ridiculous. For some reason, he really thought that shouldn't be reported. I don't know if he saw me speaking to Theo [Epstein] and [owner] John Henry and tried to assume we were talking about him.

"He really thought I was against him, which is an absolute joke. How are you going to ignore [his reduced velocity] in spring training?"

Martinez and Shaughnessy had a famously hot and cold relationship. Throughout Martinez' final two seasons with the Sox, Shaughnessy would regularly refer to him as a diva and often criticized him for operating on his own schedule. Martinez was unhappy with Shaughnessy when the columnist suggested Martinez seriously harmed his future by saying he'd brush back Ruth. Martinez also believed Shaughnessy was not ". . . held accountable for anything that he writes" and that he grew personal in criticizing both himself and Nomar Garciaparra.

"I didn't think he was professional, what he did, and I don't agree with it," Martinez says.

Like other columnists, Shaughnessy regularly lauded Martinez' talents on the mound and believed he would end up the best pitcher in Sox history (Shaughnessy wrote as much in the April 11, 2003 column which so angered Martinez). He generally wrote of Martinez in a positive light and complimented him on his efforts to maintain a real relationship with Sox fans and the community.

"How could you not like Pedro?" Shaughnessy says. "He was so smart. Even the last year, we would say hello and stuff. He was always [saying] that I didn't respect him, but he never made any public demonstrations towards me and I don't remember him ever refusing to talk to me. He probably didn't like the diva thing, but it was true. I can't help it.

"But, boy, '99 and 2000, what a privilege it was to watch him. I enjoyed him. [The Sox] got that big Cuban pitcher Arrojo and Pedro translated for him. Had this guy making $10 million a year and he's translating for a new player. I loved his brilliance. He was a gentleman. He never made a big show of his dissatisfaction."

While Martinez grew tired of Boston's unyielding spotlight, he lauded the Boston media for respecting his request to not write about his private life or, especially, his family. Reporters were far more obliging to Martinez than Williams, who was livid at reporters who attempted to speak to or examine his relationship with his family.

He was criticized by the press for not attending the premature birth of his daughter—one paper even ran a poll asking readers if Williams was qualified to be a father—and for not returning home to visit his mother following his rookie season in 1939. When Williams suffered a season-ending elbow injury in 1950, reporters wondered if he was fishing in Maine during his rehabilitation.

However, Martinez felt that desire for privacy resulted in some unfair coverage, especially during his final season with the Sox. Martinez was usually among the last Sox players to arrive for spring training, and 2004 was no different. Various stories circulated that Martinez arrived late because he was home in the Dominican Republic celebrating his father's birthday.

At the time Martinez was supposedly cutting the cake with his dad, he was actually in a hospital room in Boston, watching over a seriously ill family member. "I never explained why [he arrived in Ft. Myers late]," Martinez says. "I was so upset. I was in a hospital watching through the TV on the monitors and people [were] speculating about me being in a party. And I was in the toughest situation, probably, I've ever been in. I'm not going into details, but that was probably the worst moment of my life. I would have never gone to spring training until that problem was taken care of.

"I didn't like it and I'm not going to like it and I will never hold a grudge, but I just think it was so unfair. A lot of those comments that came were out of ignorance because people didn't know."

Judging by the 2003 and 2004 seasons only, newcomers to the Red Sox beat could assume Martinez was unapproachable, difficult to deal with for the media and impossibly prideful. Those who covered him throughout his Red Sox career were more forgiving.

"The general media perception of it is 'Pedro's a jerk, he won't talk to us,'" Massarotti says. "It's always unfair—always. But at the same time, you can't expect people who are just showing up in the clubhouse to have the same understanding as the people who have covered him for five, six, seven years. It's just not the same."

Nor, of course, was Martinez' view of the media. He was far more cynical and suspicious of the press at the end of his Red Sox tenure than he was at the beginning. After the 2003 season, he told *Herald* beat writer Michael Silverman that he did not like the press.

He didn't feel much better about dealing with the media a little more than a year later, after he'd signed a four-year deal with the Mets. "Yes, it is part of my job," Martinez says about talking to the press. "But I hate it. I hate it. I hate it."

There was little doubt, long before 2004, that Nomar Garciaparra felt the exact same way.

"I never understood Nomar's . . . hostility is not too strong a word," *Boston Herald* beat writer Sean McAdam says. "This was a guy who, for the first six seasons of his stay in Boston, you could take the critical copy written about him and fit it comfortably on the head of a pin. And yet he felt that he was under siege."

"Nomar hated us with the power of a thousand suns," *Boston Globe* columnist Dan Shaughnessy says. "He was irrational. It was never going to change.

"He would always look at you like you were standing in shit. And God forbid, I can't even imagine what he would say when you weren't around. It was unfortunate, because Jesus, he was Joe DiMaggio for a while there and we certainly wrote it up that way."

Pedro Martinez was determined to allow fans to get to know him via the media. Garciaparra had no such desire.

"That's who Nomar is, it's in his DNA," *Globe* columnist Bob Ryan says. "He never felt that it was a necessary part of the process. He never saw the need for it, never saw why we were necessary."

While his experiences with the Boston media would, in many ways, resemble those of fellow introverted superstar Carl Yastrzemski, Garcia-parra also had a knack for hearing the one shred of criticism among a cacophony of praise—just like Ted Williams, whom Garciaparra befriended during the legend's later years.

Austen Lake of the *Boston Evening-American* wrote Williams received far more praise than criticism but ". . . such is the youth's supersensitivity that he forgets the cheers and remembers the blurts." Harold Kaese sarcastically wrote he felt bad for Williams because five percent of his press was bad.

In a profile of Garciaparra that appeared in the *Boston Globe Magazine* in 2004, Garciaparra's father, Ramon, recalled his son's aborted pursuit of the magical .400 mark in 1999. "He hadn't had a hit in three at-bats," Ramon Garciaparra told the *Globe.* "He hears a fan yell 'C'mon, Nomar. You stink!' It's weird, but behind all the cheering you always hear that one person."

Garciaparra had obvious franchise-player talent: He signed a seven-year contract extension following his Rookie of the Year season, a record for a player with such minimal service time. And he exceeded 20 homers, 90 RBIs, and a .300 average in each of the six seasons in which he played at least 135 games.

Yet as a shy perfectionist who dreaded the thought of uttering something he'd regret, Garciaparra was ill-equipped to serve as the symbol and face of a franchise in a city that loved to lionize its sporting figures. "Everybody wanted to know everything they could about him because he was a superstar," says Garciaparra's close friend and former teammate Lou Merloni. "People are trying to get into his life—'What's it like being you? What is this like?' And he just wasn't willing to give any of that up."

During his formative years in California, Garciaparra displayed the attention to detail and pursuit of perfection which would later manifest itself in his maniacal pregame preparation and ritualistic actions in the batter's box. Speaking to the *Globe Magazine* in 2004, Garciaparra recalled how he'd receive a 90 on a paper or a test in school and wonder what he could have done in order to get a higher score.

"I would ask myself, Why couldn't I get a 93, a 94? Why couldn't I get a 100?" Garciaparra said.

Garciaparra's wariness only increased after his first unpleasant experience with the press as a professional. In 1995, as a member of the Sox' Double-A affiliate in Trenton, New Jersey, Garciaparra made a series of spectacular plays in the field. Asked after the game if he thought he'd energized the crowd, Garciaparra, in a story recounted in the *Globe Magazine*, said "You mean when you could hear the crickets in the stands?

The next day, a headline in the local paper read "Nomar Blasts Fans."

Garciaparra worried fans in Trenton would believe he was blaming them for his wariness with the media. "So you're in a no-win situation, no matter how you phrase it," Garciaparra told the *Globe*. "That's why I don't talk much. Because you're damned if you do, damned if you don't."

Globe beat writer Gordon Edes said he wondered how Garciaparra would have turned out had he not been drafted and developed under the tutelage of Dan Duquette, whose paranoia and disdain for the press was well-known.

"We got a glimpse of Nomar unplugged at the 1997 All-Star Game and he was just so relaxed and he was so funny and candid and revealing," Edes says. "And you know what? That curtain came down right after that and we only caught rare glimpses of it. And I've often thought that part of it was him sensing and hearing the message from the front office that the media in Boston [was] something to keep at an arm's length."

During his first three years with the Sox, Garciaparra's reticence was less obvious thanks to the presence of Mo Vaughn, the slugging first baseman who welcomed media attention and shouldered his role as team spokesman without resistance.

Vaughn would hold court at his locker before and after games, never turning down an interview request and sticking around until every last question was answered. He was rarely offended by hard-edged baseball questions and even remained calm and unflappable in the face of personal scandals when he was involved in a bar brawl and charged with DUI.

"I found that it's just as hard for the media to ask me those hard questions," Vaughn said during a subpar 2002 season with the Mets. "No one likes asking hard, tough questions. No one likes to see guys failing—media too. But when it doesn't work out, they've got to report it. And that's the nature of the whole thing."

But Vaughn departed Boston on acrimonious terms following the 1998 season, and signed a six-year deal with the Anaheim Angels. His exit left a giant void in the Sox clubhouse, one Garciaparra was unwilling and unable to fill.

Garciaparra's approach to baseball, and his personality did not lend themselves to the type of self-examination and analysis reporters expected out of superstars. Garciaparra had a strict pregame routine and speaking to reporters who wanted a minute here or a minute there was never part of the plan.

As a result, interviews with Garciaparra turned into torturous exercises for all parties. Garciaparra would give only the most vanilla of clichés and would not view his accomplishments through the prism of history, frustrating those who wanted some color for their stories.

"The guy who probably benefited the most from Mo Vaughn being here was Nomar, and they were only together for a couple years," Massarotti says. "There's just very few [players] who have the personality and the real sense of security to communicate and know that their message is not going to be mis-communicated."

Massarotti believed Garciaparra was "terrified" of making such a mistake. And in a rare moment of candor, the shortstop once told *Hartford Courant* beat writer David Heuschkel how much he feared saying the wrong thing.

"He came up to me one day in spring training 2003—nobody was in the clubhouse, everyone had gone home—and he flagged me over and he asked me something about a question some other reporter asked him," Heuschkel says. "Nomar asked my opinion, if I thought that it was a stupid question. I told him not really, someone's just soliciting your opinion.

"And he proceeded to say there's a lot of times where he looks up and there's a bunch of people and he sees faces he doesn't know. And he'll say something before a game, and then, during the game, it's the third or fourth inning, he's at shortstop and he thinks 'God, what if I said that wrong?' He was always thinking he might say something [wrong]."

Garciaparra was not the first Sox superstar to harbor such fears.

"I never covered Yaz, I did the book after he was done, but from everything I've heard and those who did cover him [say], I think it's a very accurate statement [to say] there are a lot of similarities," says *Providence Journal* columnist Bill Reynolds, who authored *Lost Summer*, a look back at the 1967 Red Sox. "Not the most social people in the world. Did not really want to be leaders. Kind of disagreeable at times. Both perfectionists. Very intense, very driven. I think there are a lot of similarities."

Yastrzemski had enough to worry about during his first few years with the Red Sox in the early 1960s, when he replaced living legend Ted Williams in left field. During his rookie season in 1961, the *Globe* regularly ran a stat box comparing Yastrzemski to Williams.

Yastrzemski spent a few spring trainings with the Sox and Williams before being promoted to the majors and observed the poor relationship between Williams and area writers. And Yastrzemski, a naturally quiet person, was determined not to follow in Williams' fiery footsteps.

As a result, Yastrzemski kept a polite distance from the Boston press, speaking on his schedule before games and not saying much of note when he was interviewed. "[If] it was a night game, once I went on the field to take batting practice, I wanted to focus on the game," Yastrzemski said during an interview at spring training in 2005. "Hey, you want to talk to me, get there a little early, before batting practice. I didn't like to talk as batting practice went on. I wanted to focus on this pitcher—did he pitch me different in some way in his home ballpark? Stuff like that."

Some reporters perceived Yastrzemski's approach as aloof and believed it set a negative tone for media relations in the clubhouse, but for him, it was a decision born more out of caution than contempt. Wrote Yastrzemski in his autobiography *Yaz: Baseball, the Wall and Me*: "I never really expressed my own feelings, but said what I thought would look right in the newspapers. I think that's why, for a long time, I was very guarded against the press. It was because I could never be myself. I don't think I ever really relaxed with the press until my last year."

Yastrzemski grew up on the East coast, but far from the white-hot intensity of Boston. He was born and raised in the small town of Bridgehampton, New York, on the eastern end of Long Island. Working on the family farm instilled Yastrzemski with an inexhaustible work ethic, and he'd often be the first to arrive at the ballpark, several hours before the first pitch, and the last player to leave the locker room after the game. He was so consumed by baseball, he admitted in his autobiography that he sometimes wept during his early career struggles.

After struggling on the field and at the gate for the first several years of Yastrzemski's career, the Sox exploded in popularity and prominence in 1967, when Yastrzemski won the American League Triple Crown and led the Sox to their first AL pennant in 21 years. As the Sox fended off the Tigers down the stretch, Boston radio stations broke into news coverage to update listeners on the Sox games. There were more stories in the local papers about the Sox than Boston's mayoral election.

New England's thirst for news on the Sox only increased after the "Impossible Dream" season. And while Yastrzemski grew accustomed to the media culture of Boston, he never became fully comfortable with it.

"You lose three or four in a row, the season was over," Yastrzemski says with a laugh. "It's just the way the fans and the Boston press were. You win four, five in a row, you're going to win it all. It was a lot of ups and downs by the press."

He observed, without rancor, the penchant of the local press to second-guess everything Sox-related and was more bemused than annoyed by the area's obsession with the Sox and the tendency of the press to make a headline out of seemingly innocuous occurrences.

"I became hardened to what was said about me and the club," Yastrzemski wrote in his autobiography. "I learned too quickly that there was nothing I could say or do to squelch a rumor or a false report in a newspaper."

Like Garciaparra, Yastrzemski never intended to turn into the face of a franchise, believing it emphasized his own accomplishments over those of the team's, and felt he could lead better by example than by delivering impassioned speeches at odds with his personality.

Yastrzemski felt this reluctance was often misinterpreted by the press as lack of interest, especially when the Sox were struggling. "The thing I always said is it's easier to play on a winner because you're not the focal point," Yastrzemski says. "It's the team. When you're not [winning]—like my first six years with the Red Sox—it's a very difficult place to play baseball, because the focus was on the individual and not the team because you're in last place."

That was never a problem for Garciaparra: The Sox made the play-offs three times in his seven years with the club and remained in the race deep into the season the other four times. But despite the success enjoyed by Garciaparra and the Sox, tensions bubbled over—between him and the club as well as between him and the media—during his final two seasons with the Sox.

During spring training in 2003, Garciaparra lashed out at reporters for the negativity he perceived in their coverage. The previous September, *Herald* columnist Steve Buckley wrote that Garciaparra didn't deserve to play in Boston, criticized him for complaining about a media corps which ". . . seek[s] out the Johnny Damons and Lou Merlonis for postgame quotes, and we only talk to you when you deign to speak to us" and also wrote that Garciaparra would argue calls with the official scorer.

"I've had to stand up for myself when something comes out blatantly lying and someone makes up stuff to make me look bad," Garciaparra told reporters. "People can criticize what I do on the field, but when you start criticizing my character and have a personal attack, I'm going to have a problem with that."

Reporters walking into the Red Sox clubhouse on Opening Day were greeted by a red line that was applied on the floor in front of the lockers, signifying a player's personal space. No one ever took credit for the idea and many reporters believed it was of Garciaparra's doing, even though the line remained there long after Garciaparra's departure and even though Garciaparra wasn't the only superstar who rarely or never spoke to the press in 2003.

"I didn't hear any other players complain about it," Massarotti says. "So it had to be more than just him."

Garciaparra also instituted a policy in which reporters had to request interviews with him through the club's media relations department at least a day ahead of time—making him, now more than ever, a modern version of Yastrzemski.

Teammates such as Jason Varitek and executives such as spokesman Glenn Geffner defended Garciaparra's new policy, but reporters were bothered by it and growing increasingly annoyed with Garciaparra's seemingly selective interpretation of privacy, as he dated celebrities, appeared as himself on episodes of "Saturday Night Live" and the ABC sitcom "Two Guys, a Girl and a Pizza Place," and served as a corporate pitchman for Gatorade and Dunkin Donuts. He also opened up to *Sports Illustrated* about his exhaustive training regimen and talked about the possibility of hitting .400 during an expansive cover story in 2001.

"To me, he was a guy full of contradictions," McAdam says. "He would complain that he wanted to be low-key and he didn't like being in the spotlight, and then you turn on your TV and he was on 'Saturday Night Live' or he was dating a celebrity actress or TV personality. What I think Nomar meant was he didn't like to be asked tough baseball questions and resented that intrusion."

Throughout the 2004 season, Garciaparra's actions and body language were those of a player who did not plan to be in Boston beyond the season. He missed the first 57 games of the season with a strained Achilles tendon he said he suffered when he was hit by a batted ball during an exhibition game. But no one recalled seeing a ball hit Garciaparra, whose protracted recovery—he was initially expected to miss only a handful of games—led many to wonder, in print and privately, if he was milking the injury to get back at the Sox for trying to trade him the previous winter.

Before he came off the disabled list, he held his annual "Nomar Bowl" benefiting numerous local charities. It was the fifth Nomar Bowl—and the last according to the superstitious Garciaparra, who said his charity does "everything in fives," presumably in honor of his uniform number.

Once Garciaparra finally donned the familiar no. 5, he seemed to withdraw from his more boisterous teammates. He rarely spoke or interacted with anyone in the home locker room at Fenway Park, preferring instead to sit facing his locker. On July 1, he was the only non-catcher position player to sit out an extra-inning classic against the Yankees in which Yankees shortstop Derek Jeter dove into the stands and bloodied his face in pursuit of a foul ball. While the rest of his entranced teammates leaned over the dugout railing, Garciaparra remained seated. He told *Feeding the Monster* author Seth Mnookin he stayed seated out of superstition.

Shaughnessy was one of the few writers to grow friendly with Garciaparra, but on July 3, he called for the shortstop to be traded in response to his inactivity against the Yankees. Exactly four weeks later, the one-time franchise icon was sent to the Cubs in a shocking three-way trade executed just minutes before the trading deadline.

He departed Boston detached from his teammates as well as the media, yet he had more defenders than he did detractors among both groups.

"A lot of members of the media didn't want to put in the effort with Nomar," Massarotti says. "It took a lot of effort. Everybody talks to Kevin Millar, because it's easy. It doesn't take any effort. That's why everyone likes Millar. You get five minutes, you want an easy answer, [Garciaparra's] not going to give it to you. Most reporters walked away saying 'This guy's an asshole,' whether it's true or not."

"Nomar came up in an organization that had a great deal of disdain for the media and I thought that rubbed off on him," Heuschkel says. "He was a friendly guy. You'd walk up to him some days and he would be very friendly. But then there were other days when you'd talk to him and he wouldn't even look at you. He'd be at his locker and he wouldn't even look at you."

Several attempts to speak to Garciaparra for this book via intermediaries were unsuccessful. But he admitted, both to former Sox executive vice president Charles Steinberg as well as to Mnookin, that he spent twice as much time worrying about his pre- and postgame interviews as he did about playing the game.

"He said 'I spend a third of my energy preparing to talk to the media before the game, a third of my energy playing baseball and a third of my energy preparing to talk to the media after the game," Steinberg says. "That broke my heart.

"My sense is that he's a good guy who passionately loves to play baseball and might love the profession even more if it didn't come with that required responsibility."

Chapter 3

Lou Gorman and Dan Duquette: Different Approaches—Same Result?

The only two men to occupy the general manager's chair in Boston from 1984 through 2001 were distinctly different individuals with correspondingly divergent media relations philosophies. But the tenures of Lou Gorman and Dan Duquette were marred and, in many ways, shaped by the tensions between their teams and the press.

Their similar experiences raised the question: Was the acrimonious nature of the Red Sox-press relationship the result of an organization-wide distrust of the media that started at the very top? Or was it proof that the relationship between the team and the press was doomed to wither under Boston's white-hot magnifying glass regardless of how a general manager approached the media?

The two were New England natives who arrived in Boston at opposite stages of their careers. Gorman was a well-traveled executive who'd worked in various capacities for four teams and was the first person to serve as the general manager of two expansion teams (the Kansas City Royals and Seattle Mariners).

Prior to becoming the Red Sox general manager in 1984, he was the assistant general manager with the New York Mets. But growing up a Red Sox fan in New England—Gorman is a native of South Providence, Rhode Island, and grew up idolizing Ted Williams—and working four years in New York did not prepare him for Boston's cauldron.

"New York could be critical too, but I don't think there's the passion for baseball that you have in this town," Gorman said during an interview in his office in December 2005. "I never dreamed that the intensity would be as great as it was here. I never realized the intensity and the passion of the coverage would be what it was. That was a little bit overwhelming at first."

But Gorman, who described himself as a "people person," neither had trouble dealing with the attention nor with the inherent demands of the press. He believed there was little to be gained by confronting writers, even those he perceived as regularly disagreeable, and figured establishing a cordial relationship with the press was a matter of self-preservation.

It was an attitude born long before he moved to Boston and one he instilled years earlier in an up-and-coming manager in the Baltimore organization. "There was a writer that covered the club in Baltimore and [Earl] Weaver, as the Triple-A manager, would go to [spring training] every year and he realized the [Orioles players] didn't like this guy," Gorman says. "And we're sitting there and he said 'If I ever get the job, the first thing I'll do is throw that guy out of my clubhouse.

"I said 'Earl, no writer can hire you, but a lot of writers can help get you fired.' If you make that guy an enemy, then his [goal] in life will be to get rid of you. You better learn to deal with him, even if you don't like him, because you have to deal with the media and you're better off having friends, not enemies.

"And of course that guy eventually became one of his biggest boosters."

Convincing his bosses and his players of that approach was not nearly as easy. Inside Fenway Park, Gorman's candid and personable nature was sometimes viewed as less of an asset.

"I forget what year it was, but *The Sporting News* evaluated all the general managers in baseball and they had me listed as the best guy to deal with," Gorman says. "So [former Red Sox chief executive officer] Haywood [Sullivan] called me in the office [and said] 'What the hell are you doing on this list? No. 1? Too easy.' I said, no, it's not that I'm too easy, I'm very fair with them. He said, 'You should be last on the damn list.'"

Says Red Sox club historian Dick Bresciani, who was the team spokesman throughout Gorman's reign: "Lou was the most gregarious and friendly [Red Sox general manager]. He was very, very accommodating—some people might say he was too accommodating. Lou was great with them.

"Sometimes we felt that Lou was being too accessible. That's his nature. He's a great guy."

Gorman was at ease with public speaking, filled notebooks as well as the airwaves, and traded barbs with his critics when he felt he was being unfairly lampooned. He uttered one of the more famous lines in Boston sports history during the height of Roger Clemens' holdout in the spring of 1987:

"Gentlemen, I'm certain that the sun will set tonight, and I'm also certain that it will rise tomorrow morning and I'll have lunch tomorrow afternoon and we will get Roger Clemens signed."

A few months later, Gorman agreed to trade one-time starting shortstop Glenn Hoffman, who was toiling at Triple-A Pawtucket, to the Dodgers, but he forgot to put Hoffman through major league waivers prior to completing the deal. As a result, the deal was delayed (though eventually consummated) and Gorman was heavily criticized for the oversight.

The *Boston Herald*'s Mike Shalin misquoted Gorman's interpretation of the waiver process in his article, which angered Gorman as much as his initial mistake. Gorman wrote a letter to the editor in which he took responsibility for his error and wondered how capable Shalin was as a sportswriter.

Gorman walked into the press box at the Red Sox' spring training facility in 1992 and heard reporters criticizing new starting shortstop John Valentin, who was struggling offensively as well as defensively. Gorman challenged the reporters to bet him that Valentin would not turn into an All-Star with 20-homer power and the ability to play solid defense. Valentin twice hit 20 homers in a season and proved adequate at shortstop as well as second base and third base.

Gorman's philosophies represented a dramatic shift from those of his predecessors, who, with the exception of Dick O'Connell, were as reluctant to deal with the press as the Yawkeys. Indeed, Gorman's two superiors—Sullivan and CEO John Harrington—were especially tight-lipped and, in Harrington's case, sensitive to negative coverage.

"When Haywood Sullivan was GM and in charge, the media was not given much access—they were looked upon as the necessary evil and don't trust them," *Boston Herald* beat writer Sean McAdam says. "There was that sort of air of paranoia that surrounded everything. When Lou Gorman came in, by virtue of his pretty garrulous nature, he was pretty accommodating."

Gorman said Sullivan, who preceded him as general manager, was not upset by negative publicity and, indeed, barely paid any attention to the press. He also knew how to use the press to his advantage: When All-Star catcher and Massachusetts native Rich Gedman was holding out in 1987, Sullivan ordered Gorman to publicize the offers the Red Sox made to Gedman, realizing such a tactic could stem the amount of negative press directed at the Sox.

"Haywood Sullivan was tremendous, nothing bothered him—good or bad, [the attention] didn't bother him," Gorman says. "He just didn't respond to it. He would handle whatever came his way."

So, too, did Gorman, who grew to alternately admire and grow aggravated by the dogged determination of the reporters covering the Red Sox. Gorman said talking to former *Herald* Red Sox beat writer Steve Fainaru made one feel ". . . almost like the person was at the Inquisition."

Gorman often criticized the tendency of local writers for what he believed was their proclivity to accentuate the negative in their reportage. "For our media it always seemed a negative story would have greater impact," he wrote in his autobiography *One Pitch From Glory*. "And the more controversial, the better."

He was continually frustrated at their ability to unearth confidential information of varying significance. During Roger Clemens' hold-out in the spring of 1987, Gorman was shocked when he learned the media knew of Clemens' $150,000 bonus for starting the All-Star Game.

Gorman preferred to keep the details of incentive-based clauses in a player's contract secret from his manager, believing that playing time should not be influenced by finances. But as the 1993 season wound down, reporters figured out reliever Jeff Russell—on the disabled list with an ankle injury—was one appearance shy of triggering a $150,000 bonus and guaranteeing his contract for 1994.

When manager Butch Hobson asked about Russell's availability, Gorman said he believed the reliever should remain sidelined. Hobson was surprised, and not necessarily pleased, to read about Russell's clause in the papers.

"The media found it out and the media had it in the paper," Gorman says. "So now [Hobson] calls me on the phone: 'Is that true? If I put him in the game, he makes some more money?' I said 'Yes, it is true.'

"[Hobson said] 'I didn't know that.' 'I didn't want you to know that.' 'Well, how did the media find out?' 'I don't know but they did.'"

After the 1992 season, the Red Sox pursued free agent outfielder Kirby Puckett and registered him and his wife at a local hotel under an assumed name in hopes of conducting the visit and negotiations in secrecy. But a local television station figured out Puckett was arriving and the future Hall of Famer was greeted by a phalanx of television cameras at Logan International Airport.

A year later, Sullivan and Harrington were annoyed when reporters learned who the Sox were considering for the vacancies on their coaching staff. They also ordered Gorman to fire pitching coach Rich Gale, who had already been told he'd return for the 1994 season. The Sox were lambasted for their awkward handling of the dismissal, and a week later, Harrington—still upset over the coverage of Gale's firing—told Gorman he was out as general manager.

There were times when Gorman managed to keep sensitive news a secret. In 1987, he and an assistant traveled to Arizona to meet with Clemens, his agent, and commissioner Peter Ueberroth in an attempt to end Clemens' holdout. And during his final year as general manager in 1993, Gorman agreed to trade Clemens to the Houston Astros in exchange for a package of players that featured All-Star second baseman Craig Biggio. Such a deal would have ranked among the biggest in franchise history, but Houston ownership refused to part with Biggio and the trade was off.

"Only time the media never knew what I was doing," Gorman says.

Still, Gorman spoke with the media regularly throughout his tenure because he believed it was part of his job to keep the public as informed as possible. He encouraged players to speak to the media, believing a lack of cooperation was more harmful than helpful, but he had little success forging a peace between the players and the writers during the mid-to-late '80s.

Gorman was sympathetic to players and managers who could never adjust to the intensity of Boston and those who were swallowed up by it. He said a handful of players during his stewardship asked to be traded because they could not deal with the media.

Some who remained had their tenures in Boston defined by their relationship with the media—none more so than Jim Rice, the superstar left fielder who did not want to serve as a spokesman on issues, whether serious (race in Boston) or surface-deep (the performance of the Red Sox).

Rice was not the first or last Red Sox player to dislike the media, but few were more public or forceful in expressing his disdain. And no player soured quicker on the reporters than Rice, whose defenses went up during his rookie season in 1975. Rice believed *Globe* columnist Leigh Montville invaded his privacy when Montville traveled to South Carolina to speak to Rice's family and friends for a positive profile. Later in the season, writer and radio host Clif Keane grew impatient with Rice while waiting for him to arrive for an interview.

When he arrived, Rice told Howard Bryant in Bryant's book *Shut Out* that Keane ". . . looked at me and said to me 'I can make you and I can break you,' and I looked him right in the eye and I told him, 'You can't do anything to me.'

"That was it. That was the beginning."

When *Washington Post* columnist Thomas Boswell asked Rice what it was like to accidentally knock down an umpire following a 1979 game against the Orioles (Rice was trying to break up an argument between the umpire and teammate Rick Burleson), Rice told him he'd throw the next person to ask him such a stupid question into a garbage can.

Rice also had physical confrontations with at least three Boston-based media types, including Fainaru (whose shirt was torn by Rice when Fainaru told him he'd treat Rice as poorly as Rice treated him) and former *Globe* beat writer Larry Whiteside, who was lifted into the air by Rice after a profane exchange between the two in Baltimore. It took two people to pull Rice off Whiteside.

His supporters do not deny or defend his churlish behavior and say he had no interest in discussing anything unrelated to baseball. But they also say Rice is a complex person who was thrust into a no-win situation as an African-American superstar in a city with a poor history of race relations. While Montville's trip to South Carolina alienated Rice, *Providence Journal* columnist Bill Reynolds said he had a good relationship with Rice largely because he traveled to South Carolina while working on a magazine piece about him in the 1980s.

In an interview with Bryant for *Shut Out*, Rice said he sensed the racial tension in Boston and refused to comment on it because, he reasoned, anything he said would be stating the obvious. "Peter Gammons and all these other guys had all this information and held so much of it back," Rice said. "There was so much out there that you would never know about. Why did he need me to talk about what he knew? If he knew it, say it."

And stating the obvious, in any context and on any subject, was something Rice didn't enjoy. Gammons said Rice was far more cooperative when talking about his struggles than his successes, which runs counter to the instincts of most players.

"Rice is a really good guy," Gammons says. "He didn't like to talk after he hit two home runs. But he was always there if he struck out twice. And he'd always say to me: 'Hey. You can write about my two home runs better than I can say it. But I've got to stand there and say I'm horseshit [after a poor game].'"

When asked to identify the most misunderstood player they'd ever encountered on the Red Sox beat, Gammons, Reynolds, and CBS4 reporter Dan Roche all said Rice and agreed he could be expansive and agreeable as easily as he could be dismissive and argumentative.

Roche said he never approached Rice during his playing days but found him surprisingly helpful several years ago during what was supposed to be a five-minute television appearance with Roche and Gammons. "The PR people said 'You have five minutes with him, that's all he wants to do and he wants to leave,'" Roche says. "We sat down and started talking baseball. Fifteen minutes later, the PR person is behind me giving the 'cut' sign. [He said] 'Jim, they're shutting us down here, we've got to let you go.' He said 'Nope, let's keep talking. We're talking baseball. Let's go."

Today, Rice talks about baseball as a regular member of the NESN pre- and postgame shows. Rice declined an interview request for this book during the 2005 season, saying he never had any problems with the Boston press.

Rice was not considered a leader among the Sox, but his differences with the press seemed to set the tone for the relationship between writers and players during the 1980s. "One of the first things I noticed when I got there as a reporter in '83 or '84 was how basically adversarial the clubhouse was," Reynolds says. "You walk in there and there's an 'us against them' attitude. [Players wondered] 'What are you in here for?'

The perception was that veterans pulled impressionable young players aside and told them to watch out for the media. Reynolds, who regularly covered the Red Sox' Triple-A team in Pawtucket, said he noticed many previously cooperative homegrown players would turn disagreeable after a short time in the big leagues. Others, such as Ellis Burks, saw their veteran teammates spar with the press and decided to interact with the media as carefully and minimally as possible.

"You had older, established players like Jim Rice and Dwight Evans and Don Baylor, none of whom had any great use for the media," McAdam says. "Those players sort of set the pace for media relations in the clubhouse. And I think it poisoned a number of young players coming up. I remember hearing stories about Mike Greenwell as a rookie in '86 and '87 essentially being told by Rice and Baylor to shut up when reporters approached him and asked him to comment on something.

"For them, part of it was keeping rookies in their place. And part of it also was 'What are you cooperating with them for? They're the enemy.' And that kind of poisoned the atmosphere in there for a few years."

The 1986 team reached the World Series and seemed split between players who didn't mind absorbing the media attention, such as Wade Boggs and Bob Stanley, and those who wanted nothing to do with it. "As good as that team was, geez, I was miserable," says *Globe* columnist Dan Shaughnessy, who covered the team for the newspaper as a beat writer. "They just had a lot of guys that really didn't like us. The trainer was not a nice person. It ran the gamut—Vinny Orlando, the equipment guy. 'Mac' [manager John MacNamara] hated us. Rice had no use for us. [Dwight] Evans had no use for us. [Bill] Buckner had no use for us. [Calvin] Schiraldi had no use for us. We had the whole Oil Can thing. Steve Crawford, Tim Lollar—man, they had some beauties. It was awful.

"And they were really good. They almost won the World Series."

Writers found the Red Sox clubhouse an especially tense place to work during the late '80s. Clemens' breakout season in 1986, when he won the AL Cy Young and Most Valuable Player awards, led to several contract squabbles with management as well as a hot and cold relationship with the press. Dennis "Oil Can" Boyd bolted the Red Sox upon learning he hadn't made the All-Star team in 1986 and, during spring training a year later, made the front and back pages of the newspapers after it was revealed he had an unpaid bill at an adult movie store in Winter Haven.

Boggs' affair with Margo Adams earned the Red Sox plenty of unwanted front and back page headlines in 1988 and landed Boggs and his wife, Debbie, a seat on the "20/20" couch with Barbara Walters the following spring. Joe Morgan, who succeeded McNamara and managed the club through 1991, criticized players via the press while players anonymously badmouthed him.

As a fan and college student in 1989, *Herald* baseball columnist Tony Massarotti observed, the team seemed to be full of sour personalities.

"I remember reading about a game that year where Devon White stole second, third and home off Joe Price," Massarotti says. "And when he came back to the dugout, Joe Morgan said something to the effect of 'Did you give any thought of trying to hold any of those guys on?' Price told him 'Go fuck yourself.'

"And I remember thinking 'This is a bad team.'"

Gorman even found himself breaking up near-fights. He once had to stop pitcher Al Nipper and Fainaru from going after one another a mere 10 minutes before a game. Gorman also recalled interrupting a player who was going after a writer with a baseball bat behind the batting cage.

As for Gorman, his open door policy remained in place throughout his days as general manager and far beyond. When the Red Sox were sold to a group headed by John Henry after the 2001 season, Gorman was asked to stay on as a goodwill ambassador. He regularly ate supper inside the press dining room, where he conversed with reporters new and old and even asked some to critique his second autobiography.

Indeed, explaining in *One Pitch from Glory* why he understood Rice's reluctance to speak to the press yet disagreed with his handling of the situation, Gorman unwittingly summarized a key factor in the demise of his successor, Duquette:

"'To ignore the media, even though there is often great cause to do so, unfortunately courts disaster.'"

Like his press-friendly predecessor, Duquette was a New England native and lifelong fan of the Red Sox, so the hope was he would come into the job already understanding how passionately the New England media covered the Red Sox.

He was born in Dalton, a small town in the Berkshires about two hours west of Boston, and grew up in a close-knit family which loved baseball and the Red Sox. Duquette would tell stories of how he learned to read by poring over box scores, and his family regularly read Peter Gammons' exhaustive news and notes column in the Sunday edition of the *Boston Globe*.

Duquette played baseball and football at nearby Amherst College, and on October 2, 1978, he and several football teammates convinced their coach to push practice back to the evening so they could skip class and attend the one-game playoff for the AL East flag between the Yankees and the Red Sox.

Bucky Dent's rare homer over the Green Monster gave the Yankees a 5–4 win and broke New England's heart. "I remember how quiet it was in Fenway when [Carl Yastrzemski] popped up to end the game," Duquette told the *Globe* in 1996. "And I remember the long drive back. It was very quiet."

In 1991, the Montreal Expos made Duquette the youngest general manager in baseball. Duquette enjoyed success with the Expos, who finished second in the NL East in 1992 and 1993, but he embraced the opportunity to replace Gorman following the 1993 season.

Upon leaving hockey-mad Montreal, Duquette said he was looking forward to joining the Red Sox because of ". . . the knowledge of the fans and the knowledge of the press. People are interested in what you're doing."

Yet less than a month into his tenure, reporters covering the Red Sox already sensed a distance between Duquette and the press that did not exist during Gorman's decade-long tenure. In the February 24, 1994 edition of the *Globe*, Dan Shaughnessy wrote that a reporter could walk into Gorman's office uninvited and expect Gorman to offer him a donut. But a visitor to Duquette's office would be asked if he had an appointment.

Shaughnessy also invoked the Boston College football team in comparing the two executives. Whereas Gorman reminded Shaughnessy of talkative coach Jack Bicknell, Duquette was more like Bicknell's successor, Tom Coughlin, who so disliked dealing with the media that he would put an hourglass on the podium during press conferences.

"Dan Duquette, at times, could barely conceal his contempt for us and our profession," Sean McAdam says. "Whatever he could do to circumvent us, he attempted to do. He once pretty famously said that for fans following the Red Sox, their two best avenues [for] reliable information were the team's website and his pregame radio show, which was a stretch, to put it mildly. That's all sort of managed information and they tell you what they want and nothing more and everybody puts a happy spin on everything."

Gordon Edes, who joined the *Globe* following the 1996 season, said he was "appalled and taken aback at the level of hostility" between the front office and the media. "The first week I was in town was when [Roger] Clemens signed with Toronto," Edes says. "And that afternoon, I came over to Fenway to come in and talk to Duquette. It's raining outside and it's cold. They wouldn't even let me come into the PR office. That was a shock. I had always encountered a different level of cooperation in other places."

Those who covered Duquette believed he may have entered office already suspicions of the press because of the negative treatment received by Gorman, who was often the subject of scathing criticism despite his New England background, the success he enjoyed in Boston, and the open and honest relationship he tried to cultivate with the press.

Why would Duquette go out of his way to accommodate a press that would criticize him regardless of his cooperation? And wasn't it counterproductive to be open with reporters when doing so made it impossible for the general manager to conduct vital business in an under-the-radar manner?

Wrote *Globe* columnist Will McDonough June 28, 1997: "There is no nicer guy than Lou Gorman and he paid the price for being cooperative. Duquette knew about Gorman's fate and made the conscious decision not to get caught in this same trap."

Others wondered if Duquette was difficult to deal with on orders from above. The Sox didn't hire Duquette for his cautiousness with the media, but given how Gorman's gregarious nature sometimes annoyed his superiors, ownership presumably didn't mind a more distant personality occupying the general manager's chair.

"Maybe [Duquette] was just being loyal to his superior who wanted him to act that way," Associated Press reporter Howard Ulman says. "In that sense, loyalty is a good characteristic. I tend to give [Duquette] a benefit of the doubt, even though he wasn't helpful."

The Sox had already operated under a cloak of secrecy for more than six decades prior to Duquette's arrival. Tom Yawkey bought the team in 1933 and owned it until his death in 1976, yet he remained a mystery to most reporters. An initially friendly relationship with the press deteriorated once Yawkey sided with Ted Williams during the slugger's legendary battles with reporters, and Yawkey once told a particularly bothersome scribe he'd love to buy his newspaper just so he could fire him.

Jean Yawkey, who inherited the team, made even fewer public appearances and granted even fewer interviews than her husband. And when it came to dealing with the media, John Harrington—who began working with the Red Sox in 1973, became a trustee in the Jean R. Yawkey Foundation in 1981 and assumed CEO duties following her death in 1992—was similarly silent with most reporters (powerful *Globe* columnists McDonough and Gammons were the exceptions) despite being far more involved in Major League Baseball business than the Yawkeys.

"There were years when I literally saw John Harrington no more than three times in the course of a calendar year," McAdam says. "He was that impossible to talk to. It was deliberate on his part. He did not want to make himself available to the media . . . even though he was a man of enormous power, not just as CEO of the Red Sox, but given where he grew to in the game on a national scale.

"He was, in the early and mid '90s, a central figure in labor negotiations, the realignment issue, wild card playoff expansion, team expansion—you name it, he was on a committee and had a hand in it. Yet we couldn't talk to him about that or his own team. That was frustrating."

Nor could Harrington ignore the negative coverage he received, à la Sullivan. "He resented criticism bitterly," Gorman says. "He did not like the criticism at all and that bothered him a great deal."

However, at least one person who worked in media relations during Duquette's regime believed he was acting on his own. "Dan had his own definite ideas about his accessibility, which was not good," says Dick Bresciani, who was promoted to vice president of public affairs in 1996 after spending the previous 24 seasons in various media relations capacities. "And he ended up in a confrontational situation with most of the media, which was to the detriment of the team, I believe. I don't think his methods were the right methods at all. How he dealt with the media and some of his beliefs about the media, I didn't agree with them.

"Don't believe one bit he was acting on orders from above."

During the 1996 season, beat reporters requested a meeting with Harrington in which they aired their concerns and asked him to step in and alleviate the tensions between the two sides. But Harrington declined to get involved.

"Duquette wasn't returning phone calls and the beat writers were complaining so Harrington agreed to meet with the beat writers and he asked 'What do you guys want?'" says former *Hartford Courant* beat writer David Heuschkel, who was not on the beat at the time but was informed of the meeting by his predecessor. "And they told him 'We want your GM to interact with us, return our calls, take our calls.' And Harrington basically said 'He's the GM, he can do what he wants' and got up and stormed out of the meeting. And from there on in, it was all downhill."

Jim Duquette, the former general manager of the New York Mets and Baltimore Orioles and Dan's cousin, believed Dan's interactions with the Boston press did not reflect his true personality, only his belief that the general manager should not be the face of the team.

"I don't think he's shy, he's obviously bright, he's well-spoken," Jim Duquette says. "One of Dan's philosophies was that the attention and focus should be on the players on the team and not on him as an individual or as a personality. I think there are periods of times where I believe that is the case and there's a lot of truth to that. In the offseason, obviously, the general manager is the spokesman of the ballclub and you're trying to improve the team.

"But once the season starts, at spring training and once, especially, when the season starts, the main focus should be on the manager, the coaches and the players. And I think sometimes he felt he became more of a focus than he should be."

But Duquette's strained relationship with the press would increasingly become a focal point of the Red Sox. Midway through a tumultuous 1996 campaign—the Sox began 3–14, their worst start ever, yet recovered to finish 85–77, just three games behind the wild card-winning Baltimore Orioles—Shaughnessy made a wistful call for Gorman to return and criticized Duquette for running the Red Sox ". . . like the Nixon White House." It was not the first time Shaughnessy compared the Duquette to the notoriously paranoid Nixon nor the last time Duquette's administration would be described in presidential terms.

The *Globe*'s Bob Hohler moved from the White House beat to theRed Sox beat in 2000. Soon after, a running joke developed among the writers that Hohler spent more time in Bill Clinton's office than Duquette's.

"It's true," Hohler says. "I've been in the Oval Office a couple times, but I was never in Dan Duquette's office."

Duquette began fielding more criticism for his handling of personnel and personal matters—particularly in 1997, when Roger Clemens, whom Duquette said the Sox hoped to retain for the "twilight of his career" signed with the Blue Jays as a free agent. Though Duquette did not appear to mean to insult Clemens, the comment fueled the fiery right-hander and Duquette was roundly mocked for his word selection when Clemens went on to win the Cy Young Award in 1997 and 1998—the fourth and fifth of his record seven Cy Youngs.

In June, Sox infielder Wil Cordero was arrested and accused of hitting and threatening to kill his wife. It was eventually revealed that Cordero's first wife also accused him of abuse during their three-year marriage earlier in the decade.

The issue became front- and back-page fodder in Boston for months and the public outcry against Cordero was so drastic the Red Sox sat him out of several games as they tried to figure out if they could place him on the restricted list or release him. Duquette, who signed Cordero with the Expos in 1988 and acquired him for the Sox prior to the 1996 season, was heavily criticized as well for not knowing more about Cordero's past, and many thought the coverage of the Cordero controversy was inflamed by the media's contempt of Duquette.

Wrote Gammons in the June 22, 1997 edition of the *Globe*: "Dan Duquette doesn't believe it, and John Harrington did his best to discount the notion, but the side issue in the extensive coverage of the Wilfredo and Ana Cordero affair was Duquette himself. Fair or unfair, the vitriol and lampooning that accompanied the repugnant and very serious charges were clear indications of the way the media feel about Duquette, who is the personification of what is perceived as the Yawkey Way Pentagon."

Duquette's personnel moves were often mocked, even though his methods of player evaluation were quite similar to those later employed by Theo Epstein. When Mo Vaughn left as a free agent following the 1998 season, Duquette replaced him at first base with Jose Offerman, a second baseman who had never exceeded 10 homers in a season but whose ability to get on base impressed Duquette. At the time, Offerman's career walk-to-strikeout ratio was nearly 1:1.

Five years later, Epstein would be lauded for his ability to pick up overlooked players with impressive on-base percentages. And one of the first people hired by the new Red Sox regime in 2002 was Bill James, whose *Baseball Abstract* books inspired a generation of sabermetricians such as Epstein.

But James was not the first sabermetrician to work for the Sox. That person was Mike Gimbel, a voracious reader of James' work in the 1980s who attempted to fill the gap left by James' sabbatical from book writing in the early 1990s by publishing Mike Gimbel's *Player and Team Rankings*.

Gimbel served as a consultant to Duquette from 1994 through 1997, but he was dubbed "a Rotisserie-inspired stat geek" (in reference to Rotisserie baseball, better known as fantasy baseball) and a "Nutty Professor technocrat" in a *Globe* article. He was also criticized for admitting that he thought the Sox should trade the popular and productive John Valentin.

The Sox finished fourth in 1997 and Gimbel's contract was not renewed. "The media was really after Duquette, and they used me as the whipping boy to get at him," Gimbel told ESPN.com's Rob Neyer.

The relationship between the Sox and the press grew increasingly poisonous during the final three seasons of Duquette's tenure. It proved impossible to find someone who could fill Vaughn's role as a team spokesman as well as difficult to find players who could even tolerate the media.

"You guys fucked me up," Offerman told reporters in declining comment following his release in August 2002.

The player who seemed most likely to replace Vaughn as a go-to guy in the clubhouse ended up having the most contentious relationship of all with the press. Carl Everett, whom the Sox acquired from the Astros following the 1999 season, was candid on any number of topics: During his first spring training with the Sox, he said he believed the moon landing was staged and that dinosaurs did not exist because there was no mention of them in the *Bible*. He was also particularly disdainful of the Yankees, who drafted him in 1990 but traded him to the Florida Marlins two years later.

"When he came in there, he had us eating out of the palm of his hand—everybody, the first day of spring training," Heuschkel says. "Carl was ahead of his time. He was a pioneer: He hated all the Yankees."

Everett's relationship with the press fell apart rapidly, though, in July. He had to be pulled away from Shaughnessy, who wrote July 1 that Everett got into a shouting match with teammate Jeff Frye.

During a game against the Mets July 15, home plate umpire Ron Kulpa told Everett, who always stood at the back edge of the batter's box, to move his feet inside the chalk. The two argued and Kulpa ejected Everett, after which Everett head-butted Kulpa during a nose-to-nose screaming match. Three members of the Sox restrained Everett from further attacking Kulpa.

The next day, Edes—who covered Everett during his two years with the Marlins for the *Sun-Sentinel* in Fort Lauderdale, FL—wrote a column detailing Everett's history of outbursts with the Marlins and Mets. Everett, who was suspended for 10 games, felt he was portrayed unfairly in the aftermath of the clash with Kulpa and generally stopped speaking to reporters.

He saved his most venomous displeasure for the *Globe* and Shaughnessy and Edes in particular. While Shaughnessy called Everett "Jurassic Carl," Everett dubbed Shaughnessy Edes' "curly-haired boyfriend."

Into this maelstrom stepped Hohler, the new *Globe* beat writer. Hohler's first interaction with Everett occurred in Detroit shortly after the All-Star Break, when Hohler saw Everett—who was known for his tardy ways—criticizing clubhouse manager Jack McCormick for not holding the team bus for him at the hotel. It cost Everett $25 to take a cab to the park.

Hohler wrote a story noting Everett's behavior. Once the Red Sox returned to Boston, Everett made it clear he didn't appreciate Hohler's story.

"He goes 'Everybody from the *Globe*, get the fuck away from me,'" Hohler says. "It was the classic rant. Gordon was there [and Everett said] 'You're the same motherfucker you were in Florida and you and your curly-haired boyfriend . . .

"That whole rant was really directed at me. And [he's thinking] 'Oh my God, what did I get myself into? Is this the way it's going to be? If you did something like that in Washington, [writing something about Ted] Kennedy being duplicitous about something, he'd call me up and say 'Geez, what'd you do that for?' It wasn't that kind of hell."

Everett politely declined comment when approached for an interview during the 2005 season, saying he doesn't talk about or to Boston-based reporters. Edes, though, admitted earlier in 2005 that he had spent a lot of time thinking about Everett, how he handled the relationship and what role race may have played in Everett's disputes with the press.

"I believe that there probably are some things I could have done differently, and I regret that I didn't," Edes said during an interview at spring training. "Even though I had a very antagonistic relationship with him, I think I was fair more often than not. But nonetheless, he was a complicated guy and I'd love to have—and maybe it'll happen when he's out of the game—an opportunity to sit down and talk to a guy like that, just hear it all from his side, where it wouldn't be just motherfucker this and motherfucker that and he actually said 'All right, here's where I was coming from.'

"When it's an African-American player like Carl Everett, there's a racial component to it because of the history in Boston that makes things even more charged than they otherwise would be in other markets . . . some of the accusations made about racial bias on the part of Boston media—I cringe at the thought that there may be some truth to that, but I'm not naïve enough to deny it in every instance, because we're a reflection of our culture too."

Duquette's last season as general manager was the most tumultuous. With the franchise in the process of being sold, Duquette loaded up on depth in hopes of making one last run at the World Series, but many of the players he acquired were starters at their previous stops and were not happy with their irregular playing time in Boston. Infielder Mike Lansing was famous for flipping off the lineup card if he wasn't starting as well as yelling at reporters for watching TV in the clubhouse.

Manager Jimy Williams was fired in early August, but players and writers alike quickly soured on interim manager Joe Kerrigan, who was viewed as imperious and uncommunicative. Kerrigan didn't tell anyone he was replacing Derek Lowe as closer until he called for Ugueth Urbina in the ninth inning of his first game as manager.

"Considering his relationship with the press and his relationship with the players I think it was a bad combination from the beginning," catcher Doug Mirabelli says. "When your head guy doesn't have the respect of the players, and all he does is try to force his respect on to the players—it doesn't work like that."

Later, Kerrigan said the tensions within the roster were the fault of eavesdropping reporters. "That year set media relations with the team back to the days of Ted Williams," Ulman says.

"There were expectations, we had a manager fired—just turmoil," former Sox catcher Scott Hatteberg says. "It was just one of those tough years. Tempers just spilled over into the media. Tough situation. Tough year."

It got much worse on September 11, when a spate of terrorist attacks occurred on the east coast. Major League Baseball postponed six days' worth of play as America mourned. After the attacks, it took the Sox two days and various modes of transportation to get home from St. Petersburg. En route, mild-mannered pitcher Tim Wakefield reportedly got into a fight with Urbina.

The Sox and every other team in baseball held workouts the following weekend in preparation for the resumption of the schedule on September 17. But the Sox were the only team in baseball to bar the media from its workouts—which, it was later revealed, featured arguments between Kerrigan and both Carl Everett and Pedro Martinez.

"By the end of the year, I can't remember particular numbers, but I want to say there were four players left speaking to us," former *Herald* beat writer Jeff Horrigan says. "Nasty people. A lot of people who were brought up in Boston through that system were given carte blanche to treat people like dirt. That included rookies—coming up, you saw someone called up, you could watch him change before your eyes, get tainted. It was pretty pathetic."

Heuschkel says former *Hartford Courant* columnist Jack O'Connell, who was the secretary of the Baseball Writers Association of America, told him that the BBWAA received more complaints from the media regarding the Red Sox than the other 29 teams combined.

"No question, in my six years on the beat, it was by far the worst," Heuschkel says. "It was so bad that a guy like Chris Stynes, who was very accommodating all season long, walked in the clubhouse for the final home game of the season and told the press to get the fuck out of the clubhouse. And he was one of the good guys on the team.

"Rod Beck got so worn down by all the dysfunction. He was a guy who loved to chat, probably the best player to go through Boston as far as for our purposes. He finally threw up the white flag with about two weeks to go in the season. He said 'You know what? There's nothing more I can say. Just another day in Red Sox kingdom.' He said anything that happens between now and the end of the season, just say another day in Red Sox kingdom and attribute it to me. Which I would."

Duquette, meanwhile, was fired on February 28, 2002—less than 24 hours after John Henry's ownership group officially took over the Sox. Shortly after the news broke, Duquette invited reporters to his spring home, where he delivered a farewell address and shocked those in attendance by breaking down in tears. His surprising show of emotion did not elicit much sympathy from the press corps he'd battled over the previous eight seasons.

"It all comes down to this," Heuschkel says. "Be nice to the people you meet on the way up. Because they're going to be the same people you meet on the way down."

More than half a decade later, Duquette's legacy remains a contradictory one. He arrived with the reputation as a savvy trader and evaluator of amateur talent, but the Sox farm system was among baseball's worst at the time of his firing and the 2004 club had just one homegrown starter (Trot Nixon). Yet his bargain-basement signing of struggling knuckleballer Tim Wakefield in 1995, his fleecing of the Mariners (for Derek Lowe and Jason Varitek), and the one-sided trade he made with the Expos to acquire Pedro Martinez in 1997 played a huge role in shaping the eventual world champions.

He is also viewed as a brilliant person who nonetheless made things unnecessarily difficult between the Sox and the press. Duquette either could not or would not reveal the warm and funny side so often seen by his friends and family.

"I think Dan made a lot of mistakes in the sense that he would be quite abrasive, or just didn't show maybe what he should have shown," says CBS4 television reporter Dan Roche, who grew friendly with Duquette when he hosted the pre- and postgame shows on WRKO. "What I was told years and years ago, when I started in radio—the best advice I was ever given—was be yourself. And if Dan was himself a lot more, then maybe it wouldn't have been so hard for him at times."

"Dan's a smart guy, did a lot of great things," Gammons says. "He just withdrew too much from the public. And it was too bad, because Dan's a very funny guy."

Duquette has not worked in Major League Baseball since his firing by the Sox. He founded a sports academy in his native western Massachusetts and is also the director of baseball operations for the Israel Baseball League.

He responded almost immediately to an email requesting an interview for this book in January 2005. But he avoided direct questions about the media, instead speaking in generalities about his tenure with the Sox. Duquette mentioned the press only twice in a 398-word message: He complimented Sox fans for understanding the media and expressed gratitude to reporters for naming him Major League Baseball's executive of the year in 1995.

Phone calls and emails to Duquette requesting specific comment about the press went unreturned over the next two years. And so his theories on why his tenure was pockmarked by such a difficult relationship with the press remain unknown, even to his closest confidants.

"I don't know where that philosophy came from, if that was an organizational philosophy, if that was his own personal philosophy—I have never spoken to him about that particularly," Jim Duquette says. "I came of the feeling that was not the right way to do battle—you can't win the battle against the media, they're going to have the last word.

"From a distance, I think there was a wall that was put up between Dan and the press. I'm not sure where it emanated from."

Chapter 4
The Boston Media: The Ultimate Insiders

I read sportswriters all over the country and it saddens me when somebody reaches the broadcast media, because almost without fail—and I will qualify it because there are a few rare exceptions—their print work suffers.—Glenn Stout

As the national baseball writer for *The New York Times*, Jack Curry has covered the Red Sox enough to understand that the Boston writers who regularly chronicle the team sometimes end up as unique celebrities themselves. But it took a cab ride from Fenway to his Boston hotel following an annual baseball game between Boston and New York writers to confirm the stature of media members in the city.

"[The cabbie asks] 'What's up? What were you doing in here today?'" Curry says. "[He said] 'I'm a member of the New York media. We're playing the Boston media.

"He started basically giving me the Red Sox media lineup. 'Was Dan Shaughnessy there? Was Tony Massarotti playing? Where was Steve Buckley playing?' You caught a cab outside Yankee Stadium, maybe they'll know who Mike Lupica is. That's as far as they're going. He listed eight or 10 guys in the Boston media and knew the guys who would be the more athletically inclined.

"These people are really followed closely."

They'd been followed closely long before Peter Gammons and Will McDonough—two long-time *Boston Globe* writers and personal rivals—made the leap to become national television personalities in the 1980s. But their emergence no doubt furthered the perception that Boston writers are the ultimate insiders—and created even more hunger for news, information, and analysis by the sportswriters providing the coverage in Boston.

McDonough and Gammons had already played vital roles in one

journalistic revolution as newcomers to the *Globe* in the 1960s. The presence of Gammons, McDonough, Bob Ryan, and Leigh Montville—rising young talents who arrived at the paper within two years of one another in the mid-to-late 1960s—quickly turned the *Globe* into the most decorated and powerful sports section in the land and one of the true destination papers for sportswriters.

"The *Globe*'s section in the '60s and particularly the '70s, when you had Will McDonough as the football beat writer, Bob Ryan as the basketball beat writer, Peter Gammons as the baseball beat writer, and Ray Fitzgerald and Leigh Montville as your two columnists—that's your Hall of Fame staff right there," *Boston Herald* Red Sox beat writer Sean McAdam says.

The *Globe* vaulted to prominence along with the Red Sox, who snapped a streak of eight straight losing seasons by winning the closest pennant race in history in 1967 before they lost the World Series to the Cardinals in seven games. In the subsequent years, the *Globe*'s young writers—all of whom were either born and bred in New England or, in Ryan's case, schooled in the city—would mirror Boston's youthful passion for the Sox.

"The whole fanaticism that we have today with Internet followings and blogs and sites and everything that we know, right up to and including Jerry Remy's astonishing cult status—it all flows from '67," Ryan said in early 2005. "The *Globe* became a great sports paper in the '70s. All sports in town benefited from our new vigorous approach to sports. But I don't think any of them benefited more than baseball.

"I don't think we can claim any great help for the Red Sox. They've done that for themselves and it all goes back to '67. Now both papers cover the team in a way that was unimaginable [40] years ago. The Red Sox kind of made this necessary, if you will."

The impact of Gammons, Ryan, and McDonough went far beyond their beat work. Eventually, they became known as the most authoritative baseball, basketball, and football columnists in America. Gammons, whose Sunday baseball notes column has been imitated in countless newspapers nationwide, is often dubbed "The Commissioner" and players and executives regularly approach him for information instead of vice versa.

During his final years at the *Globe*, Gammons was known as the only reporter who could speak to reclusive general manager Dan Duquette with any regularity. Today, Gammons remains one of the few writers in regular contact with current Red Sox general manager Theo Epstein, who has grown more withdrawn as his profile increases.

Gammons' recounting of Game Six of the 1975 World Series—the classic contest that was capped by Carlton Fisk waving fair his game-winning home run—is considered one of the greatest game stories ever written. Roger Angell, the longtime *New Yorker* baseball columnist, told Dan Shaughnessy he believes Gammons is ". . . as important to New England baseball as a Yastrzemski or a Fisk."

"Go back and read the *Globe* in 1967," former Sox vice president of public affairs Charles Steinberg says. "It's as though you were there. They tell you the story of the ballgame. The number of writers who tell you the story of last night's game the next day, I think, is few."

McDonough was known as "Mr. Pro Football," a title as legitimate as it was laudatory. At the time of his death in January 2003, he was one of only a handful of reporters to have covered every Super Bowl.

Boston's biggest names were some of McDonough's closest friends. He co-authored a book and co-hosted a radio show with former Patriots coach Bill Parcells. McDonough was one of the last people to speak to Tom Yawkey prior to the longtime Red Sox owner's death from leukemia in 1976. Later in his career, he was the only writer to speak regularly with notoriously press-wary Sox CEO John Harrington.

"Almost everyday you answered the phone and it would be [late NFL commissioner] Pete Rozelle or [Oakland Raiders owner] Al Davis or [broadcasting legend] Howard Cosell," says McDonough's son, broadcaster Sean McDonough, who was the Sox' play-by-play man from 1986 through 2004. "I remember one time when I was a really young boy, I was out in the yard raking leaves with my dad. He said, 'The phone's going to ring, I'm expecting an important call. When you answer, make sure you politely ask who it is and come get me.'

"So the phone rang and he wanted me to answer it because he knew it would be [Baltimore Colts quarterback] Johnny Unitas. It was a big thrill for me to answer the phone and talk to Johnny Unitas."

Their status as insiders was aided by their interest in areas other than sports. McDonough had political and business contracts throughout the city. In 1960, he was the campaign manager for fellow South Boston native William M. Bulger when Bulger ran for state representative. Bulger would later serve as the president of the University of Massachusetts.

Gammons is an avid rock-n-roll fan who released an album in 2006. Three decades before Bill Simmons married pop culture with sports in his "Sports Guy" columns, Gammons was lauded by sports and music fans for filling his work with references to musicians and songs both popular and obscure. Gammons had a natural in with fellow music fan and guitarist Epstein.

The two rivals cultivated sources in a remarkably similar manner that would be difficult to replicate today. McDonough and Gammons traveled with the teams they covered during the bulk of their *Globe* careers, which helped create a less antagonistic atmosphere.

They were among the first to arrive and the last to leave, which made them no different than current writers covering the Sox and the other Boston-area teams. But Gammons readily admits he had more pregame time to spend with players—and fewer writers with whom to compete for this time—than today's writers.

Gammons could get to the park several hours before the first pitch and either talk to players in the locker room or head to the field with them. Such casual interaction is unimaginable today.

"One of the great things for me, and it helped me immensely with baseball in the '70s and early '80s when I traveled with the Red Sox, there weren't as many writers," Gammons says. "I would go out and I would shag [fly balls]. I would go to the clubhouse like noon or 1:00 and I knew players on that basis and developed a lot of good relationships. They knew if they had a complaint, I was right there to listen to it. [Jim] Rice used to hand me a clipping with something underlined. He'd say '[Do you] think this was fair?'"

"I remember throwing batting practice to Wade [Boggs] or backing up [Rick] Burleson and [Jerry] Remy and guys like that. I don't think it clouded my coverage, it just gave me a much better understanding of the game. And you also see how human they are—it's not just 'This guy's a bum.'"

Much of this time was spent talking off the record. Like with McDonough, players knew they could vent to Gammons without worrying that their true thoughts would end up in the paper. The two managed to strike a delicate balance between regularly breaking news and earning the trust of their subjects with patience and restraint.

"I think the people that he covered liked him, respected him, trusted him," Sean McDonough says. "They knew that he wouldn't burn them. For every scoop that he had, every big story that he knew and broke, there were probably 25 others that he never wrote or said anything about."

"I think one of the most important things for anyone in the media is trust," Gammons said. "Not that you cover up something, but if someone says to you 'You can't use this,' you don't use it. There are some people you kind of inherently know if it's off the record."

Of the two, McDonough was the more confrontational writer—both in print and in person, most famously in 1979, when he slugged Patriots cornerback Raymond Clayborn. Clayborn pushed McDonough as well as a television reporter. McDonough responded by punching Clayborn, who fell into a laundry bin. A few hours later, McDonough—with one eye red and almost completely shut—filed a column on the incident.

"I remember it as a pretty big deal," then-Patriots quarterback Steve Grogan says.

The knockout inspired admiration from McDonough's children and his fellow journalists alike. Players had been elbowing writers aside for years. Finally, someone fought back.

"When you're a kid, I think everybody got into conversations with buddies: 'My father can beat up your father,'" Sean McDonough says. "I said to my friends 'Not only can my father beat up your father, he can beat up NFL players. I've got the article to prove it!'

"It did make him a hero. I can remember an enormous number of phone calls and several columnists around the country saying 'Will Mc-Donough's my hero, because all of us have wanted to knock out an athlete at one time or another. And he's the only guy who did it.' I loved it—when you're a kid [and] it makes your father out to be that tough guy."

Gammons and McDonough were also able to deal as easily with everyday folks as well as the most powerful people in sport. Gammons is as likely to strike up a conversation about music with Lenny DiNardo—a pitcher who bounced between the Red Sox and Triple-A Pawtucket from 2004–2006—as he is to talk with a superstar such as David Ortiz or Curt Schilling.

McDonough was famous for passing a story scoop on to a younger reporter trying to make his or her name. He'd often pass along tickets to local sporting events to the blue-collar workers at the *Globe* who otherwise wouldn't be able to attend. Though he earned his fame chronicling the major leagues, he was an ardent supporter of local high school and youth sports.

When the Charlestown High School boys basketball team won the state title yet did not have enough money to purchase commemorative rings, McDonough wrote a column encouraging people to donate money to the school. Not only did the program collect enough to buy rings, they had enough left over to buy uniforms as well. When McDonough died, the team attended his funeral in uniform.

The obituary in the *Globe* mentioned how McDonough's co-workers ". . . marveled at the names of people—figures from sports and politics and just plain folk—who returned his calls, or just called him up to talk, knowing their names would be protected if that was what they wanted."

The ascent of Gammons and McDonough did not come without disapproval from others or a strain in their own relationship. As noted by Howard Bryant in his book *Shut Out*, the two trailblazers were from the opposite side of the tracks and would, Bryant writes, ". . . grow to despise each other."

Gammons was born and raised in suburban Groton and attended the University of North Carolina. He began interning for the *Globe* in 1968, and his first story—on which he shared a byline with fellow intern Bob Ryan—was a front-page story on the reaction of the local sports teams to the assassination of presidential candidate Robert F. Kennedy.

McDonough was from hardscrabble South Boston and attended Northeastern University, where he interned at the *Globe* as part of a co-op between the school and newspaper. Though McDonough began his career covering high school sports, it didn't take him long to race up the ladder, and the 25-year-old McDonough was assigned to the Boston Patriots beat when they began play in the fledgling American Football League in 1960.

Gammons and McDonough were often criticized for getting too close to their subjects. When the Red Sox were for sale at the start of the decade, McDonough championed the cause of his close friend Joe O'Donnell, who was the president of Boston Concessions Group. O'Donnell lost out in the bidding for the Sox and McDonough traded barbs with Larry Lucchino, the president of the new Sox ownership group, until his final column. McDonough also remained a steadfast supporter of William Bulger, whose brother Whitey is one of the FBI's most wanted criminals.

And it often appeared McDonough was speaking on behalf of Red Sox ownership when he criticized Roger Clemens and Mo Vaughn during their contentious negotiations and subsequent free agent departures in the 1990s.

Gammons, a season-ticket holder at Fenway Park, and McDonough were also unable or unwilling to take the Sox to task for their poor record of race relations. Wrote Bryant in *Shut Out*: "Peter Gammons did not seem to own much of a personal or moral passion for the race question, while McDonough simply did not believe that race in Boston was a story at all."

McDonough, a longtime confidant of Yawkey and Harrington—the latter of whom served as the Red Sox CEO from 1992–2001 and was the last link to the Yawkey family—criticized books and articles that painted Yawkey as a racist.

"My father got a lot of criticism and I guess, depending on your definition of how the job should or shouldn't be done, for being too close to some of the people he covered—[some thought it] wasn't appropriate to have close friendships with guys like [Boston Celtics patriarch] Red Auerbach or Bill Parcells if he might be covering those guys," Sean McDonough says. "He didn't care what the rules were. He didn't want anyone to tell him who his friends should or shouldn't be. He knew those friendships were access to stories. His number one job at the *Globe* was to get them inside information, and to me, he did it better than anyone in the history of sportswriting."

The access to and relationships with sources that Gammons and McDonough enjoyed are tough for writers to build and obtain today. Public figures are more cautious than ever in their dealings with the print media. Access is more regimented than it was 20 or 30 years ago and there are more writers and broadcasters battling for the players' attention.

"It wouldn't be the same for me covering today, because you only get like, what, half an hour to an hour in the clubhouse?" Gammons says. "And most of the time, it's like a neutron bomb. [The players are] hiding out and they're out of there. I don't blame the players, either, because there's so much more media now that it's intrusive. You can't go in there and sit around and talk to people."

In addition, there's an ever-widening financial gap between players and the media and writers are under an increasing amount of scrutiny for any perceived biases in their coverage.

"I have relationships with Larry [Lucchino] and Charles [Steinberg] that go back to the '70s in Baltimore," says *Boston Globe* columnist Dan Shaughnessy, who used to cover the Baltimore Orioles for the Baltimore *Sun*. "Somehow it's bad to have relationships now. Back in the day, Will McDonough was a god for that. Now something's wrong with it."

By the 1980s, the influence of the *Globe* and its writers reached far beyond newspapers. Ryan briefly became the lead sports anchor at a local television station. Gammons, who had returned to the *Globe* after a stint as a hockey writer at *Sports Illustrated*, was hired by the all-sports cable network ESPN in 1989. Montville went to *Sports Illustrated*, where he replaced Frank Deford as the magazine's lead columnist.

McDonough worked as a sideline reporter and NFL insider at CBS and NBC. When he accepted his first job with CBS, neither he nor the network's executives figured McDonough's move would pave the way for his fellow writers to move into television.

"He was invited down as a guest on 'The NFL Today,'" Sean McDonough says, referring to CBS' pregame show. "He had written a couple columns on topical subjects in the NFL at that time and the producer of the show and [host] Brent Musberger thought it would be a great idea to have him on to talk about those things. When he was done there, he knew a lot about other things that were going on and they invited him again. That's when the mindset was formed: It might be a good idea to have this guy on as a regular.

"He didn't have any great desire to be a TV personality. It wasn't from an ego standpoint. I think the thing that was appealing to him at that point was money. He had a young family—I was in college and a brother and sister right behind me [were almost ready for] college—and the real benefit to him was the financial reward. Even though he was a highly regarded sportswriter, sportswriters in that era were not being overwhelmed with cash by their employers. It made a big difference to our family when he got that opportunity."

At ESPN, the hiring of Gammons signified the network's growing commitment to programming and reportage centered around the four major pro sports. Gammons arrived at ESPN two years after it began airing NFL games on Sunday nights and one year before the debut of Sunday Night Baseball.

"Basically, I'm doing the same thing—I'm a baseball reporter," Gammons says. "But [executive editor] John Walsh at ESPN saw that information was king and that ESPN had to become an information vehicle."

Gammons and McDonough were not the first Boston-based reporters to make the leap to national television: *Globe* tennis writer Bud Collins worked for CBS as an on-air commentator at the U.S. Open in 1968 and was NBC's top tennis broadcaster for 35 years.

But in a medium where style often won out over substance, the sight of the decidedly ink-stained Gammons and McDonough providing field reports indicated networks realized they had to deliver news. "I proved once and for all you don't have to be pretty to be on television," McDonough once quipped.

"I was always, and still am, proud of the fact he's a pioneer—the first newspaper guy, information man who made the crossover into TV," Sean McDonough says. "When he died, [*Sports Illustrated* writer and HBO Sports commentator] Peter King came up to me at the funeral and said 'When I got hired in TV, your dad was the first person I called. I thanked him because he had done such a great job as a pioneer. None of the rest of us would have the chance to do this.'"

Broadcasters were making the leap from the Boston stage to a national one well before Gammons and McDonough blazed a trail for writers. Dick Stockton, who was the play-by-play man on Sox telecasts from 1975 to 1978, became a mainstay at CBS and Fox for more than a quarter-century and broadcast baseball games for Turner Sports in 2008. Jon Miller, who broadcast Sox games on the radio in the late 1970s, is the voice of the World Series on ESPN Radio and the play-by-play announcer for ESPN's "Sunday Night Baseball."

McDonough, who has also served as CBS' lead play-by-play baseball man and is currently a college basketball and football broadcaster for ESPN, believes Boston writers and broadcasters land national radio and television appearances because of the city's proximity to New York, the media capital of America, and ESPN studios in Bristol, CT, an hour-and-a-half south of Boston.

"We get advantage, in terms of other opportunities," McDonough says. "These executives are more familiar with our work. I was on WSBK [Channel 38], which was at the time a superstation [and] on cable all over Connecticut and New York and Long Island. So executives at ESPN and CBS saw me regularly and I guess I made a positive impression."

More than two decades after Gammons and Will McDonough forayed into television, it has been suggested, only half-jokingly, that it's more difficult to find a Boston writer who doesn't dabble in or move entirely to another medium. And the multi-media success of so many Boston-based writers means fans no longer have to wait for their insider information to land on the doorstep.

Gerry Callahan parlayed his work as a *Herald* columnist into a move to *Sports Illustrated* and regular appearances on the CNN / SI network. In 1997, he moved full-time to powerful all-sports talk radio station WEEI, where he and John Dennis manned the 10–noon shift, and two years later, they moved to the drive-time slot (6–10 a.m.) and eventually toppled Howard Stern in the local ratings. (Callahan also continues to pen a weekly column for the *Herald*.)

The explosion of the Internet created plenty of freelance writing opportunities. Numerous city and suburban writers make regular appearances on WEEI, which has a studio adjacent to Fenway Park. The station is not embraced by everyone: The *Globe* barred its writers from appearing on WEEI after one of its writers, Ron Borges, used a racial slur to describe Japanese pitcher Hideki Irabu in the late 1990s. And writers for smaller daily and periodic publications regularly appear on television and radio programs throughout the state.

For writers, appearances on radio and television serve a dual purpose: They raise one's profile while also often lining the wallet. Beat writing won't make anyone rich, so any additional income from radio or television appearances is appreciated.

"I take on the work because I enjoy it [and] because it's a good income stream for me," says Sean McAdam, who, in addition to his radio appearances, said he appears on television an average of twice a week. "It's a sad fact of the newspaper business that you don't get rich working for a newspaper, and it's hard to pass up the opportunity to make extra money when it's presented to you.

"There's an enormous amount of work out there if you can handle the load."

Globe writers appear regularly on New England Sports Network, which carries most of the Red Sox regular season games and is partially owned by the *Globe*'s parent, The New York Times Company. *Herald* writers appear on talk shows, including the nightly *Mohegan Sun Sports*

Report on Comcast SportsNet. Writers from both papers appear weekly on multiple Red Sox-themed magazine shows.

The reputation of the city's sportswriters is further legitimized when beat writers and columnists make frequent appearances on ESPNews, where they often examine the latest breaking news, as well as the network's library of topical programs such as "Outside the Lines," "The Sports Reporters," and "Around the Horn."

"The print reporters bring credibility to these shows—those are the people who are around the team the most," former *Hartford Courant* Red Sox beat writer David Heuschkel says. "If it wasn't for the print media, those talk shows would just be like circus acts and a bunch of guys yelling at each other."

McAdam said writers from other cities can't believe the amount of appearances he and his fellow Sox writers make on radio and television. "We kind of take a ripping from guys who cover other teams who come into Boston and they're in the cab and they hear one of us on the radio," McAdam says. "And they get to the hotel and one of us is on the TV. Get to the ballpark and someone's doing a satellite interview on the field before the game."

This omnipresence created an unusual culture in which the local writers and columnists became celebrity figures, albeit on a smaller level than that experienced by the city's athletes. Writers had their own informational "wiki" pages at sites such as Sonsofsamhorn.com while female writers and fan clubs and blogs were devoted to female writers and television personalities such as Amalie Benjamin, Tina Cervasio, Heidi Watney, and Hazel Mae.

Ex-players who moved into the media following retirement weren't immune from this unique celebrity, either, as they went from the chronicled to the chroniclers. Jim Rice, whose relationship with the press was famously strained during his playing days, became a regular member of the Sox' pre- and postgame show on NESN. Other popular mainstays on the pre- and postgame show included former Sox such as Dennis Eckersley, Lou Merloni, and David McCarty.

Nobody enjoyed a wave of post-career popularity quite like Jerry

Remy, a Massachusetts native who was a fan favorite as the Sox' starting second baseman from 1978–84. Remy began broadcasting Red Sox games in 1988 and soon provided to the television generation the type of familial comfort radio voices gave fans decades earlier.

Remy's voice—thickly accented and hardened by years of cigarette smoke—was instantly recognizable and often mimicked by viewers. And his camaraderie with partners Sean McDonough and Don Orsillo made for some hilarious interplay during broadcasts.

Remy parlayed his fame in the booth into numerous successful business ventures, including a hot dog stand outside Fenway Park and a sports bar at Logan Airport. He served as a spokesman for Sovereign Bank, was voted the first president of Red Sox Nation, wrote three books, and created "The Remy Report" website, on which he sold "Rem Dawg" apparel as well as replicas of the scorecards he kept at Sox games.

Some writers, meanwhile, were not nearly as comfortable with their celebrity, even if they recognized it as a byproduct of accepting assignments in multiple mediums. During the 2007 season, one beat writer was particularly uncomfortable, from a journalistic point of view, with being nominated for the president of Red Sox Nation because "running" for the position could be construed as having a personal stake in the team's fortunes.

Former *Globe* beat writer Chris Snow says he only went on the radio as a favor to friends or his former classmates at Syracuse University. Jeff Horrigan, the former beat writer for the *Herald*, says he does not make many radio or TV appearances and is glad because it means he's "very rarely" recognized in public.

"It's unbelievable—everywhere we go, every city, people will come up to the press box and say 'Hey, I'm so-and-so, originally from Malden, I just want to shake your hand,'" Horrigan says. "Everywhere. It's a lot less for me—not many people know what I look like. Shaughnessy, Ryan, Massarotti, McAdam, Howard Bryant—it's non-stop. I'm kind of uncomfortable with attention. When I'm walking through a ballpark and I'll hear someone say my name, I have an uneasy feeling about it. It's strange."

But fans were fascinated by the media and the coverage of the Red Sox long before writers were bolstering their profile with television and radio appearances. Readers had, for decades, seen beat writers and columnists as much more than just anonymous bylines atop a story. They were a tangible link to a world that was otherwise hard to visualize.

McAdam says Gammons ". . . kind of brought the rest of baseball to your kitchen table" every Sunday. "His passion for baseball definitely had an effect on people my age growing up," McAdam said. "You're forming your reading habits, and I was a teenager in the '70s and I couldn't wait to read Peter every Sunday. You don't have to get into this business to have that same viewpoint of him in that time."

As teenagers, Theo Epstein, the future general manager of the Red Sox, and his twin brother Paul were thrilled to learn they were attending the same tennis camp as the son of Leigh Montville.

"I don't know what it is about Boston that makes the media so important and part of the story," says journalist David Scott, who authors an online media column called "Scott's Shots." "But I do believe it has something to do with the fact that in the heyday of the *Globe* sports section, those guys like Leigh Montville and Bob Ryan were really the names that you saw day in and day out. And it became, to me anyway as a Boston fan, they became part of the story just because they were telling [it to] you. I couldn't really separate the fact that they were simply writers."

The *Globe* contributed to that confusion: During its ascension in the late 1960s, the newspaper provided an additional layer of insider information by turning the spotlight on the reporters and tapping former copy editor Jack Craig to write the nation's first sports media column.

It was an immediate hit and a sports media column is now a staple of daily big-city newspapers. And nearly 40 years after Craig's debut, Boston fans had grown accustomed to reading as much about reporters as about the Sox, Patriots, Celtics, and Bruins.

"I have never seen anything like [this], where people wonder and are as aware of who we are," Gordon Edes says.

Scott said he considers the media Boston's ". . . fifth major sport," and he treated it as such by regularly breaking news about personnel moves at the local media outlets. He wasn't alone in wanting to cover the media like the Sox, Patriots, Celtics, or Bruins: The traditional media was a perfect topic for the burgeoning alternative media to mine on the Internet—and the perfect time to do so with so much scrutiny being placed upon reporters and media companies.

Appearing on radio or television carries with it some journalistic dilemmas for writers, who must be careful to save their "scoops" for their print employer. And for a beat writer, who is supposed to play things down the middle and report the facts with no opinion, the immediacy of talk radio and live television can lend itself to spontaneity and the risk of one revealing his true feelings on the team or players he or she covers.

"In spring training 2003, I was talking to [ex-Sox infielder] Shea Hillenbrand and he was ripping the team for signing Bill Mueller because Shea made the All-Star team in 2002," Heuschkel says. "The next day, three or four radio stations call me up, want me to come on. Sean McDonough calls me up, [he] goes on [McDonough's radio show at 1510 The Zone]. Being a beat writer, I'm not supposed to incorporate my opinion in any of my copy.

"So McDonough has me on and I preface the whole interview by saying 'Sean, I want to make it clear that I've got to be careful here not to give my opinion about certain questions, because I don't want to compromise my objectivity as a beat writer.' And McDonough says 'Well, I think that's very admirable. We don't have enough of that in Boston. We've got too many beat writers giving their opinions.' I was a little stunned."

The perils of live television were revealed in 2003, when Ryan told Bob Lobel during the "Sports Final" show on WBZ-TV that Joumana Kidd, the wife of New Jersey Nets point guard Jason Kidd, needed to be "smacked" for putting her and her children in a position where they could be booed at a Nets-Celtics playoff game. In 2001, Joumana Kidd had filed domestic violence charges against her husband; they were later dropped. Ryan was suspended from the *Globe* and barred from appearing on television or radio for a month.

"It's such a rabid sports market and people and TV stations have found there's money to be made," McAdam says. "And there's kind of an unholy alliance between the print media to supply that talking head element and the information that's needed to keep this going."

The double- and triple-dipping can also lead to the perception of a divided focus. How, critics wonder, can a writer excel at his full-time job at the newspaper when he's making regular appearances on radio and television? And how much does burning the candle at both ends affect his print work?

"The ubiquity of the media, I think, is the reason why a lot of people despise the media," Heuschkel says. "[Writers are] all over the place, and I think fans resent the fact that some of these people are drawing more than one paycheck. They figure, look, if your job is a newspaper guy, that's what you should do: Be a newspaper guy."

Author Glenn Stout, who is the series editor of the annual *The Best American Sports Writing* anthology, believes the multi-tasking is hastening the decline of the print product.

"The perception is that the money's in radio or TV and I think that's really been horrible for both newspapers in town," Stout says. "I think they've both suffered egregiously. Words on the airwaves or on TV are disposable. You don't last. There's no living archive.

"I read sportswriters all over the country and it saddens me when somebody reaches the broadcast media, because almost without fail—and I will qualify it because there are a few rare exceptions—their print work suffers."

Given how so many Boston reporters have parlayed their writing into well-paying full-time work in television or radio, some players view current writers as opportunists who are trying to make a name for themselves in multiple mediums so they can eventually follow in the footsteps of Gammons, McDonough, and others.

"Half of the guys in this market are trying to make a name for themselves in another format, whether it be radio or TV," Red Sox pitcher

Curt Schilling says. "So they make themselves the story more so than the actual story itself. You've got a ton of guys in this market who are trying to make themselves the story."

New Hampshire resident and lifelong Boston sports fan Bruce Allen didn't mind writers appearing in multiple mediums. "I've got no problem with them making some money on the side," Allen writes in an email. "There is obviously a demand for their opinions and their appearances."

Instead, he founded the BostonSportsMediaWatch.com website in the spring of 2002 because covering the media sounded like a dream job as well as a necessary one. Bill Simmons, whose wildly popular site "Boston Sports Guy" featured daily links to stories about the Boston-area teams, had just moved to ESPN.com. And in addition to providing a one-stop shop for links, Allen also felt there was a need to chronicle what he and many fans felt was the local media's negative and agenda-driven coverage.

In addition to the links, Allen's site features essays and blogs—Scott's column is hot-linked there—as well as a message board where fans dissect the coverage much like they would a game. Several hundred posts per day are not uncommon, providing further proof of the passion which area fans bring to appraising those who cover the sports they love.

"I always thought that guys like [former *Herald* media critic] Jim Baker and [former *Globe* media critic] Bill Griffith had the ideal job," Allen says. "They watch sports on TV, listen to the radio, read the papers, and get paid to give their opinion of it. It was something that intrigued me.

"I had plenty of frustrations at observing misstatements, errors, and flat-out agendas and wanted an outlet to sort of point those things out," Allen says. "Even though I have a technical background, this idea of creating a website was a bit overwhelming. Then I came across this new phenomena—this was way back in 2002, remember—called blogging. It made it super simple to set up and get your own space on the Internet to voice your opinion. I tried it out, not thinking anyone would actually find me, but soon, the visitors were coming from all over."

Allen's site was just the latest and most obvious example that the

Boston fan is closer to a participant in the media than merely a passive observer. The degrees of separation that existed when Gammons brought baseball to the kitchen table no longer existed. In dissecting the media, a fan could feel as if he was as much of an insider as a writer covering the team.

"They'll say they distrust [the media], but they pay more attention to it than they do anywhere else," Stout says. "They love to complain about it, but people are addicted to the dirt. Boston is a place, too, that's always been much more of a 'who you know' town than a 'what you know' town. And I think with the fans sort of participating with the media to the degree that they do, it sort of gives everybody this faux connection."

Allen's site also quickly became a must-read for local media, some of whom found it an invaluable resource and some of whom found it overly critical and believed it wasn't fair to be criticized by someone who was not in journalism—the exact criticism often leveled by players to reporters. (Allen says the feedback from reporters has been "overwhelmingly positive.")

"I don't think there's enough [watchdogs]," Massarotti says. "If you ask the players, the one thing they'll tell you all the time is the media's not accountable. And they're right: When does anybody really pound us for being wrong on something?"

The presence of websites and message boards devoted to covering the coverage in Boston also presented writers with a dynamic most often dealt with by athletes: How to respond to the coverage they received. Ignore it? Pay close attention to it? Preach the former but practice the latter?

Snow said during the 2005 season that he doesn't think writers should check out the media watchdog sites on a daily basis—just as he doesn't think players should read the papers every day to see what people are thinking and writing. Still, just like many athletes didn't always heed the advice they imparted to one another, Boston Sports Media Watch and other media watchdog sites were a frequent topic of conversation in the Fenway Park press box.

"It's not a healthy thing for them to go back and read everything," Snow says. "And where people write about us everyday—I don't think it's healthy to go on there everyday and read if they think I'm doing well or poorly."

It was also viewed by some as a valuable reminder of both the passion for Boston sports as well as the scrutiny that athletes are under on a daily basis. "The more the merrier," former *Herald* columnist Michael Gee says. "It's tremendous to work in a city where some fans read enough to support a site criticizing writers. They care."

"I remember when I did that first book and the criticism started coming on message boards," says WEEI.com writer/editor Rob Bradford, referring to his 2004 book *Chasing Steinbrenner*. "That hit hard. Then you realize this is what the players get all the time. So you can see a different perspective. That's one thing that you have to be ready for, and a lot of guys aren't. A lot of guys are very thin-skinned.

"It's a great thing—a lot of writers before us didn't have this and a lot of writers in the country still don't have this. But there's always a flip side. That's why I try to remind myself if something good is happening, a good story or whatever, and I get a lot of credit for something, there's going to be something around the corner. So I better be ready."

Moments later, Bradford asks if he could continue the interview later in the evening. "I've got to go on TV myself," he says with a laugh. "Juxtapose that however you want."

Chapter 5
"Gehrig38" and the Bridge Between the Mainstream and Alternative Media

"You have the right to remain silent. Anything you say will be misquoted, and then used against you."—T-shirt worn by Curt Schilling

Curt Schilling had been a member of the Red Sox for just 136 days when he made his first Fenway Park start April 11, 2004. Yet he was far closer to an icon than a newcomer thanks to the immediate and lasting bond he'd established with Sox fans before he even officially donned the uniform.

It was a perfect marriage: The computer- and media-savvy player and the fan base which was skeptical of the mainstream press and eager to use the Internet to generate its own in-depth coverage of the Sox.

"I've always been a fan of the game and the game interests me when I'm not at the park," Schilling said in September 2004. "[There's a] pretty significant chunk of fans in this market that are smart, that are intelligent, that do get it, do understand the game. To hear what they have to say is enlightening sometimes."

Late on Thanksgiving night 2003, a poster with the screen name "Gehrig38" logged on to the SonsOfSamHorn.net, the best-known and most popular of the many message boards devoted to in-depth discussion of the Red Sox. Gehrig38 went into a chat room and identified himself as Curt Schilling.

That, figured SonsOfSamHorn.net founder and moderator Eric Christensen, was impossible. Schilling had spent Thanksgiving hosting a pair of important guests at his Arizona house: Red Sox general manager Theo Epstein and his assistant, Jed Hoyer. The Sox and the Diamondbacks had agreed upon a trade that would send Schilling to Boston—contingent on the Sox signing Schilling to a contract extension—and Epstein and Hoyer traveled west for the holiday to try and hammer out a deal with Schilling, a fly ball pitcher who was skeptical about making half his starts at homer-happy Fenway.

With all that going on, Schilling couldn't possibly have time to chat with Red Sox fans. "I thought it was a bunch of horseshit," Christensen says. "I didn't think it was actually Schilling."

But a little detective work by Christensen revealed this was, indeed, Schilling. And soon, the rest of the posters realized "Gehrig38" was anything but a phony as Schilling began sharing intimate details of his contract negotiations with the Sox and asking members about the intricacies of pitching at Fenway Park.

"People [were] in there giving the full court press as to why he shouldn't be concerned about pitching at Fenway Park—why that Green Monster is actually his friend, [how] the right field is one of the deepest in all of the major leagues and how left-handed hitters that maybe he struggled with in previous years wouldn't [do as well against him] at Fenway Park," Christensen says. "And then, in the middle of the night, he'd be like 'Hang on, I've got a phone call.' And everybody [would say] 'who is it?'

"[Schilling would reply] 'It's Theo. Hang on a minute.'"

Those inside the chat room at that moment couldn't believe their good fortune. In an era in which the gap between ballplayer and fan is larger than ever and growing by the day, here was a star pitcher—a potential Hall of Famer—logging on to gauge the pulse of Red Sox Nation.

What transpired was improvisational and instant; an advertisement for all that is rousing about the Internet. In addition to discussing various Sox-related issues, Schilling and the posters argued good-naturedly about which animal would win a fight, a bear or a shark.

"That's one thing we found out in a hurry: That Curt Schilling puts his pants on the same way you and I do—one leg at a time," Christensen says. "He's a normal guy, he's got a great sense of humor. He allowed us to get to know him through fun stuff like that shark-bear debate. He gave his two cents on some of the more irrelevant stuff that goes on in a chat room after-hours. It wasn't long when the celebrity glow kind of wore off and they treated him like everyone else on the site."

Landing a big-name player as a poster was the last thing Christensen had in mind in 2000, when he formed the SonsOfSamHorn.net—or, as it came to be called, the SoSH—out of the ruins of the Dickie Thon Fan Club, a website named after the former National League middle infielder which had message boards devoted to every major league team.

When that site went under in 2000, Christensen contacted the regulars at the Red Sox message board and invited them to join his new site. That it was named after former Sox first baseman/designated hitter Sam Horn—who hit 14 homers in just 158 at-bats as a rookie in 1987 but hit just .148 with two homers and 36 strikeouts in 115 at-bats before he was released in 1989—was symbolic of the uncommonly enthusiastic and intelligent fans who frequented the site.

"It just seemed like everyone was on the same page—the quality of the content [and] the discussion, it was just a bunch of real diehards," Christensen says. "It was unlike any other discussion group I'd been around on the Internet.

"ESPN, AOL, CNN—all those sites had their own Red Sox forums, and the signal-to-noise ratio was just terrible. We had a bunch of like-minded [posters] and passed the link to others of the same ilk."

SoSH was the most popular of the many message boards and websites founded by fans and born out of a passion for the Sox and a desire to dissect the club more than the daily newspapers could. Christensen never intended to expand the message board beyond 100 members, but it didn't take long for the site to grow far more popular than he ever expected. SoSH's membership quadrupled in a matter of days in 2001 after Bill Simmons—a Red Sox fanatic whose popular "Boston Sports Guy" column at AOL Digital City spearheaded the alternative media revolution—included SoSH among his daily links.

Interest in SoSH reached unimaginable levels once Schilling and the Sox agreed to terms on a two-year contract extension—with an option for a third season that would automatically be triggered if the Sox won the World Series in 2004—the day after Thanksgiving. Sox owner John Henry, a frequent visitor to Sons of Sam Horn and even more computer-savvy than his new no. 2 pitcher, believed SoSH played a vital role in convincing Schilling to come aboard, and he expressed his gratitude by logging on to the site and announcing the news a few minutes before the Sox officially issued a press release to the mainstream press.

Such a move was as unprecedented as it was a sign of things to come in 2004—as well as another symbol of the ever-tenuous relationship between Red Sox fans and the media.

"Certainly those few days were eye-opening as a means of illustrating how the business has changed and is changing and constantly evolving," *Boston Herald* beat writer Sean McAdam says. "You had a pitcher negotiating a contract extension and posting periodic updates on an Internet message board and a principal owner who took to providing updates in the same fashion. That's one of those moments where you perhaps don't recognize it as it's happening, but you look back and say 'This is different. This is not the old way of doing things.'

"That's when you realize that things don't stay the same. There are new media, and they can be a force to be reckoned with."

Every major professional sports team has numerous unofficial websites and message boards devoted to it, but none had quite the voracious following of the Sox. "The business of caring is more pronounced here than anywhere," says Boston native and ESPN.com columnist Howard Bryant.

Those who created and visited these sites believed the booming alternative media was as much a byproduct of the Sox' wide-spread popularity as it was of the well-educated nature of New Englanders.

New England has been dubbed the "intellectual capital" of America. The six-state region is home to some of the oldest and most respected colleges in America, including four Ivy League schools. Massachusetts was the epicenter of New England education, with exclusive schools dotting the landscape from North Adams to Boston, the latter of which is considered one of the best college cities in America.

Out-of-staters who matriculated in Massachusetts were quickly exposed to the romanticism of the Red Sox: the lyrical bandbox that is

Fenway Park, the team's star-crossed history and the passion with which fans followed the franchise.

"I always found it an interesting juxtaposition," says former Mets and Orioles general manager Jim Duquette, a native of western Massachusetts and the cousin of former Red Sox general manager Dan Duquette. "Because you do have a highly intelligent area with all of these colleges. Why people would respond so emotionally at times and so negatively at times over—I'm just trying to put it in perspective—just a baseball game? I always found that interesting. I don't know if it's explainable."

For those who grew up in less baseball-intensive environments, the pull of the Red Sox was hard to resist. "A lot of people come from all over to go to school here," Christensen says. "And I think once you've had your first taste of Boston baseball—your first experience at Fenway Park or first experience around the fans who live and die with the team—it's hard not to get drawn in."

"If you've never been a real diehard fan of another team or maybe somebody who is just a casual baseball fan—they come and go to school someplace in New England and they take it back home with them," says Steve Silva, the founder of the popular weblog "Boston Dirt Dogs." "So I think that's helped to make it more of a global thing."

In addition, no sport transcends academia quite like baseball. The literary likes of George Will, Doris Kearns Goodwin, and A. Bartlett Giamatti—the latter two of whom were particularly partial to the Red Sox—were all inspired to wax poetic on the sport. The sabermetric revolution was about finding new and more revealing statistics about baseball. Even the most basic of baseball acts—throwing a pitch and taking a swing—were scrutinized by physicists.

And an inquisitive, scholarly fan base also believed it could scrutinize the Sox better than the beat writers assigned to the team.

Boston fans had long figured they were better-informed than fans in other cities. In his book *Shut Out*, Bryant wrote that the *Boston Globe*, in emerging in the late 1960s as one of the nation's best sports sections on the shoulders of talented young writers such as Peter Gammons, Leigh Montville, and Bob Ryan, also grew to mirror Boston's reputation as ". . . a place known for its insider behavior." Led by Gammons, the Sunday paper was filled with page-long notebooks that contained the latest news and rumors about each of the four major sports.

New Englanders—and even former Red Sox players—marveled at how much better and comprehensive the coverage was in Boston than elsewhere. "We definitely have higher standards here," says New Hampshire native and Boston Sports Media Watch founder Bruce Allen. "I'm always amazed when I travel somewhere else and pick up the sports section."

"We were spoiled," says Paul Epstein, Theo Epstein's twin brother. "We didn't realize the *Globe* was the best sports section in the country until you get old enough to travel to different cities and you pick up the newspapers in those cities and are horrified by what you see.

"We didn't know what else was out there. We thought it was kind of normal. We thought that was the way every city looked."

"If you've ever been anywhere else, you miss the Sunday papers— at least I did," says former Sox player and coach Tommy Harper, who played or coached for nine other clubs. "The Sunday papers weren't the same as the *Boston Globe* and the *Herald*—not anywhere I've ever been."

For the modern Red Sox fan, coverage of his or her favorite team is as available as oxygen. Prior to home games, the *Globe* and *Herald* each sell their newspaper at reduced rates on the streets surrounding Fenway Park. The *Metro* newspaper, which is published by the *Globe*, is available for free in vending boxes.

Fans can choose from three game programs, including *GameDay*, a free tabloid published under the *Metro* moniker and in conjunction with the Red Sox. The Sox also sell their official game program, *Boston Red Sox Magazine*, inside the park while vendors outside the park hawk *Boston Baseball*, an upstart magazine unaffiliated with the Sox that costs $2—three dollars less than the Sox' official program.

Upon taking their seats, fans gaze to the field and see dozens of reporters and cameramen milling about. NESN's pregame show— which always features a *Boston Globe* reporter—airs live from in front of the Red Sox dugout. After the game, an hour-long postgame show airs on NESN followed by multiple rebroadcasts (usually condensed into two hours) that bridge the gap until the next game. NESN also airs classic Red Sox games as well as various Sox-themed shows—including "Sox Appeal," in which Sox fans go on blind dates at Fenway.

Fans realized there probably wouldn't be message board discussion of the Sox and the media covering the team without the access garnered by newspaper writers and the resultant coverage. "I think the Boston sports media is absolutely critical to following the Red Sox," Christensen says. "We can talk all day about an issue, but you really don't get a seed for a discussion unless you've got something that crops up in the news. A rumor could surface that the Sox may be looking for a better defensive shortstop or a defensive upgrade at first base, and now all of a sudden, we've got some food for thought that we can really ignite a discussion on."

And to some degree, the fans whose passion fuels the intense coverage could grow as burned out on the ubiquitous media as the players. "There is obviously a demand for their opinions and their appearances," Allen says. "It only bothers me when I might hear the same person say the exact same thing on four outlets in one day. They write in the paper, then have a stint on WEEI that same day, then might appear on NESN or New England Sports Tonight, and then finally on CN8 or NECN to round out the day.

"It's probably not an issue for those who don't witness all four appearances, but when you do catch it, it's a bit overboard and you're not learning anything new."

Yet even though a case could be made that the Red Sox were the most chronicled team in baseball by the turn of the 21st century, there was a large segment of Sox fans who were not satisfied, for a variety of reasons, with the too-much-is-never-enough coverage of their favorite club.

Following the 2004 championship season, Montville authored a book about Red Sox fans titled *Why Not Us?* That same three-word query also applied to the attitude of the fans regarding the news-gathering process: Why not us? Why can't we emerge as a viable media force?

The days of the newspaper providing the most immediate coverage of a game were long gone. Decades before television was invented, Boston fans counted on newspapers to provide the closest thing to live game coverage.

When the Red Sox traveled to New York to take on the Giants in the 1912 World Series, crowds gathered along newspaper row on Washington Street and gazed upwards, watching and listening to the recreated game. A man with a megaphone was informed of each at-bat's result via telegraph and announced it to the enraptured crowd. As the action unfolded, wooden figures constructed to look like baseball players were moved along a billboard to show the progress of the runners on the bases.

Red Sox games began airing on the radio in 1927 and on television in 1948. Even in the infancy of these mediums, fans still relied on the newspaper to break the game down and bring the players to life.

Newspapers are still able to provide far more space to a subject than television (though Boston's broadcast journalists were as dogged and thorough in their reporting as their print counterparts). But by the 21st century, the Internet allowed fans to chronicle the game as it evolved without waiting several hours for game stories to be posted online—or even longer for the newspaper to land on their doorsteps. Even the most thorough recap could not capture every ebb and flow of a nine-inning game. And with no deadlines, no word counts and no editors, there was no limit to how extensively a game could be parsed on a message board.

In the days before the Internet, insider status was reserved for those who covered the Sox on a regular basis. But now, anyone with a high-speed modem could circumvent the traditional media and feel as if he, too, could become an insider.

"Everyone thinks they're an expert, and when you start, by virtue of new media avenues and vehicles, start having some access to information, I think that coupled with the passion and the interest level combines for that sort of 'Hey, I could do this too. I'm on the inside now,'" Sean McAdam says.

Some writers believed the "anything-the-press-can-do-we-can-do-better" attitude among the new media was a natural byproduct of base-ball's universality. Not everyone who watched football had run a cross-ing pattern or spent hours studying an intricate playbook.

But almost everyone who watched baseball had, at one time or another, played the game, whether it was in a competitive venue such as Little League or American Legion or in a setting as casual as a back-yard Wiffle ball game. As a result, fans could watch baseball and assume, based on their own experiences, they could play or manage the game as well or better than those doing the actual playing and managing. Why else, Terry Francona wondered during a west coast trip in the summer of 2004, was the manager of the Red Sox the most second-guessed per-son in New England?

So if fans had played the games their entire lives, couldn't they cover and analyze it better than the area beat writers? Such a phenomenon was not limited to Boston.

"I remember one time in Cincinnati, this guy telling me that he knows more about the Reds than me," says Jeff Horrigan, the former Sox beat writer for the *Boston Herald* and a former Reds beat writer for the *Cincinnati Post*. "And I said 'How do you know more about the Reds than me?' He said 'Because I watch every game and I read everything that's written about them.'"

Replied Horrigan: "Who writes that stuff?"

In addition, many of those who created and visited the alternative Red Sox sites were inspired not only by natural curiosity and confidence but also by the belief the area's writers did not reflect the interests of Sox fans.

"The Massachusetts and Boston areas have the highest percentage of college-educated graduates in the country," Horrigan says. "And every-one, with good reason, feels very self-assured about themselves and their intelligence. And people around here don't like being told what to do and what to feel."

Most of the Red Sox beat writers believed the team needed to be cov-ered by a New Englander, because someone born outside the region couldn't quite understand what the Sox meant to New England, yet Sox fans were dissatisfied with much of the local media and convinced it was obsessed more with negativity and turning the Sox into a daily soap opera than straight reportage.

The Sox' off-field matters had always served as fodder for the writers covering the team. Even by the Sox' standards, though, the first few years of the 21st century were remarkably theatrical. Indeed, between the media boycotts staged by Manny Ramirez, Pedro Martinez, and Nomar Garciaparra, the perception Martinez was operating by his own rules, the increasingly bitter battle between Sox management and the press, Carl Everett's public meltdowns in 2000 and 2001, and Ramirez' flighty acts, the Sox made as much news off the field as on it.

"I think things that really shouldn't be stories become stories," Christensen says. "Manny Ramirez, he's out with the flu [during a series against the Yankees in 2003] and Enrique Wilson happens to be staying in the hotel Manny lives in. Manny says hello to Enrique, who is an old friend of his from Cleveland, and all of a sudden there's a lynch mob burning stakes outside. In so many other cities where maybe the media exposure isn't so great, that's not even newsworthy."

Many fans felt as if a cynical press was preparing them for an inevitable October failure and as if the media was trying to create a sense of inferiority by constantly reminding fans of the Sox' historic struggles against the Yankees. "I think the media can be accused, in some regard, of just being incredibly pessimistic whenever the opportunity presents itself," Christensen says.

During the 2003 season, Trish Saintelus, the moderator of the message board at "The Remy Report" website, organized a petition in which site members, disgusted with what they perceived as overwhelmingly negative press coverage, expressed support for the Sox and said the media's perception of the team did not match their own. Saintelus gave the petition to Remy, who gave it to the players.

"Jerry said they hung it in their clubhouse and a couple of players, from time to time, told Jerry how much they appreciated it," Saintelus says. "They say the players don't read the papers, but the players read the papers, and what a guy like [*Globe* columnist Dan] Shaughnessy writes is just food for fodder on WEEI later in the day. And the negativity just abounds. That's the most frustrating thing that any one of us feels about the media.

"As a fan, I've always felt frustrated that the media [claims] to represent how the fans feel, which is very far from the truth. And the message boards and the Internet have given us a voice."

Shaughnessy, who had long been a polarizing figure in the city thanks to his opinionated takes, and tendency to volley with Boston's sporting icons, was the top target for fans in the days before the Internet as well. In his autobiography *One Pitch From Glory*, former Red Sox general manager Lou Gorman recalls appearing at seminar at the Boston Public Library in 1992 and feeling as if he was under fire from the audience until someone stood up and said he didn't read the *Globe* because it was too negative and Shaughnessy—who was appearing on the podium with Gorman as well as Peter Gammons—was the main offender.

The blog Dan Shaughnessy Watch regularly critiqued his columns and had at its slogan "We read him so you don't have to" and a Boston *Phoenix* feature about Shaughnessy in 2007 was titled "The Most Hated Man in Boston." One woman was quoted in the *Phoenix*—a trained emergency medical technician—said she wasn't sure if she would administer CPR to Shaughnessy if he collapsed in front of her.

And in the years before the Red Sox finally won the World Series, fans believed Shaughnessy—author of *The Curse of The Bambino*—profited from the Sox' championship drought and wanted it to continue because it was good for business. Shaughnessy appeared in an HBO documentary of the same name and, at the premiere in a Boston sports bar, sat next to a woman who booed every time he appeared on screen.

"It was only like the last three or four years when people started to blame me, like I invented Red Sox history," Shaughnessy says. "And this whole idea that he's just perpetuating this to sell books—anybody that knows anything about books knows I wasn't making any money off the books in the last 10 years. It was dribs and drabs, but nothing where [I'd urge my editor] 'Let's put it in the paper to sell another million books.' Please."

Those who covered the Sox believe the most rabid members of the anti-media contingent were, like many players, sensitive to anything other than overwhelmingly positive coverage and too quick to believe there was a bias or ulterior motive behind anything that didn't paint the Sox in an appealing light.

"It seems to me sometimes there's a real knee-jerk component to some of the media bashing that goes on," says Gordon Edes of Yahoo! Sports. "It's almost like they're very protective of the players. There's a sense of we're out there trying to tear the team down. I certainly haven't felt that's my function, to tear the team down."

Says McAdam: "There seems to be this sense that we're too negative, that we dwell on what's going wrong instead of celebrating what's going right. And I've said to [the critics that] it's not our job to cheerlead or to root or have a vested interest in how they do one way or the other. Our job is to report the news that is going on around the team and be the eyes and ears of the fans that don't have the access that we do."

Informed of the comments made by Edes and McAdam, Allen says his ". . . first instinct is to say that they're simply being protective of their own livelihood with that sort of comment, but I do think there is a kernel of truth to the notion.

"However, fans probably wouldn't feel the need to be protective of their teams if they didn't perceive that the media, in many cases, seemed to be out to get them. It's lessened quite a bit now that there have been so many championships this decade."

And one of the players most responsible for the Red Sox' first championship in 86 years would provide fans with the type of access once thought unimaginable.

Curt Schilling was not the first Red Sox superstar to attempt to communicate directly with fans and echo their skepticism with the mainstream media covering the club. Ted Williams penned columns in the *Globe* and *The Saturday Evening Post* at times throughout his career. In writing a feature about Williams' final game in 1960, *Sport*'s Ed Linn overheard Williams say the Sox ". . . should let everybody in" the club-house if they're going to give access to the writers.

The letters to the editor at the local newspapers were almost entirely critical of the press and in support of Williams, who realized the fans were forever on his side when he received a standing ovation for mimicking his famous spit towards the press box in 1956.

But Schilling's off-field interests made him more qualified than anyone to become the first Sox player to embrace alternative media as a viable form of communication. An avid gamer his entire life—he regularly played Dungeons and Dragons in high school—Schilling enthusiastically jumped on the information superhighway in the 1990s, when he participated in on-line computer games with his former Phillies teammate Doug Glanville.

And following the 2006 season, Schilling began to prepare for his post-playing career by founding a gaming company, 38 Studios. According to its website, 38 Studios aimed to become ". . . the undisputed leader in online entertainment."

Schilling's hobbies symbolized the independence that separated him from most of his peers, particularly when it came to his handling of the press. Most teammates had a hard time putting a writer's name to a face and had no interest in developing a relationship beyond the locker room, but Schilling knew for whom beat reporters and broadcasters worked and counted as one of his best friends ESPN.com columnist Jayson Stark, who covered Schilling as a columnist for the *Philadelphia Inquirer*.

Schilling was not shy about expressing his opinion about anything, whether it be about himself, the team, baseball's burgeoning steroid problem, or even the world at large. Shortly after he was acquired by the Sox, he wrote on Sons of Sam Horn that reporters ". . . had no idea what the state of our clubhouse is, or isn't." A year later, he made campaign appearances on behalf of President Bush in the days leading up to the election, and in 2008 actively stumped in New Hampshire for Republican presidential candidate John McCain.

And whereas most players said they didn't read the newspapers or listened to the radio—"Most of them are lying," Schilling says—Schilling not only absorbed as much coverage as he could but challenged writers and hosts whose stories he believed were inaccurate or unfair. During his first summer with the Diamondbacks in 2000, Schilling became embroiled in a feud with *Arizona Republic* columnist Pedro Gomez, whom Schilling believed was criticizing manager Buck Showalter in an attempt to raise his own profile. Gomez eventually landed at ESPN and he and Schilling remain disdainful of one another.

"I didn't realize just how much Schilling disliked Pedro until driving back home from a state sports editors meeting one day," former *Arizona Daily Sun* editor Chris Lang said. "Schilling called into one of the local sports talk radio shows and just proceeded to rip Gomez, questioning his objectivity and credibility."

Schilling and Dan Shaughnessy sparred throughout Schilling's tenure, beginning in April 2004 over Shaughnessy's column criticizing Pedro Martinez for leaving Camden Yards before the season opener was over. In September 2004, Schilling called into WEEI and argued with host Butch Stearns, who said Schilling didn't get along with Martinez because they rarely interacted on the field.

"It's a stupid idiotic comment to make," Schilling said on the air. "We get along awesome. Because you don't see us playing grab-ass on the field doesn't mean a thing."

Said Schilling in October 2004: "Outside of the small handful of people in my life I'm going to meet face-to-face [and] shake hands with, the rest of the world sees me through a picture frame that you guys write, paint, and talk about. When I hear people lying about things—like I'd heard Butch Stearns lying about Pedro and I's relationship—it bothers me and you want fans to understand that you guys aren't the experts."

Such outspokenness could annoy those in his organization. Ed Wade, the Phillies general manager for the final two years of Schilling's tenure in Philadelphia, referred to Schilling as ". . . a horse every fifth day and a horse's ass the other four." And Schilling was nicknamed "Red Light" while in Arizona for his comfort in front of the camera and his perceived love of publicity.

Schilling was also unpredictable in terms of both what he would say and how he would respond when approached by reporters. Schilling could be expansive and thoughtful and eschewed the easy clichés in favor of in-depth and honest analysis about the craft of pitching—as he did in August 2006, when, three months before his 40th birthday, he discussed the challenges of getting older and no longer being the dominant workhorse he'd been even two years earlier.

"I feel like from a command standpoint, I can still dot a gnat's ass, you know?" Schilling said. "I feel like I'm consistent. I feel like [Terry Francona] can count on me giving a minimum six or seven innings every time he gives me the ball. And I've never looked at that as being a great attribute. But you take what you can get when things are not going the way you want them to go."

Yet Schilling could also be dismissive and elusive. While he unfailingly met with the media after each start, trying to set up an interview with him between starts—when he followed a meticulously planned workout schedule—was a challenge for all beat writers.

Before the Sox played the Phillies at Fenway Park June 25, 2004, he seemed to enjoy taunting the Philadelphia-area writers who gathered near his locker. Schilling would walk near the group, appear as if he was going to stop at the locker and then, at the last second, veer off and disappear into a back room without making eye contact as Derek Lowe cackled.

Schilling felt as if he'd been misrepresented several times in the past by the media and often wore a T-shirt which read "You have the right to remain silent. Anything you say will be misquoted, and then used against you."

"For the most part, I've never been misquoted," Schilling says. "I've been misinterpreted a million times. And that's the problem with the media: A lot of things don't translate well to print. A lot of guys in the industry don't care to translate or get intent across because it doesn't make as good a story."

When speaking to print media, Schilling was worried writers would shape his quotes to fit the stories they'd already written. And when he spoke to broadcast media, he was certain anything he said would be condensed into a 30-second sound bite for the late local news.

However, calling into radio talk shows—and posting on message boards—allowed Schilling to deliver his message in an unfiltered manner. After all, "Curt from the car phone" was not going to be cut off by the hosts, who would let Schilling speak as long as he wanted because a star player calling in made for great radio.

And Boston-area writers figured Schilling knew that "Gehrig38" would face a far different audience and line of questions online than he would at his locker. To them, his foray into message boards and blogs—in addition to posting at Sons of Sam Horn, Schilling participated in regular Q&As with the "Boston Dirt Dogs" blog throughout the 2004 season, including one during the World Series—was a self-serving way of controlling the message and currying favor with fans already suspicious of the media.

"Let's face it: When Curt Schilling posts on SoSH, he's not getting cross-examined," author Glenn Stout says. "He gives his statement—boom. Total control. I think that's why that took place. He's no dummy."

"He clearly rode into town and just tagged me as the guy—the one he would use to fortify his agenda," Shaughnessy says. "It's tantamount to standing up at the Democratic national convention and saying 'George Bush sucks.' He knows he has an audience that's going to go 'Yeah, he does.'"

Schilling said in October 2004 that message board posters warned him of certain reporters and surprised him with the venom they had for the media in Boston—"I think there's more dislike for members of the media than any place I've ever been"—but that he didn't enter Boston with preconceived notions of any writer or columnist.

"I never really had a discussion or talks with them about it," Schilling says. "They said 'Hey, watch out for so-and-so, these guys are bad people.' As a player, I'm going to find that out on my own anyway. You go in with your eyes open."

Schilling and the alternative media spent several months opening a lot of eyes and generating plenty of discussion in the traditional media—as opposed to vice versa. "Boston Dirt Dogs" was the first outlet to report that shortstop Nomar Garciaparra had suffered a serious Achilles injury in March 2004. Garciaparra, initially expected to miss only a few days, didn't make his regular season debut until June 9.

Schilling regularly posted in a members-only area of SoSH after his starts and shared with the message board information he hadn't provided the traditional media, including his take on the coverage of the purpose pitch he seemed to throw at Kevin Millar during a spring training intrasquad game—before stepping into the batter's box, Millar reminded Schilling that he was 1-for-9 with a home run against Schilling; the hurler responded by throwing his first pitch behind Millar's head—as well as news about the ankle injury suffered in April that would bother him all season.

Some of the posters perceived a critical tone in comments made by WEEI hosts as they discussed the news that was broken at SoSH—perhaps, they thought, betraying a bit of envy or pique. After Schilling's acquisition was announced on the message board, *Herald* columnist and WEEI regular Tony Massarotti said players who wanted to communicate via message boards could promote their charities there as well. And in discussing the Millar purpose pitch, Glenn Ordway said ". . . the nerds are like reeling us in right now."

The hosts said it was all in good fun while those on the message boards believed it was another example of old media's condescending attitude for the new media. "They were just frustrated that they spend hours trying to seek out these athletes and they're snubbed by them and they coming running to a place like us to, quote unquote, tell the truth," says Trish Saintelus, who, along with Schilling, called in to WEEI shortly after Schilling's arrival to defend the message boards and those that frequent them. "Their egos were definitely knocked down a peg, which I think they should [have been]."

Beat writers eventually aired their concerns with Schilling, who did not offer any exclusives to the online message boards the rest of the season. However, Schilling indicated in an interview with the *Herald's*

Karen Guregian in June he decided to cut down on his message board activity because he was annoyed by the coverage his private posts were receiving in the mainstream press.

Schilling says he didn't interact with fans on message board in order to shut out the mainstream press or to annoy beat writers. He did believe some in the traditional media were threatened by the emergence of the alternative media and that it forced some writers to work harder to uncover scoops.

"I think there are some guys who don't like [the alternative media]," Schilling says. "I think it's jealousy, in a sense. There are a lot of guys who try and write their stories in the past, and online media is making guys actually have to walk the beat, so to speak, to get their stories, get their scoops."

Schilling's participation in online media was ground-breaking, but it was not the beginning of a revolution in how players communicated with the masses. "I got all excited—I thought Curt posting on SoSH and "The Remy Report" would start this flood of players who were just clamoring to talk to the fans via the computer," Saintelus says.

She laughs. "But what I found was most of them are computer illiterate and they don't have the time to do this. I think Curt is a truly a rare breed . . . I don't think that there's going to be a huge influx of players running to Internet sites at all."

The reluctance of other big leaguers to participate in online media hasn't deterred the enthusiasm of those running the sites nor the creation of new ones. Indeed, with new media sites and personalities emerging into the mainstream, fans are more energized than ever to create the next big thing.

By 2004, the "business of caring" that Howard Bryant discussed was profitable—particularly for Bill Simmons, who re-invented the wheel and disproved the usual rules about access and objectivity by finding a worshipful national audience for the decidedly Boston-centric columns he penned from his living room.

A generation earlier, perhaps Simmons would have followed in the footsteps of a Shaughnessy (who attended Holy Cross, like Simmons) or a Peter Gammons (who attended a private high school, like Simmons) at the *Globe*. But Simmons, who began working at the *Herald* as a clerk after he got his graduate degree at Boston University, felt it was nearly impossible to get an opportunity as a columnist and was disillusioned by the interoffice politics.

Simmons did not reply to numerous interview requests sent to multiple email addresses, but he told online media columnist David Scott in November 2005 that he would have loved to have taken the traditional path to a writing career. "So when someone like Shaughnessy is bitching behind the scenes that I (or any other internet columnist) 'never go in the clubhouse,' well, you know what?" Simmons wrote in the email exchange with Scott. "I would have loved to have gotten a column that way. But all the dead weight was blocking my way.

"Clearly, I was good enough to do this for a living, but there was no way I was ever getting a chance doing it conventionally. That's what pisses me off. I never even had a real chance."

After leaving the *Herald*, Simmons began penning a column called "Boston Sports Guy" for AOL Digital City. He remained there for five years, building up a loyal cult following with pieces that merged pop culture with sports and were original, often hilarious, and completely unlike anything in a newspaper.

In the summer of 2001, he went to ESPN.com, where he was re-dubbed the "Sports Guy" and became the lead "Page 2" columnist. He quickly became the site's most popular columnist and established a lasting connection with the hard-to-satisfy young male adult demographic.

Simmons eventually parlayed his success at ESPN.com into a gig as a writer for comedian Jimmy Kimmel's late-night talk show, though he left the show and returned to ESPN.com and *ESPN The Magazine* (for whom he penned a biweekly column) full-time in 2004. And his book about the long-awaited Red Sox world championship, *Now I Can Die In Peace*, became a best-seller in 2005.

"I think there's a lot of Simmons disciples out there that have a web connection and a word processor that think they can try and do something similar," Scott says. "Let's face it: Bill has tremendous, tremendous talent. He would be one of the best columnists in the nation whether he was doing it from the living room, which he does, or if he was going out to the game and covering it."

Simmons wasn't the only alternative media icon to eventually find himself squarely in the mainstream. On the afternoon of Game Seven of the AL Championship Series, a thread was started on Sons of Sam Horn called "Win It For . . ." in which posters implored the Sox to complete the greatest comeback in baseball history by beating the Yankees in honor of loved ones, alive and deceased, who were passionate for the Sox. Those posts were collected in a book, also titled *Win It For . . .* , whose foreword was authored by Schilling.

In June 2004, the "Boston Dirt Dogs" blog was bought by The New York Times Company, which owns the *Globe*. The "Boston Dirt Dogs" page was given a prominent place on the boston.com website and BDD creator Steve Silva was hired as a sports producer for boston.com.

The irony didn't escape those in the traditional media: Alternative sites which once reveled in their outsider status were now part of old media companies.

"It doesn't get much more mainstream than being an off-shoot of *The New York Times*," McAdam says.

The arrangement between the *Globe* and BDD—a site which often produces parody headlines and news—led to some awkward moments when Silva appeared on conference calls for beat reporters, penned report card-type pieces for Boston.com and was credited with a byline on the *Globe*'s Red Sox blog, "Extra Bases," for pieces that were largely culled from Sox press releases or wire reports.

During spring training in 2005, BDD was embroiled in controversy when it ran what proved to be a false story from a fan in Chicago who said she'd heard Nomar Garciaparra, the former Sox shortstop who had a bitter falling out with management before he was traded to the Cubs July 31, 2004, say he didn't care if the Sox gave him a 2004 World Series ring.

"What do you do when a legit, quote unquote, news organization like us puts bloggers on the same website?" then-*Globe* beat writer Gordon Edes asked in March 2005. "I don't know. For me, it's confusing."

Edes believed "Boston Dirt Dogs" contributed to an awkward introduction between him and new Sox pitcher David Wells in February
2005. Wells told Edes he had no interest in speaking to him because he'd
seen on BDD a photo taken immediately after Wells was beaten up in a
fight at a Manhattan diner in 2002. On Wells' forehead was stitched no.
3, his uniform number with the Sox.

"Wells kept insisting it was on the *Boston Globe* [and saying] how
many *Boston Globes* are out there," Edes says.

While there was only one *Boston Globe*, there was no shortage of fan-
generated media emerging to dot a media landscape in which the newspaper's role seems to diminish by the day. Boston.com acquired
"Touching All The Bases," a popular blog by *Globe* copy editor and former *Concord Monitor* columnist Chad Finn, in the spring of 2008 and
prominently placed it on the website.

The alternative media still lacked beat reporter-type access, but its
access was improving, albeit incrementally. Sox season ticket holder
David Laurila—whose interviews with Sox players, prospects, and executives as well as fans and media members appeared on the message
board RedSoxNation.net—had his Q&As published in a book called
Interviews from Red Sox Nation. Laurila later became a regular contributor to the popular website BaseballProspectus.com.

SoxProspects.com and the Sons of Sam Horn each conducted Q&As
with farmhands. SoSH collaborated with Maple Street Press to publish
Red Sox Annual, a preseason guide to the entire organization, in 2007 and
2008.

"There's a feeling in Boston that people want to elevate themselves
here because they see the opportunity," Bryant says. "The Red Sox are
a profitable entity if you can somehow align with them. If you run a
website in Philadelphia, chances are it'll just be your website in Philadelphia. Look at Bill Simmons' career—this is an example of how powerful an outlet the Red Sox really are and how powerful the entire Boston
dynamic really is. There's money to be had there."

Chapter 6
New Ownership, Familiar Suspicions

"I told the writers regardless of what we might accomplish in Boston, I sought one legacy: Indoor plumbing."—Charles Steinberg on the threadbare media facilities at the Red Sox' spring training facility

Charles Steinberg entered the University of Maryland in the fall of 1976 expecting to pursue a career in dentistry. Twenty-six years later, Steinberg had his doctorate in dentistry and arrived in Fort Myers, FL, the spring home of the Boston Red Sox, and began fixing the biggest cavity of his professional life.

After nearly seven decades under the stewardship of the Yawkey family and its trust, the Red Sox were purchased for $700 million—by far the highest price ever fetched for a baseball team—by a group headed by John W. Henry in December 2001.

Henry made his fortune in the futures market, but he and his partners knew that in order to maximize their investment, they first had to look to the past and begin repairing the frayed relationship between the Red Sox and the New England media, which had deteriorated throughout Dan Duquette's eight-season reign as general manager and bottomed out during a tumultuous 2001 season.

At the same time, Henry realized he and his partners had to answer the suspicions of fans. Such a problem is not typically one encountered by a fresh ownership group, but Bostonians were wary of Henry's bid from the moment his interest became known. Provincial pride was wounded and fans wondered if Henry's group would understand the importance of the Red Sox in Boston.

At best, they were viewed by fans as out-of-town businessmen unworthy of owning a sacred local trust. At worst, they were considered carpetbaggers who cultivated enough political capital with baseball's powers over the previous decade to earn ownership of one of the most valuable franchises in sports.

ESPN.com columnist Howard Bryant found such a sentiment unintentionally ironic considering that long-time Sox owner Tom Yawkey lived in South Carolina and returned there every winter.

"Nothing more than the usual Boston suspicion—when I say that, I mean it was the usual Boston hypocrisy," Bryant says. "'How can you sell this team to an outsider because these guys are carpetbaggers?' Well, Tom Yawkey wasn't here either. Tom Yawkey only hired one general manager who was from here, Dick O'Connell. So to try to hold this new ownership to that standard was totally hypocritical."

The distrust of out-of-town bidders was fueled by the late and legendary *Boston Globe* columnist, Will McDonough, who aligned himself with the bid of local businessman Joe O'Donnell and wrote several columns praising O'Donnell and criticizing the other potential owners.

Fans who didn't enjoy the air of uncertainty and desperation hanging around the club since CEO John Harrington announced plans to sell the club in October 2000 were also fearful the new owners were not in this for the long haul. Operating a baseball team was nothing new to the top three men in the ownership group—Henry, chairman Tom Werner, and CEO Larry Lucchino—and all three had shown a knack for maximizing their investment in a relatively short amount of time.

At the time he purchased the Red Sox, Henry was the owner of the Florida Marlins, and in order to buy the Sox, he had to agree to sell the Marlins—whom he'd owned since 1998—to Montreal Expos owner Jeffrey Loria. Werner owned the San Diego Padres from 1992–94 and oversaw a fire sale in 1993, when, in response to the operating losses he said the team suffered the previous season, he traded stars Fred McGriff and Gary Sheffield for minor leaguers. Lucchino was a top executive with the Baltimore Orioles (1988–93) and Padres (1994–2001) and left each franchise shortly after he helped it land a new stadium.

"If someone had done an analysis of qualifications, experience, collective ability to run a successful baseball franchise, I think we would have won the contest," Lucchino said during an interview in February

2007. "That should have been, in many ways, what people cared about, as long as they wanted a successful team, a successful Fenway Park or a replacement for Fenway Park."

The media's suspicions of the new owners were heightened by the perception that Major League Baseball commissioner Bud Selig steered the Red Sox to Henry's group instead of another competing group headed by New York businessman Charles Dolan.

Six days before baseball owners approved Henry's purchase, the Associated Press reported a Red Sox lawyer told Dolan on December 19 that a $660 million bid would win the franchise. Dolan upped his bid to the supposed magic number but still lost out to Henry. Dolan was told Henry's bid was more complete, but after Henry was awarded the team, Dolan offered to pay $750 million for the team.

However, Dolan's bid was fraught with numerous potential conflicts of interest. His brother, Larry, owned the Cleveland Indians. Dolan was the CEO of Long Island-based cable giant Cablevision, which was famous for charging the highest cable rates in the country, and did little to hide the fact he viewed the Red Sox as an opportunity to expand his media empire. The Red Sox sale included an 80 percent share in the New England Sports Network, which carried the majority of Red Sox games in 2001.

"If there was anything that gave the reporters any type of fuel, it was the fact that the Dolans had offered more than the Henry group and Bud Selig still gave them the team," Bryant says. "And that was the one thing: the fix, essentially, was in. And everybody knows that the fix was in, because the Henry group didn't offer the highest bid until Bud Selig made them offer higher. Otherwise, the Cablevision Dolans would be owning the Red Sox right now."

Henry's shyness presented another public relations obstacle. He struck most he met as kind and benevolent, but his appearance and personality were anything but bombastic. Tall and extremely thin, his air of fragility was enhanced by his soft speaking voice. He was the first to admit he was far more comfortable communicating from behind a computer than in front of a packed auditorium.

In baseball terms, the new ownership group was in a 0–2 hole even before it stepped to the plate in Boston. It only had one more strike to repair its image and begin fixing decades of media relations damage. It needed a spokesman to tirelessly and happily convey its message and usher in an era of positivism and cooperation.

And Werner and Lucchino knew Charles Steinberg—a Renaissance man with a doctorate in dentistry, three decades in public relations, and a passion for the written word—was the perfect person for the task.

The son of an orthodontist, Steinberg was already envisioning a career in dentistry when he accepted a public relations internship with his hometown Baltimore Orioles during his senior year of high school in 1976.

Yet Steinberg found his true passion with the Orioles. He quickly earned the trust of Orioles public relations director Bob Brown, who instilled into Steinberg the importance of accuracy, a sense of mutual respect for the press and its job, and an ability to think not only of the story but the person behind it.

"All along the way I'm absorbing the lessons of media relations that Bob Brown is teaching, overtly or inadvertently," Steinberg says. "How you bust your tail to look something up at a writer's request, because that writer's on deadline. How you realize that that writer not only has a job to do, but has an editor to please, has a family to support, has pressures that they don't speak about—deadlines, family issues, tough editors.

"They are not fans in your world. These are people whose livelihoods and whose ability to send their children to good schools depend on their ability to write news or opinions that are accurate, credible, interesting [and] newsworthy. And it was instilled the way breathing is instilled."

Steinberg was especially impressed by Brown's work during the 1979 World Series against the Pittsburgh Pirates. Brown, aware most beat writers loved to eat crab cakes during their visits to Baltimore, arranged for crab cakes to be served at each of the Orioles home games.

The concept of satisfactorily filling writers—literally and physically—stuck with Steinberg. "If they're hungry, feed them," Steinberg said during an interview over dinner at Fenway Park's Crown Royal Club in May 2005. "If they're thirsty, quench their thirsts. You're not to judge whether you agree with their opinions. Bob Brown said freedom of the press is one of the greatest elements of American life, and when you work for the company, you are on the side of freedom of the press."

"So the principle is evident to you that you must help these journalists with their stories. You must provide them access because you have a bounty of stories in your organization. Some may be too sweet and soft to satisfy that hard edge that some journalists may seek, but no matter what, you know that a journalist can't call his editor and say 'Yeah, I didn't come up with anything today.' Can you come home as the bread winner and say 'I'm sorry, I didn't bring any food?' No, you've got to come up with something."

Steinberg shakes his hands. "And if you help the writers with their access, then you're helping them meet the fundamental professional need of not only telling the story but also keeping their jobs. And if, when it comes to stories, the writers are hungry, then feed them. You don't force them to become vultures because they must get their food. It's their job. It's not Shangri-La in which they say, 'Hmm, I think I'll write a story today.' It's a 12-hour and then some gig that is both literary and intensely competitive. The last thing they need is for the subject to be an adversary. This is not common sense."

Steinberg served in a variety of roles for the Orioles and was running the public relations department before he accompanied Lucchino to San Diego, where he became the club's executive vice president of public affairs.

Even working in San Diego, Steinberg had a sense of the adversarial relationship between the Red Sox and the area press. His Boston baseball education began just before Christmas 2001 in a mall in San Diego and continued over the next two weeks on the beaches of Aruba.

Steinberg was 12 hours away from departing for his annual vacation when Lucchino called him and told him the Henry group landed the

Red Sox. Lucchino wanted Steinberg to join the new Red Sox front office in a capacity similar to the jobs he held in Baltimore and San Diego. So Steinberg went out, bought six Red Sox hats and "every Red Sox book I could find," and spent most of his vacation reading up on the history of the Sox.

"I studied those books the way I studied in dental school," Steinberg says. "I made index cards. I wrote out lists. I memorized every Red Sox manager from 1901 to 2001. I devoured the stories and the history. It was a throwback to the intensive study of dental school, only more delicious. It was an impassioned saturation in an ocean of stories that I absorbed like a giant sponge. And I knew I needed that credibility upon arriving in Boston."

In January, Steinberg joined the new ownership group in Arizona for the baseball owners meetings, where the sale of the franchise was approved. Beat writers walked up to Steinberg and vented about the poor relationship they had with upper management.

"One by one, they would give me an assessment of the media relations atmosphere, and every story was the same regardless of who was the orchestrator of the culture," Steinberg says. "The culture was not just one of adversarial-ism, but they described a three-way adversarialism: An adversarial nature between the media and the player, between the media and the front office [and] between the players and the front office. It was a dysfunctional triangle.

"And you say to yourself 'It can't be that bad' and you say it out loud and they go 'Ohhhh just watch.'"

In mid-February, Steinberg traveled to Ft. Myers for his first spring training with the Red Sox. One of the first things he saw upon arriving at the team complex February 16 was the media headquarters, which was housed in a wood-paneled trailer on the grounds adjacent to the team offices.

It looked like a bare-bones operation. But Steinberg was shocked to walk inside the trailer and learn just how rudimentary it really was.

The only amenity was a water cooler. There was no food available. The bathroom did not work and the Red Sox didn't allow writers to use the team's facilities. The only option for writers who needed to use the bathroom was a portable toilet next to the trailer.

"Steve Buckley of the *Boston Herald* would drive to a market up Edison Avenue [the street housing the complex] to go to the bathroom so that he could wash his hands," Steinberg says.

The sale of the team was officially completed on February 27. The next day, ownership fired unpopular general manager Dan Duquette and opened the new media trailer. It was a new era in Red Sox media relations, one unimaginable a season earlier.

"I told the writers regardless of what we might accomplish in Boston, I sought one legacy," Steinberg says. "Indoor plumbing. And when the sale of the club was completed at 5 o'clock on February 27, 2002, we arranged on February 28, 2002 a ribbon cutting of the doorway that would take them inside to the bathroom. And once that was established, a barbecue with food and drink."

The firings of Duquette and manager Joe Kerrigan, the latter of whom was dismissed March 5, and new ownership's openness with the local media provided Henry, Lucchino, and Werner a lengthy honeymoon period. As spring training began, the trio not only informed the press of its introductory meeting with Red Sox players but also allowed a photographer to shoot the final few minutes of the get-together.

Such access was symbolic of a new era, one in which Steinberg wanted to make the media relations department the "nerve center" of the Sox—as it had been with the Orioles—instead of detached from it. When he arrived in Boston, he was surprised to see the Red Sox were redesigning the media office because they didn't want the writers passing through on their way to the press box.

Under Tom Yawkey, the Sox generally ignored the press, which created a mutually tense relationship. The club's first publicist, Ed Doherty, disliked the media but got the job because he was friends with manager Joe Cronin. Doherty's successor, former Sox coach Larry Woodall, harbored similar feelings for the writers.

Dick Bresciani, who has served in the club's public relations department for more than 30 years, was popular with writers and the organization alike. The Boston chapter of the Baseball Writers Association of America awarded him its "Good Guy" award for his cooperation in 1987 while the national writers awarded him the Robert A. Fishel Award as the game's top media relations executive in 1997. He was retained by the new ownership as team historian and inducted into the club's Hall of Fame in 2006.

But relations between the club and the press again turned ice cold once Dan Duquette took over as general manager in 1994. Those who covered the Sox during that time alternately sympathized and sparred with Kevin Shea, who was the club spokesperson under the reticent Duquette.

"I think Kevin was a good guy—he was working for a guy who wanted him to behave that way," Associated Press reporter Howard Ulman says. "Everyone said he was a decent guy and he sort of had to run interference for Duquette. Kevin was taking orders—he was a loyal employee and it ended up hurting him."

So the writers were surprised when the Henry group, led by Steinberg, exuded warmth and an eagerness to accommodate. "That David Spade commercial? 'No, no, no?'" former *Hartford Courant* beat writer David Heuschkel says, referring to the Capital One bank ad where Spade comes up with new ways to decline loan requests. "This was the exact opposite."

Woodall was famous for not giving players' phone numbers to reporters who were hoping to write feature stories. Decades later, Glenn Geffner—a former Padres broadcaster who accompanied Steinberg and Lucchino to Boston and became the club's head spokesman in 2003—was more available than anyone had a right to expect.

"I called Glenn, [thinking] there might have been some developments with [the trade talks involving] A-Rod, and he answers the phone," Ulman says. "I said 'Where are you?' And he said 'Well, I'm in the hospital. My wife is about to give birth. Can I help you?'"

The larger scope of the media in Boston didn't intimidate Steinberg and his staff, which thought it was easier to disseminate the message to many rather than just a few. And while Boston was well-known for its controversial columnists, Steinberg figured mathematics made it better for the Sox to clash with one or two writers in Boston than one or two writers in San Diego.

"I viewed the large quantity of media in Boston as baseball's biggest microphone," Steinberg says. "The media is the medium to communicate to your market. The media seeks to communicate accurately to their market. The opinionates will be on the mark far more often if they are knowledgeable.

"And with so many writers and TV reporters and radio broadcasters, if there's one who's unpleasant, if there's one who has an agenda, if there's one who demonstrates some kind of bias—I'd rather have that be one out of 25 than one of the four who covered us in San Diego."

The openness and approachability was a no-lose proposition for the new owners, who realized the best way to diffuse the notion they were interlopers unworthy of owning the Red Sox was to face their critics and make peace, sometimes in a pointedly humorous manner.

Meetings with WEEI, the powerful all-sports talk radio station, and the publisher of the *Herald* were particularly memorable. "We went to meet with WEEI—we went over there in January for a breakfast," Lucchino says. "I remember saying at that first meeting 'Listen: I know we weren't your first choice to be the new owners of the Red Sox. But frankly, you weren't our first choice to be sports talk show hosts either. So why don't we just agree to get along and try to get along.'"

On the way to a meeting with the *Herald*'s Pat Purcell, Lucchino decided to literally bury the hatchet with the newspaper. "We passed a hardware store and I screamed out to the driver 'Stop the car! Stop the car!'" Lucchino says. "I said to John Henry 'I've got an idea. Let's go in there. I'm going to get a hatchet and we'll take the hatchet over there and ceremoniously and literally and metaphorically bury the hatchet.' So we did. We brought a hatchet to Purcell and we buried it in a clump of dirt in his office plant. I think that made a joke out of the hostility rather than being too offended by it."

Later in the spring of 2002, ownership facilitated a clubhouse meeting between the *Herald*'s Tony Massarotti and the players in hopes of making a fresh start between the parties and letting each side know what the other expected from it. There was no avoiding the fact the writers and players would share the same space for the next seven or eight months and would see each other more often than their families.

Finally, writers and players seemed to agree life would be a bit easier for all if everyone made an effort to get along.

"We've tried—and it's not only from the organization's standpoint, but also from the player's standpoint—[to get] together and tried to create a more friendly atmosphere to work in for both of us," Red Sox pitcher Tim Wakefield says. "Because we both understand that everyone has a job to do that's in there."

Says Jeff Horrigan, formerly of the *Herald*: "I think they knew coming in that there was a cynical New England view that these guys were carpetbaggers. Henry was from Florida, Werner was from California, and Lucchino had bounced around a little bit. The conventional wisdom was, 'What do these guys know about Boston?'

"And as if to combat that, I think they realized the more we put ourselves out there, the more we get people to know us, the more we can shoot that perception down. I think that, in combination with the realization that the previous administration had had an ongoing war of sorts with the media, they understood that it was perhaps better to take on a more conciliatory tone."

But the openness of Henry, Werner, and Lucchino did not spare the trio from criticism or suspicion. After so many years of dealing with a distant ownership, some writers assumed the new group's friendly ways concealed an ulterior motive.

As interest in the Red Sox increased with every title-less season, Bryant wondered if the Sox benefited as much from the frantic coverage of the championship pursuit as those who provided it.

Phrases that were concocted by writers to describe the Sox' Quixotic pursuit of a championship not only became part of the American lexicon but part of the Sox' internal fabric: In the 2002, 2003, and 2004 media guides, the ownership group listed a handful of objectives, the last of which was to "Break the Curse of the Bambino and bring a world championship to New England."

Interest in the Red Sox increased with every title-less season, peaking with a litany of headline-grabbing events leading up to the 2004 season. The Sox suffered their most agonizing defeat yet against the Yankees in the 2003 ALCS, after which they traded for ace Curt Schilling, signed closer Keith Foulke, and came within a stroke of the pen of acquiring superstar Alex Rodriguez, who was later obtained by the Yankees. The Sox were entering a win-or-else season with several impending free agents, including franchise icons Nomar Garciaparra and Pedro Martinez, and a new manager in Terry Francona.

Boston writers and personalities were in demand nationwide. As the season opened, a number of Sox-related books were in the works. Bryant believed that some of the Sox' slogans—both of the marketing and internal inspirational variety—were direct descendants of *The Curse of the Bambino*.

During 2004, the Sox implored fans to "Keep The Faith." Led by Schilling, players wore T-shirts that read "Why Not Us?" After the Sox won the championship, former *Boston Globe* and *Sports Illustrated* columnist Leigh Montville authored a book titled *Why Not Us?*, while the Sox issued a DVD called "Faith Rewarded." And Schilling penned the foreword to *Win It For . . .* , a collection of message board posts from the Sons of Sam Horn message board.

"Everyone that gets on [Dan] Shaughnessy's case for it—a lot of people rode that gravy train that ended up being the Curse gravy train," Bryant says. "Dan Shaughnessy wrote *The Curse of the Bambino*. How different was that than *Why Not Us . . .* ? How different is it even if you don't use the word 'curse?' How different is that than *Faithful* [a book about the 2004 season written by and from the vantage point of noted authors Stewart O'Nan and Stephen King], than all these other entities that are coming up—keep the faith, Red Sox Nation, reverse the curse. [Shaughnessy's] not getting 10 cents off the dollar for all that stuff. It became part of the Red Sox dynamic and the Red Sox themselves profited from it. So this whole culture kind of closed in on itself.

"What does that do to the dynamic of holding the team accountable and what does it mean?" Bryant asks. "Do you run the risk of not covering the team in a way that you would normally because you stand to lose money by angering certain people in the organization?"

The Sox were also criticized for not renewing the contract of NESN announcer Sean McDonough, the son of the noted columnist Will McDonough. Sean McDonough aired his concerns over the new ownership group's ability to spend money upgrading the Red Sox after they spent more than $700 million to acquire the club. One day, Henry took the unusual step of driving to the studios of 1510 The Zone—where McDonough hosted the afternoon drive show—and arguing with McDonough on air.

McDonough believes it was finances—and not opinions or reverse nepotism—that led the Sox to cut ties with him.

And with the *Globe*'s owner, The New York Times Company, holding a 17 percent stake in the Red Sox—and the Red Sox owning 80 percent of NESN, the network that aired all but a handful of the Sox' regular season games—there were those inside and outside the media who were concerned the Sox' ties to big media companies could allow them to shape their message via the two most powerful outlets in town.

It wasn't the first time Sox ownership was connected to the *Globe*: In 1904, John I. Taylor, the son of *Globe* publisher General Charles Taylor, bought the Boston Americans from Henry Killilea for $145,000. John Fitzgerald, the publisher of the *Republic* newspaper, a former and future mayor of Boston and the grandfather of future President John F. Kennedy, was willing to pay any price to land the Americans, but American League founder (and former sportswriter Ban Johnson) steered the Sox to Taylor for $5,000 more than Fitzgerald's supposed best offer because he thought Taylor would be easier to control than the independent Fitzgerald.

One hundred and one years later, Bryant called the relationship between the Sox, The New York Times Company, NESN, and radio station WEEI—which has no financial connection to the Sox but was, at the time, the Sox' flagship radio station—a "growing synergistic cartel."

That term quickly gained popularity among not only observers of the Boston media scene but also non-*Globe* writers. The relationship between The New York Times Company and the Red Sox was even criticized within the pages of the *Globe* itself. When the paper ran a front-page story about a new Red Sox travel service in May 2006, Shaughnessy wrote it was an example of what can be perceived as the *Globe* going out of its way to paint the Sox in a positive light.

"It's bad, we can't win," Shaughnessy says. "What's really unfortunate is the way it impugns the work of Gordon Edes and Chris Snow [the beat writers at the start of the 2006 season]. They're working their ass off and no matter what they do, WEEI is going to say they're being spoon-fed because they're [affiliated] with the club. It's really unfair, it puts us in a no-win position."

Sox executives said there was no directive to the *Globe* to spin Sox-related news in a positive fashion. "It never registered very much with me one way or the other, because I thought it was just so wrong," Lucchino says. "The notion that we were somehow dealing preferentially with one media outlet over the others.

"Charles Steinberg would have put his body on the tracks to stop that from happening because it was he who was constantly talking about equal access, equal availability. I cannot remember a single instance when he was motivated by a desire to sort of repay *The New York Times* for investing in the ballclub."

Says Steinberg: "I don't want a tabloid yelling negative things about the Red Sox. That's not in our best interests. What advantage is there to that? It doesn't make sense. I want them praising the Red Sox with the same voice that the broadsheet does."

Come the fall of 2005, there would be minimal praises sung about the Sox, its front office, and its intentions.

The relationship between the Red Sox and the media was healthy in 2004, but players and writers alike were wondering if the new ownership group was exploiting the good faith it had built up to turn public opinion against team icons Nomar Garciaparra, Derek Lowe. and Pedro Martinez, all of whom were expected to depart as free agents following the season.

Such accusations against ownership were nothing new in Boston. Messy exits were particularly plentiful in the 1990s, when Wade Boggs, Roger Clemens, and Mo Vaughn all departed in acrimonious fashion after putting up Hall of Fame-caliber numbers for the Red Sox.

Questions about their character dogged each player during his final season in Boston: Boggs, a five-time batting champion whose quirky personality made him a favorite of writers, was criticized for his perceived obsession with his average and booed by fans as he hit a career-low .259. At the end of the season, a *Globe* poll revealed fans overwhelmingly preferred that the Sox hand third base over to prospect Scott Cooper instead of re-signing Boggs, who went on to sign with the Yankees after the season and played seven more seasons. Cooper made a pair of All-Star teams but played his final game in 1997.

"The best way to get a player out of town is to start dogging him in the paper," Boggs said shortly after he was elected to the Hall of Fame. "Because when the fans start reading it, then they start booing. And then after that, it's just a matter of time. It's happened all the way back to Ted Williams.

"They know who they are and how they treated me. When you have a player that's honest and accessible and you take advantage of that and then turn around and dog him, I think that's not right. They know who they are."

Clemens was criticized for his expanding waistline as well as his mediocre—by his standards—performance in Boston over his final four seasons (40–39, 3.77 ERA). After Clemens left the Sox for the Blue Jays as a free agent following the 1996 season, McDonough reminded readers Clemens had once said he'd never leave the Sox except to go back home to Houston and he'd never want to come back and pitch against the Red Sox.

McDonough also called Clemens "Roger (The Dodger) Clemens" and "The Texas Con Man." Clemens was perhaps the most-hated visiting player at Fenway over the next seven years, especially once he joined the Yankees in 1999.

Vaughn, a New England native who was the go-to guy in the clubhouse for writers for most of his six seasons in Boston, was also a frequent target for McDonough, who called the first baseman "Mo Money" and lambasted him so fiercely during Vaughn's final year in Boston in 1998 that Vaughn's father asked McDonough why he was so critical of his son.

Former *Herald* writer Joe Giuliotti told Howard Bryant in an interview for Bryant's book *Shut Out* that he believed the Sox wanted to use the media to ". . . turn the people against [Vaughn] and in a way, it worked. They said he was fat, out of shape."

The seismic separations between the Sox and Boggs, Clemens, and Vaughn symbolized a complicated relationship in which writers, while not necessarily carrying out the wishes of ownership in boiling the player-team relationship down to a simple and lopsided case of us vs. them, tended to nonetheless mirror the sentiment of fans who are unhappy with the player who has left town.

"They'll never do it while he's here, because they want to keep that small sliver of hope that when they need him for something, they'll talk to him," *Globe* columnist Tony Massarotti says. "As soon as they leave, they'll kick the crap out of them. And fans here do the same thing. Roger Clemens won more games here than anyone but Cy Young, but he left here and he was the biggest jerk ever. It's always the player leaving, it's never the team holding the door open.

"At the same time, in any divorce, it's never easy to pick one side. And that's what these things are: They are ugly divorces."

Says Bryant: "The writers seem to know, very acutely, that the team comes first. There are very, very few instances where, during the negotiations, the writers took the players' side. And the player knows this."

Garciaparra, Lowe, and Martinez all believed the team was greasing the skids for their departures long before they entered the final year of their deals in 2004. Lowe thought the Sox were floating stories about his penchant for enjoying the night life. In September 2004, it was

125

reported Lowe and other players were out deep into the night following a dramatic come-from-behind victory over the Yankees at Yankee Stadium. The next day, Lowe lasted just one inning and gave up seven runs in a 14–4 loss.

"You're in such a high media market and they are so conscious of what people say because people in New England have such strong opinions, good and bad," Lowe told Sporting News Radio after the 2004 season but before he signed a four-year deal with the Dodgers. "So if they make it ugly, and kind of drag your name through the mud, people will say 'Well, now I see why they're not bringing him back.' But if they leave on good terms, people will be wondering why they didn't bring this guy back."

That quote was read to Steinberg during an interview in February 2007. "I insist it neither has to be ugly nor should it be ugly," Steinberg says. "I think so fondly of my time with Derek Lowe. After we did "The Tonight Show" November 1, 2004, we all went out to eat. That brings a smile to my face today. It's only in our best interests to always celebrate the virtues of the people we have in our organization. I have not found in my career that there is any value in the denigration of anyone's name.

"We're all in this together—the media and the players and the front office are all in this together—and the popularity of the game is in the best interests of all those parties."

Martinez believed, as far back in 2003, that there were potential spies in the press corps; those he believed were acting in concert with management to drive him out of the city. And in announcing April 30, 2004 that he would not negotiate with the Sox until after the season, he accused the Sox of whispering that his right shoulder was unhealthy.

"That bothered me that they did that just to bring my salary down or make things more difficult for me go to in a free agency year," Martinez told reporters. He signed with the Mets following the season, and his introductory press conference in New York—four hours south of Boston—was attended by just two Boston-based reporters: the *Herald*'s Silverman and CBS4's Dan Roche.

Garciaparra, meanwhile, was reportedly convinced in 2003 that the Sox were bugging his phone as well as making the dirt around shortstop rougher in order to make it more difficult for him to field grounders. He told author Seth Mnookin that the Sox told the *Globe* following the 2003 season that he had turned down a four-year extension worth $60 million. Garciaparra told Mnookin he believed the two sides were still negotiating when that news leaked.

Relief pitcher Todd Jones, who joined the Sox during the 2003 season and befriended Garciaparra, signed with the Reds after the season but believed the Sox and the media conspired in 2004 to paint Garciaparra in a negative light as his departure approached.

"I always talked to Nomar about his situation," Jones said in September 2004. "If he didn't sign back with the Red Sox, he was gonna be the bad guy and the media was gonna pick up on it. They were gonna make Nomar the bad guy because the Red Sox can't afford to lose Nomar. I said all that pre-trade.

"He was too big to let the Red Sox just let him walk away, so there were going to have to be attacks on his personality, attacks on his character. If you look back at any player that was comparable [in importance] to the team, [they] had to go through some kind of character assassination right before the deal."

Garciaparra was traded to the Cubs on July 31, 2004. Shortly thereafter, Massarotti wrote: "Shame on the Red Sox. Shame on them for mistreating one of the greatest players in their history . . . some members of the club leaked information about negotiations to make Garciaparra look bad, proving that this administration, like the old one, is fully capable of running what Mo Vaughn once termed a 'smear campaign.'"

The previous August, Massarotti also wrote that Sox ownership was not criticized for its tactics because ". . . these guys talk to us," words which stung both Lucchino and Steinberg.

Said Massarotti in March 2005: "I think that in terms of dealing with the media, the Red Sox versus Nomar was a complete mismatch. The media was getting information strictly from the Red Sox, who are much more cooperative and forthcoming than previous ownership and management. And Nomar had never cultivated a relationship with any members of the media. So on the whole, he got slaughtered.

"I thought it was a lousy way to treat a guy you put on the billboard at the beginning of the year. They put his image up there to sell tickets and then, literally and figuratively, tore it down. I just thought it was lousy. Take the high road."

Says Lucchino of Massarotti's written criticism: "I do know that he said something about how we made Nomar look bad on his way out, but I didn't know that he attributed it to because 'they talk to us.' I will acknowledge that that sometimes happens: That the media people tend to trust the people that they can question and examine and have access to more than those they don't."

Lucchino and Steinberg would eventually believe that a lack of access was the cause of the biggest controversy either man would face with the Red Sox.

Midway through the 2005 season, Lucchino came to Steinberg and told him there needed to be a concerted effort to keep in-house the news of the increasingly tense contract negotiations between Lucchino and Theo Epstein, whose three-year contract was due to expire October 31.

"The cold simple truth is Lucchino told me at some point in 2005 when, I'm guessing, his discussions with Theo were beginning or intensifying [that] 'This won't be something that we'll be discussing,'" Steinberg says. "'We must stay quiet on this issue.'"

And while Steinberg said Lucchino didn't explicitly declare that, for the first time in their nearly 30 years together, he needed to keep Steinberg uninformed about a vital team matter, Steinberg inferred as much from his discussions with his long-time friend.

And for months, little, if any, news trickled out about Epstein's negotiations with Lucchino. John Henry told the *Globe* in July that the possibility of a new contract for Epstein was not an issue for himself, Epstein, or anyone else within ownership.

Once the season ended, Epstein did his best Dan Duquette imitation in deflecting queries about the negotiations. "That's an issue that's coming up and something we're going to have to deal with," Epstein said the morning after the White Sox swept the Red Sox in the AL Division Series. "But, again, that's another issue that I don't think we'll be discussing publicly."

Over the next few weeks, Epstein and Lucchino conducted negotiations in secret. Finally, on October 28, the *Globe* reported the two had neared an agreement and that a new deal was imminent.

Shaughnessy spoke to both men that night. Two days later, he penned a column in which he wrote the clash between Lucchino and Epstein was ". . . as old as the *Bible*" but that it was discouraging that Epstein appeared eager to ". . . distance himself" from mentors such as Lucchino and Steinberg, each of whom had worked with him in Baltimore as well as San Diego.

Shaughnessy also wrote that Lucchino took the heat when the Sox pulled out of a trade with the Rockies at the trade deadline three months earlier and that Epstein did not necessarily know more about baseball than Lucchino, who reached the Final Four as a member of the Princeton men's basketball team and began working in the Orioles' front office while Epstein was in kindergarten.

Shaughnessy thought the column provided proof "The Cartel" did not exist. He wrote that neither Epstein nor Lucchino would discuss their contract discussions because of their self-imposed media blackout. Wrote Shaughnessy: "So much for the *Globe's* home-court advantage . . . So much for the cartel."

Bostonians picking up the *Globe* Halloween morning were greeted with the news that Epstein would ink a three-year deal. But even as the news was hitting the stoops and computer screens, Epstein was in the process of resigning. The *Herald* was the first outlet to report Epstein's departure that very afternoon.

Shaughnessy's column inspired a torrent of criticism aimed at him, the *Globe*, and the Sox. Writers, fans, and media critics, already concerned with the Sox' connection to the city's biggest media outlet, believed the Sox teamed up with "The Cartel" to turn fans against an exiting icon—

in this case, not a player but the universally respected general manager. And the columnist responsible for the controversial piece was the most popular target for fans who thought he symbolized the negative Boston sports media.

"In my case, it was the hat trick of hatred," Shaughnessy says. "It played to WEEI—they hate the *Globe*, they hate me. That's good. And then the *Herald* was on it right away blaming me. That's good for them. They want us to die. And then the bloggers. So hence the hat trick."

Many connected the dots, privately and publicly, and theorized Lucchino and/or Steinberg—each of whom Shaughnessy had known since he covered the Orioles for the *Baltimore Sun* in the late '70s—were the source(s) for the column. When WEEI hosts would criticize Lucchino for his role in Epstein's departure, the sound of a dentist's drill—an obvious homage to Steinberg—could be heard in the background.

In his book *Feeding the Monster*, Seth Mnookin wrote "several sources confirm[ed]" that Shaughnessy, a week prior to the release of his column, met with Steinberg and another writer and that Steinberg ". . . said many of the things that ended up in Shaughnessy's column."

Steinberg denied that charge to Mnookin and numerous times thereafter, as did Shaughnessy. "There were very few new things in there— 70 percent of the column was all documented in the book [*Reversing the Curse: A Look at the 2004 Season*]," Shaughnessy says. "I've known Larry Lucchino since 1979, I met Theo for the first time as a sophomore at Yale. And the background of those two men—I thought this was a good day to get it out there. And [Lucchino accepting the blame for the aborted Rockies trade] was apparently the hand grenade in the thing— three different people had told me that. I thought it had been out there already.

"Apparently he felt betrayed and went thinking that he was getting sandbagged by Dr. Charles and Larry and others, but they weren't the source on that. It had been out there."

Steinberg kept a low profile throughout the winter—he was not present for Epstein's press conference on November 2, nor was he quoted in the 2,031-word press release announcing Epstein's return on January 24. He was aware his absence made it look as if he was being frozen out and/or punished, but he said he disappeared from view to show support for the fellow executives who were getting hammered in every medium.

"If Larry's not saying a word and he has no complaints as he takes cannonballs, who am I to complain about taking bullets?" Steinberg says.

Said Lucchino in February 2007: "I thought it was superficial and melodramatic and unfair to a few people, but I think it's ancient history now. I don't want to sound like a chip off the old Red Sox block, but there were members of the media that had their own particular agenda, and to that extent, I do think the coverage was somewhat unfair and somewhat misleading to the public."

Neither Lucchino nor Steinberg—nor anyone else within the Sox front office—identified the writers and media members whom the club felt exploited the drama of the 2005 offseason for their own gain, though the *Globe* reported July 11, 2006, shortly after *Feeding the Monster* was released, that team executives ". . . did send out an e-mail instructing Fenway folks to be 'dismissive' of its claims."

But the entire experience both proved and disproved Steinberg's theory, stated early in the 2005 season, that the media would be correct if it was kept informed by the team and that Boston's massive media presence made it easier for the organization to deal with a renegade writer or writers than it would be in San Diego or Baltimore.

The experiences of 2005 resulted in an organization-wide effort to be more careful and wary in the following seasons. There were no projects chronicling a year in the life of the organization in 2006 or 2007. Ownership abided by the one-voice philosophy preferred by Epstein, while Lucchino said those whom the organization suspected of providing leaks in the fall of 2005 were nudged aside in the subsequent months.

"We've had a change in personnel—people who were here then, many of them are not here now," Lucchino says. "Not necessarily because they were sources or leaks or whatever, but there are some people who have a natural inclination to talk more than they should about things that they shouldn't be addressing."

And Bryant, who was critical of the *Feeding the Monster* project, wrote for ESPN.com during the 2007 season that ". . . these Red Sox seem more buttoned-down" and ". . . less reality TV" than the pre-2006 clubs.

Steinberg, meanwhile, gradually emerged again as a key public figure for the Sox in 2006—capped in December, when he organized and emceed the gala, international-themed press conference introducing star Japanese pitcher Daisuke Matsuzaka—before he left following the 2007 season to become the chief marketing officer of the Los Angeles Dodgers.

During an interview in February 2007, he said he would not judge the entire media by ". . . the scuttlebutt and rumor mill and talk radio gossip mill [that was] filled with speculation" in the weeks and months following Epstein's departure. Steinberg also said he had no regrets over the events of 2005 and believed any fallout and controversy from the organization's vow of silence regarding Epstein's contract negotiations were worth it in order to preserve friendships within the front office.

"What is the consequence to the media when the usually open Red Sox leaders go mute?" Steinberg says. "If you're the writers, you still must write your stories and you will be resourceful. And if you're not going to get information from the primary sources, you'll get it from secondary sources or tertiary sources.

"We made it hard for the media to chronicle that story. And yet we had to do that out of respect to each other."

Chapter 7
From "The Hawk" to "Cowboy Up"

There was much more to the drought-busting 2004 World Championship team than merely the Red Sox having multiple players who were comfortable in the spotlight and dealing with the media. But it is difficult to imagine that a different group could have created the type of history that the Sox made in October.

The goofy Kevin Millar and the kindly Johnny Damon symbolized the element of comfort Sox had with each other as well as the media. Such calm had rarely been enjoyed by the franchise, particularly in the years prior to the arrival of Millar and Damon.

Millar and Damon were far from alone in their ability to handle the voluminous Boston press. "I don't think every player has to [talk]," former Red Sox vice president/public affairs Charles Steinberg says. "But it is to the team's advantage for some players to do so. And you watch how Varitek does, how Millar does, how Lowe does, how Schilling does, and they provide the words that relieve some of the pressure on the ones who aren't as comfortable doing that.

"I watched players praise Derek Lowe for standing in the middle of the clubhouse when he wasn't doing well as a closer [in 2001] and taking it. I watched Jason Varitek say, 'If you screw up, say I made a mistake so there's no second question.'"

Varitek preferred to speak in generalities and often dodged questions about strategy by saying he didn't want to give away the state secrets. But as the catcher, he realized he was in a position where reporters would regularly want to ask him about the pitching staff and its performance. So he'd long ago established himself as an accountable spokesperson who would meet with reporters—a timed heat pack wrapped tightly around his throwing shoulder—after almost every game.

"Sometimes it's not easy, but you just try and respect the fact that you have jobs to do and help you do your jobs," Varitek says.

A constant plotline in 2004 was the uncomfortable tango between the press and Schilling, who embraced the Internet and the opportunity to bypass the traditional media by communicating directly with fans. But while Schilling could be elusive, he was almost always expansive and informative when he did speak, particularly at his postgame press conferences.

Like Varitek, relief pitchers Mike Timlin and Alan Embree did not seek the spotlight but believed it was part of their job to speak to reporters on a regular basis. Reserves Gabe Kapler and Doug Mirabelli proved to have an accurate read on the state of the team while rotation stalwarts Lowe and Bronson Arroyo were each entertaining.

Lowe, in particular, enjoyed a spirited give-and-take with reporters during his seven fascinating seasons with the Red Sox. He saved 40 games in 2000 and won 20 games in 2002 yet lost his closer's job in 2001 and posted a 5.42 ERA in 2004, when he asked writers why his struggles made them portray him as a "mental Gidget."

"Before Game Four of the World Series [which Lowe started and won], he was just sitting there in the dugout, shooting the bull with people before the clinching game of the World Series," Redsox.com beat writer Ian Browne says. "He couldn't help himself. He loved to talk. He loved the banter. Once in a blue moon he'd get in a little snit about something. With him, it never lasted more than a day or so."

David Ortiz, meanwhile, lockered in the same corner of the Fenway Park clubhouse as one-time team icon Mo Vaughn and emerged as a similarly popular player with writers. His speech was peppered with R-rated language, but he came off as charming instead of profane. He'd often end press conferences by spraying reporters with his cologne and telling them to ". . . go home and get some ass."

Ortiz was also beloved by teammates, particularly Pedro Martinez and Manny Ramirez. The two superstars were several years older and far more accomplished than Ortiz, yet they both looked up to Ortiz as if he was an older, more protective brother. Ortiz continually defended Martinez and Ramirez, both of whom had up-and-down relationships with the press, and it did not seem a coincidence that both players ended their media boycotts in 2004, the year after Ortiz established himself as one of the game's premier power hitters.

"I respect everybody just like I hope everybody respects me," Ortiz says, referring to his relationship with the media. "I don't get involved in any of that—I worry about the way I deal with you guys. Whatever [quieter teammates have] been doing, they have their reason. And sometimes [it's] just part of their personality, shyness or whatever."

Ortiz' ability to thrive in pressure situations and connect with teammates of different races, nationalities and personalities evoked memories of Luis Tiant, the gutsy and gregarious pitcher whom Carl Yastrzemski called "the heart and soul" of the successful 1975 Red Sox.

And like Ortiz, Millar and Damon were reminiscent of vital players from earlier pennant-winning teams who proved doubly valuable thanks to their willingness to embrace the attention showered upon the team and their ability to shield their less outgoing teammates from the glare and demands of the media.

"It's not for everybody," Millar said in 2006, after he'd left the Sox and signed with the Orioles as a free agent. "Some people don't like the media. You know what? They're not paid to talk to the media. They're paid to play baseball. So if me, Johnny, Todd Walker, [Jason] Varitek, Ortiz take some of the heat off Billy Mueller—who was a shy guy and didn't like talking—and Manny [Ramirez, who] was shy . . . we would do that."

That Damon and Millar played pivotal leadership roles in 2004 only further symbolized the unlikely nature of the Sox' championship. After all, who would have expected Millar to even reach the major leagues, never mind start for a world champion, when he signed with an independent league team after he went undrafted following his graduation from little-known Lamar University?

Who would have expected Damon—who stuttered as a youngster,

and, as a big leaguer with the Kansas City Royals and Oakland Athletics, was the picture of the clean-cut all-American boy—to become the shaggy-haired, hard-partying embodiment of the counter-culture Sox?

Damon's on-field contributions were obvious: The former American League stolen base champion also had 20-homer power and served as the perfect leadoff hitter for the Sox, who emphasized patience and professional at-bats. He walked more often than he struck out between 1999 and 2004 and was an expert at "wasting" pitches—i.e., spraying foul balls all over the ballpark, thereby forcing the pitcher to throw his entire arsenal and giving the players behind him in the lineup a chance to size up the opposition.

Damon was valuable as well off the field. He signed with the Sox following the 2001 season, and it didn't take him long in 2002 to learn he'd entered a clubhouse scarred by its previously poisonous relations with the press—and with each other. So the leadoff man, far more accustomed to setting the table for the hitters behind him, decided to set the tone for teammates by serving as a go-to guy for the press.

"I think you have a responsibility," Damon said in 2004. "I am one of the players that is somewhat important to this team. I understand the media needs to get stories."

Indeed, nothing in Damon's past suggested he was a candidate to serve as the spokesman for the most chronicled team in baseball. Playing in small-market Kansas City and Oakland, where the Royals and Athletics often played to half-empty ballparks and largely vacant press boxes, wasn't quite the optimal primer for playing in Boston.

"I never had a wave [of reporters] until I got to Boston," Damon says. "And it's not fun. But you kind of understand [it] and you kind of wait until the crowd is around you."

And while Damon says he and his family ". . . just kind of grew up in Happyland, close to Disneyworld" in a suburb of Orlando, FL, childhood was not without its challenges for Damon, whose shyness was compounded by an omnipresent stutter.

Damon, who said his tongue could not catch up with his mind when he was a youngster, cured the stuttering issue by training himself to speak slowly and softly in order to articulate his thoughts. His public speaking skills were further aided in Kansas City, where the Royals held a seminar instructing players on how to better convey their message to the public.

In addition, Damon's distinctive visage—particularly when he sported long hair and a beard in 2004 and 2005—gave him an unwanted look at the intolerance of others. Damon is half-Thai: His mother, Yome, is a native of Thailand who met Jim Damon when he was serving in the United States Army in southeast Asia. Yome gave birth to Johnny in Ft. Riley, KS, in 1973 but the family bounced around the globe for the first few years of Johnny's life as Jim completed his service.

"I'm running into people nowadays who, because of the way I dress—I go into a clothing store or a jewelry store and they just don't want to deal with me," Damon said in May 2006. "It's unfortunate, people with their stereotypes. It's happened to me, and not only recently."

Instead of embittering Damon, though, such experiences infused him with a kindness unusual in a player in any market, never mind Boston.

The Sox locker room during Damon's tenure could be an intimidating place for a newcomer covering the team. Players who weren't already naturally wary of the press were often worn down by the constant coverage of the team. And players who found it difficult to establish a familiarity with reporters who were around the team on a daily basis were particularly suspicious of those they did not recognize at all.

But Damon was as talkative and open with unfamiliar faces as he was with the beat writers. As a result, a newer writer looking to write a Sox-related story was inevitably steered towards Damon's direction. In June 2005, Damon told a first-time visitor to the Sox clubhouse he would speak to him for a magazine feature after batting practice. Upon returning to the locker room more than an hour later, Damon searched the clubhouse for the reporter until he found him.

"My parents taught me well and just taught me how to respect everybody," Damon says. "That's very important."

Writers walking into the Sox clubhouse after games during Damon's tenure were almost always greeted by the same sight: Open the door, look immediately to the left and there was Damon, holding court with the press a few feet in front of his locker—the exact pose suggested by Steinberg.

"I remember walking in there, how everybody just ran away and always put the blame on something else instead of themselves," Damon says of his thoughts upon joining the Sox in 2002. "I was one of the first ones—maybe the first one—to stick it on themselves. A lot of players can't admit that. And that's too bad.

"I just don't hide from the truth. The stats don't lie. The scorecards don't lie. So you can always look and say I struck out with the bases loaded or I came through with a big hit. As long as it stays within the realm of baseball, it's easy to talk about."

By 2004, Damon was earning attention for far more than his willingness to speak. He arrived at spring training that February sporting shoulder-length hair and a full beard. The new look earned him comparisons to everyone from a caveman to Jesus Christ—Damon walked around the locker room blessing teammates—to Charles Manson to Samson, the Greek god who derived his power from his long hair.

Damon's long hair symbolized the scruffiness of the Sox, whose goofy untidiness—several other players, including stars Manny Ramirez and Pedro Martinez, joined Damon in sporting unkempt hairdos—made them the antithesis to the corporate arch-rival Yankees.

Damon embraced the attention bestowed upon his look. His hair became the main topic of countless interviews. In May 2004, he shaved his beard for charity during a ceremony at the Prudential Center in downtown Boston. And during spring training in 2005, Damon was the headline attraction among the five Sox players chosen to appear on the male makeover show "Queer Eye for the Straight Guy."

"There's been a big deal made of it," Damon said of his look in May 2004. "I don't have my long hair for a [specific] reason, I have it just because I wanted it. The media likes it and I'm liking it. My hair's going to be staying for a while."

The long hair was part of an image overhaul by Damon, whose reputation in Kansas City and Oakland was decidedly G-rated. He sported short hair and sideburns that made him look more like a cast member of *Beverly Hills 90210* than a caveman. He was also married at age 19 to his high school sweetheart, Angie, who gave birth to twins Madeline and Jackson in 1999.

By the start of 2004, though, Damon and Angie were separated. In his autobiography *Idiot*—one of many Sox-related books published in the year following the world championship—Damon wrote of extramarital affairs he had near the end of his marriage and of lobbing water balloons and pumpkins out the window of his high-rise Boston condominium with his new fiancée, Michelle Mangan.

Damon was sensitive to those who suggested his hard-partying ways would affect his on-field performance. During spring training in 2004, he told reporters he stayed in shape the previous winter by racing against cars down his street in Orlando. He said he ran even with the cars in a 25-mph zone.

He had the best year of his career in 2004, hitting .300 for the third time, while setting then-career highs in homers, RBIs, and walks. He also delivered the exclamation point home runs in the Sox' historic postseason surge to the world championship: a second-inning grand slam in a rout of the Yankees in Game Seven of the AL Championship Series and a leadoff homer in the fourth and final game of the World Series.

With his tabloid life, penchant for telling stories that sometimes pushed the limits of believability, and impressive production out of the leadoff spot, Damon was a modern version of Wade Boggs, the Hall of Famer who made as many headlines off the field as he did on it during a decade-long stint with the Sox.

Fenway was a good fit for Damon's style of hitting, but Boggs was born to hit in Boston. The Sox weren't initially impressed with Boggs, a left-handed hitter with minimal speed and minimal power who spent six full seasons in the minor leagues, but his remarkable batting eye and an ability to tattoo the inviting left-field Green Monster wall allowed him to become the preeminent hitter of his era. Boggs ranked among the AL's top five in batting average every year from 1983 through 1991, during which he won five batting titles and hit 40 or more doubles eight times. He was the only player of the 20th century to collect 200 or more hits in seven straight seasons.

He also garnered plenty of notice for his quirky behavior. Athletes are naturally creatures of habit, but Boggs was remarkably ritualistic. His pregame meal always consisted of chicken. Every pregame activity—from leaving the house to participating in wind sprints minutes before the first pitch—was scripted to the second. For instance, his wind sprints always began at exactly 7:17 p.m. Boggs was not Jewish, but he drew a Chai sign—the Hebrew symbol for life—upon walking into the batter's box.

Like Damon, Boggs seemed to enjoy interacting with the media and did not mind being portrayed as an eccentric. His willingness to speak regularly with the press was especially vital during a tense period of Sox/press relations in the mid-'80s.

Boggs appreciated that reporters respected his schedule, which in turn made him more likely to chat during his down time. "They understood my time completely and I was very open with the press," Boggs says. "I gave them as much time as they needed and they understood that I did things at a certain time.

"Believe me, I didn't take up a whole eight hours of the day doing silly things," Boggs says. "I would do something for five minutes and then have another 45 minutes [where] I didn't have anything to do so I could talk to the media. Then I'd do something for another 20 minutes and still have another 50 minutes that I didn't do anything. So when the doors opened at 3 o'clock for the media, I was there everyday and answering questions and various things about the day before."

Off the field, Boggs displayed a knack for larger-than-life exploits. He was once robbed at knifepoint outside a restaurant, but he said he escaped injury by willing himself invisible. He once said he was run over by his wife, Debby, after he fell out of a truck she was driving—yet he was not hurt.

His most notorious tale began unfolding in June 1988, when his former lover, Margo Adams, sued Boggs for $11.5 million. Adams said

Boggs promised to repay her for wages she lost while traveling with him during their four years together.

When the story broke, Sox general manager Lou Gorman was worried it would tear apart the Sox, who were struggling to stay afloat in the AL East. Boggs and the Sox were further embarrassed over the subsequent calendar year as Adams appeared on "The Phil Donahue Show," posed for *Penthouse*, and conducted a two-part interview with the magazine. Adams' lawyers also tried to subpoena Boggs' teammates.

In the spring of 1989, Boggs—against the advice of Gorman—appeared on the ABC newsmagazine "20/20" with his wife. Boggs admitted to being a "sexaholic" during an interview with the renowned Barbara Walters.

Not surprisingly, Boggs was the target of constant abuse by fans in opposing stadiums and a popular interview request for out-of-town writers, who wondered if the news was distracting Boggs and if it caused the midseason firing of McNamara.

But through it all, Boggs had perhaps the finest stretch of his career. He hit a remarkable .380 after the All-Star Break in 1988 and finished the season with a career-high 125 walks and just 34 strikeouts. The Sox surged from fourth place at the All-Star Break to the AL East championship.

"The comments he would hear were unbelievable, and for him to totally ignore that and to have the year he had . . . he was amazingly stoic to it," Gorman says. "He just went out there and played hard and played well."

While Boggs did not appear outwardly bothered by the controversy, he hinted during a 2005 interview that the coverage wore on him. "I'm not going to get into the off-field stuff," Boggs says. "The thing about it is, when you're an athlete, you're in a fishbowl. And if something does happen off the field, then it's going to be front-page material. So I'll leave it at that."

Damon continued to follow in Boggs' footsteps following the 2005 season, when, like Boggs more than a decade earlier, he left the Sox to sign as a free agent with the Yankees. But while Damon's exit angered

Sox fans—T-shirts mocking Damon were a common sight at Fenway Park throughout the 2006 season—he harbored no bitterness and believed playing in Boston taught him valuable lessons about shrugging off and accepting criticism, on and off the field.

"Boston could really tear up a player," Damon says. "There was a lot of pressure. Every opportunity I had [to accept blame], it was always my fault, because I can deal with it. I can deal with people saying 'Oh Damon, it was his fault.' I can deal with it."

Reporters didn't show up to spring training in 2004 expecting Manny Ramirez to develop into a quote machine. Ramirez, already shy and reluctant to speak to reporters when he arrived in Boston from Cleveland after the 2000 season, didn't take long to chafe underneath the comprehensive coverage of the Sox. He missed the Sox' home finale in 2001 for undisclosed reasons and then, after getting hit by a pitch in the next game at Detroit, sat out the final nine games.

He barely spoke to reporters for more than a year after he was lambasted by the press and fined by manager Grady Little for not running out a ground ball in September 2002, which made him a worthy heir to Ted Williams in left field. In 1956, Williams was criticized by the Boston press for his reluctance to walk to first base after drawing a bases-loaded, game-ending walk against the Yankees and responded by boycotting the media in 1957.

In 2003, Ramirez missed a key three-game, late-season series with the Yankees due to what was termed a severe sore throat. But he was seen visiting Yankees utilityman Enrique Wilson—his friend and former Indians teammate—in the lobby of his hotel. And in the Sox' first game following the Yankees series—a 14-inning classic on Labor Day against the Phillies—Ramirez said he was too sick to pinch-hit during a six-run rally in the ninth inning.

After the season, the Sox tried dumping Ramirez—first by placing him on irrevocable waivers, which meant any team could have claimed him and inherited the nearly $100 million remaining on his contract, and then by nearly dealing him to the Rangers in a blockbuster that would have brought perhaps the best player in baseball, Alex Rodriguez, to Boston.

Teammates and managers defended Ramirez throughout his first three years in Boston by saying he was anything but a clubhouse cancer and really just a shy and kind-hearted—albeit absent-minded—person who enjoyed life in his own unique way and found it difficult to express himself in English.

During his rookie season with the Indians, Ramirez heard people talking about O.J. Simpson, who was in the midst of his low-speed chase with cops through Los Angeles. Ramirez asked, "What did Chad do?" He thought the topic of conversation was teammate Chad Ogea.

But much to the surprise of those covering the team, Ramirez responded to his near-exit by opening up to reporters in 2004—beginning March 7, when he went up to writers unsolicited and started chatting with them. After a few minutes, Ramirez went to retrieve Millar, who was in a back room, and returned with Millar serving as his "interpreter," even though Ramirez was conducting an English-language interview just fine prior to Millar's arrival.

"It was hilarious," former *Boston Herald* beat writer Jeff Horrigan says. "And he just got better and better."

Ramirez spoke to reporters throughout the season and would interact with them even outside of a formal interview. He'd often walk up to reporters as they interviewed other players and distract them—sometimes with a simple tap on the shoulder, other times by spraying cologne into the writer's neck.

He also displayed a thoughtful side with longtime Boston radio broadcaster Jon Miller. As he walked through the clubhouse before batting practice one day, Ramirez noticed a downbeat expression on Miller's face.

"You OK, Jonny?" Ramirez asked. "You look sad."

Miller said he was fine. "You sure, Jonny?" said Ramirez, who patted him on the shoulder as Miller repeated he was fine.

"I decided to open up more to the press because before I was kind of shy," Ramirez told reporters at a press conference during the 2004 AL Division Series. "Me and David Ortiz and Pedro, sometimes we are not comfortable in our English. But [if I try] and give you guys five to 10 minutes, at least guys are going to say, well, I think he's not that good, but at least he is trying to talk to us and get to know him."

Ramirez wasn't the first legendary Sox outfielder to find some relief in his reluctant superstardom from a relative newcomer to Boston. In August 1967, Ken Harrelson signed with the Sox, who were in the midst of one of the closest pennant races of all-time as well as winning over Boston fans who had grown apathetic following eight straight losing seasons.

Few newcomers could land on a playoff-bound team in late summer and immediately emerge as a leader. But Carl Yastrzemski, who would win the Triple Crown and Most Valuable Player awards that season, was thrilled to pass the team spokesman baton on to Harrelson, who regaled reporters with tales of how he turned down more money elsewhere to sign with the Sox and play for owner Tom Yawkey.

"Good old Hawk," Yastrzemski wrote in his autobiography *Yaz: Baseball, the Wall, and Me*. "Now he could take over all those questions from the press in the locker room."

Said Yastrzemski during an interview at the spring training complex in 2005: "Instead of coming to me if something bad happened, [reporters would] go to [Harrelson, who would] always have a story with his shoes [Harrelson said he owned 200 pairs] . . . I loved it. The press went to [Harrelson] and they got stories."

There were at least two Ken Harrelsons. One was the quiet person who feared he'd underperform in pressure situations. But the one most people knew was the "Hawk," the happy-go-lucky goofball who rarely broke a sweat in a big spot and, much to the relief of at least one introverted superstar, made himself the life of the party with his attention-getting behavior.

For Harrelson, deflecting some of the attention to himself was the least he could do after seeing the microscope that Yastrzemski—viewed as the savior of Boston baseball by many fans—was under. "To see him

144

handle the pressure of the media—I'd never seen it before . . . it was phe-
nomenal," Harrelson says. "His execution, his leadership, was in a time
that no Red Sox player had ever faced—maybe ever, including number
nine [Ted Williams]."

Harrelson said the Hawk didn't emerge until he landed in Boston,
where he was inspired by the passion the sellout crowds suddenly had
for the game. He would stand in an on-deck circle and ask Hawk to take
over, or walk on to the field for a day game following a late night on
the town and feel re-energized.

"When I got here, it was only a nickname," says Harrelson, whose
first professional manager, Dick Howser, dubbed him the Hawk because
of his crooked nose. "The Hawk took a life of its own and we became
buddies, he and I. People who know me will tell you I'm very quiet and
very introverted. But The Hawk was not. He was just the antithesis of
that.

"And that's what Yaz was talking about, and he's right. It took a lot
of pressure off a lot of the guys."

Most notably Harrelson himself, who had the best year of his career
in 1968, when he set career highs with 35 homers, 109 RBIs, and a .275
average on his way to a third-place finish in the AL MVP balloting. And
while he credited Yastrzemski's protection in the lineup for his breakout
campaign, he also believed it wouldn't have been possible if he hadn't
embraced the second personality that he felt most people possessed.

"I've talked to some psychologists about it—they said it was very
common," Harrelson says. "They said you were very fortunate to at
least recognize that, though you may not have understood it. You recognized it at an early age.

"You have multiple personalities—everyone has them," Harrelson
says. "And I was able to recognize mine. I couldn't stand the pressure. I
didn't like it one bit. Hawk loved it."

The Hawk remained one of baseball's most notable personalities
long after Harrelson retired. He pursued a career in golf and regularly
channeled Hawk during appearances on the celebrity tournament
circuit.

Harrelson has become one of the nation's best-known broadcasters, first for the Red Sox from 1975 through 1981 and from 1982 through 1985 and again since 1990 for the White Sox, where he makes headlines for his opinionated and gloriously pro-Chicago tone (ironic, considering he was fired by the Red Sox for criticizing the performance of owner Haywood Sullivan).

"He comes in sometimes, yeah," Harrelson said of the Hawk as he sat in the visitor's television booth at Fenway Park in July 2007. "I'm glad it's only sometimes. Because when he gets in, [there's] usually a lot of stuff that's written about and talked about what he said. He'll say some shit that I'd never say."

The cause of Kevin Millar's candor was far simpler: His unique buoyancy, on and off the field, was born out of his protracted path to the major leagues.

Millar laughed when he was asked on his 33rd birthday September 24, 2004 if he was going to say he was younger than his listed age in order to enhance his standing in the eyes of baseball executives.

"I've never been a prospect," Millar said.

Even after reaching the big leagues and establishing himself with the Florida Marlins, Millar had to beat the odds again to land with the Sox. Following the 2002 season, the Marlins sold his contract to the Chunichi Dragons, with whom Millar signed a two-year deal worth a reported $6.2 million.

In order to complete the transaction, Millar had to clear major league waivers. But the Sox claimed him and Millar, who said he was worried about leaving America as it prepared to go to war with Iraq, decided he'd rather play for the Sox. Several weeks of contentious negotiations later, the Dragons released Millar from his deal and the Marlins dealt him to the Sox, who signed him to a two-year deal worth $5.3 million with a 2005 option worth $3.5 million.

Millar's free-spirited nature played much better in Boston than it would have in Japan, where players are expected to be serious and conforming at all times. With the Sox, Millar almost instantly changed the image of the Sox from rigid and divided to goofy and harmonic.

A video of a teenaged Millar lip-synching Bruce Springsteen's "Born in the USA" became a popular in-game clip during the summer of 2003. During the playoffs, Millar led most of the Sox—even manager Grady Little and general manager Theo Epstein—in shaving their heads and growing beards in a show of team unity. And in October 2004, Millar led the Sox in sharing pregame sips from a bottle of Jack Daniels during the historic winning streak that took the Sox from the edge of elimination in the AL Championship Series to world champions.

Late in the 2004 season, an alternately hilarious and touching moment occurred when Millar and recent acquisition Dave Roberts sat near Roberts' locker and played Wiffle ball with Roberts' son. As the youngster hit the ball, his dad told him to imitate the home run trots of various Sox players, which he did with uncanny accuracy. One of the son's shots landed in Millar's groin, much to the amusement of Millar and those who witnessed it.

Earlier in the summer, Millar found a picture of teammate Gabe Kapler, who had posed—shirtless and flexing—for a weight-lifting magazine during his rookie season with the Tigers in 1999. With Kapler out of the room—but plenty of reporters and teammates looking on—Millar pinned the picture of Kapler above his locker. When Kapler walked back into the clubhouse and noticed everyone laughing, he looked up and saw the picture, which Millar asked him to sign. Kapler, as good a sport as there was in the Sox locker room, obliged.

Taking on Kapler was one thing, but Millar also had no problem ribbing star pitcher Curt Schilling for his perceived love of publicity. Schilling was nicknamed "Red Light" in Arizona for his ability to turn on the charm and give good sound bites when the cameras were rolling, so whenever Millar saw a camera in the clubhouse, he'd shout "Red Light!" Schilling would inevitably turn around and laugh.

Day after day, before and after games, Millar stood at his locker and met waves of reporters. Out-of-towners—especially New Yorkers—

147

flocked to him, knowing he'd say something amusing for the next day's paper.

When the Sox were in New York in late September 2004, Millar was asked about the number of players growing beards. He said the Sox were turning Amish and they'd soon get rid of electricity in the clubhouse.

Millar was quick with a quip for a reporter outside the formal interview as well. During spring training in 2005, he saw the *Hartford Courant's* David Heuschkel standing in the clubhouse waiting for Keith Foulke, with whom he had arranged an interview. Millar told Heuschkel he looked as if he'd just lost his best friend.

"In terms of the relationship between the press and the team, I think Kevin Millar was one of the most important acquisitions made under the new ownership," Heuschkel says. "Every clubhouse needs a go-to guy or two or three. And Millar was that go-to guy.

"Millar was a godsend, he really was . . . Kevin Millar doesn't have a fake bone in his body. He is the anti-fraud. He is what you see. And I think his presence in the clubhouse has done wonders for the relationship between the players and the press."

Millar was also willing to draw attention to and absorb criticism himself in order to shield other teammates from the glare and focus of the media. He was always good fodder for the media, and took some good-natured ribbing such as when the blog "Boston Dirt Dogs" dubbed Millar "Kentucky Fried Kevin" because he was a spokesman for local Kentucky Fried Chicken restaurants.

In July 2004, midway through his second season with the Red Sox, Millar expressed his unhappiness with the boos directed his way and said he ". . . hope[d] those aren't the same guys cheering when I hit a home run. I hope they sit right down in their seats, and when this thing turns around, I hope they don't show up to the park." "Dirt Dogs" then lambasted him for telling ". . . third-generation fans they suck and to stop dropping $200 a night at Fenway 'cause he knows how this works having been in Boston for a year and a half."

Said Terry Francona in 2005: "Millar is one of the greatest characters you will ever see. But some of what he does is calculated. And I mean that [in a] complimentary [manner]. Part of what he brings is taking the heat off people."

In August 2003, with Derek Lowe being criticized for not pitching through a blister and the Sox under fire for lagging behind in both the AL East and wild card races, Millar told reporters he wanted people inside and outside the media to support the Sox because they would ". . . be a fun team to root for" once they came back to win the wild card or division title.

"I want to see somebody cowboy up and stand behind this team one time and quit worrying about all the negative stuff and talking about last year's team and 10 years ago and 1986," he told reporters.

The Sox adopted "Cowboy Up" as their slogan for the rest of the season and went 23–12 down the stretch to win the wild card. In the playoffs, they came back from a two games to none deficit to beat the Athletics in the best-of-five Division Series before a dramatic seven-game AL Championship Series loss to the Yankees.

"Last year, when they were on Derek . . . I went off on the media and it was all 'Millar can't handle the media, Millar's starting to tell the fans they're too negative,' and all of a sudden I was turning into this big, bad guy," Millar said in July 2004. "But all I was saying was lay off Derek. We need him.

"Sure enough, we did get him in the fifth game of the playoffs [when Lowe recorded the save in the clinching game against the Athletics]. And all of a sudden everything was all right."

In 2005, Millar asked fans and reporters to criticize him instead of new shortstop Edgar Renteria, who was off to a slow start in his first (and, as it turned out, only) season in Boston. "I am not a very good player, but I bring some intangibles and it's my job to speak the way I feel about Edgar Renteria," Millar says. "Don't let eight years of greatness be overshadowed by six weeks of whatever you want to call it."

Nor could a fitful final season with the Sox in 2005 (.272 with nine homers and 50 RBIs, his worst performance as a full-time player) overshadow the contributions Millar made in mending the relationships the Sox had with each other as well as reporters.

"If a few superstars don't want to talk [and] you can take some pressure off that way, I'll sit at my locker and answer questions," Millar says. "I would love to shower and leave and not speak to the media either, you know? But that was part of my job on that team: being a good teammate. I think you filter some of that. If I had to stay another 10, 15, 20 minutes, then I would. And that means in the good times and the bad times."

Chapter 8
Managing the Media

Managing the Red Sox is a job in which the inherent scrutiny and tension is best symbolized by the rapid rate of turnover as well as how close Joe Cronin, the longest-tenured skipper in franchise history, came to committing felonious assault—or worse—upon a writer.

"I think the hardest thing to do is be a manager in Boston," said Dwight Evans, who played 18 seasons for the Red Sox.

Yet only one of the two managers responsible for the most seismic seasons in club history arrived to find success and failure in Boston measured by one's ability to win the World Series. Those stratospheric expectations were made possible in 1967 by Dick Williams—who, while managing the Montreal Expos in 1980, intimidated with the silent treatment a rookie outfielder named Terry Francona who, nearly a quarter-century later, directed the Sox to the championship that eluded the previous 31 men to occupy his seat.

A two-decade pennant drought dulled the passion for the Sox prior to Williams' appointment following the 1966 season. A meager crowd of 10,454 attended Ted Williams' last game on September 28, 1960. That game completed the second of eight straight losing seasons for the Sox, who bottomed out during a 100-loss season in 1965. Dave Morehead's no-hitter at Fenway Park on September 16 was one of the few highlights, but it was witnessed by just 1,247 fans. Thirteen days later, just 409 fans turned out to see the Sox post their 62nd and final win of the campaign.

"I came of age as a fan in '61 or '62, eight years old, and they were terrible," *Boston Globe* columnist Dan Shaughnessy says. "We would have liked for them to go .500. I never knew what that was like."

Shaughnessy and thousands of others would get a lot more than a .500 season in 1967, when the Sox seemingly came out of nowhere and made a shocking run to capture the pennant and take the World Series to a full seven games against the Cardinals. As he wrote in *The Curse of the Bambino*: "There was no transition. The skinny little girl next door became a *Playboy* centerfold overnight."

Leading the way was Dick Williams, a 38-year-old who was just three years removed from playing for the Red Sox yet ran the club in demanding and distant fashion. He often criticized players publicly and was unsparing and harsh in his criticism.

Williams called George Scott—an overweight and sensitive first baseman—fat. After a stretch in which the Red Sox gave up 56 runs in six games, Williams told reporters "I think some of our pitchers will have to leave town" when he was asked if he was glad to see the Baltimore Orioles leave town. And when iconic outfielder Tony Conigliaro nearly died after he was beaned by a pitch on August 18, 1967, Williams reportedly didn't visit him in the hospital.

Williams' blunt honesty was a major reason he was a Hall of Fame manager as well as a peripatetic one. He managed six teams, only two of which he skippered for four full seasons (the Expos from 1977–1981 and the Padres from 1982–1985).

Francona, meanwhile, co-existed easily with players as well as his bosses. He turned 45 early in the 2004 season and had been retired longer than he'd been active, but his personable nature resulted in the adjective "young" regularly preceding his name. He joked, conversed, and played cards with his players, interaction that would have been unimaginable between a player and a manager a generation earlier.

"Dick Williams—you get in an elevator with him, he wasn't gonna say hello to you," Francona says.

A lifetime in the game gave Francona a unique sense of every player's mindset. His dad, Tito, played 15 years in the majors, and Francona was the national player of the year at the University of Arizona before he was selected in the first round of the 1980 draft by the Montreal Expos. But several knee injuries and a lack of power ruined any chance the younger Francona had at stardom and turned him into a pinch-hitting journeyman who played for five teams from 1981 through 1990.

"I think I was a lot like anybody else [when he reached the majors]—

thought I was going to be a young hotshot, make a lot of money, retire, be a golfer, all of that," Francona said with a grin during an interview in September 2004. "[But] I also thought if I was good enough—even with the injuries—I would be productive enough [to play everyday]. And I wasn't. I just wasn't.

"And I think maybe something else [my career] taught me [was] to evaluate myself better, because it's hard to evaluate yourself. I could still get hits and singles, but couldn't run. I didn't hit for power, I didn't have a lot of ways to help teams win by playing everyday."

Francona was as unyieldingly positive with his players as he was brutally honest in assessing his own career. He was cautious never to criticize a player through the media and made sure to inform him of a decision—from something as mundane as a day off or minor lineup alteration to more serious matters such as assignments to the minor leagues or disabled list—before he broke the news to the press.

He was also willing to absorb the blame for players if it meant extinguishing a potential controversy. When Pedro Martinez left the clubhouse shortly after he was pulled from his Opening Day start in Baltimore in 2004, Francona said it was his fault because Martinez missed the team meeting where Francona explained the team's rules. On July 1, 2004, Francona told Yankees broadcaster Jim Kaat that unhappy shortstop Nomar Garciaparra told him he could not play that night. But Francona clarified his position after Garciaparra was criticized for not playing in that night's 13-inning classic.

"That doesn't sound like it came out like I would have envisioned," Francona told reporters the next day. "If I misled Jim, maybe I made a mistake."

Part of Francona's managerial style was a reflection of his personality, but it was also an indicator of the escalating player salaries and the players' corresponding sense of entitlement which made it impossible for a modern manager to enjoy a Williams-like autonomy.

"Oh, it's so different [from] when I first came up [in] 1980," Francona says. "I used to hear the phrase all the time: I want to treat people like I wanted to be treated. You can't say that anymore. You have to treat players like they expected to be treated, because times have changed. It doesn't mean you sacrifice your principles, but people have changed. Not just in baseball, it's everywhere."

Nor, in Williams' era, was a manager's ability to deal with the press a determining factor in his ability to find employment. But the media had proven to be a distraction for many recent Sox managers—an overwhelming one, in some cases—and it was essential for owner John Henry and general manager Theo Epstein to gauge how managerial candidates would handle the analysis and interrogation they'd face more than 200 days a year.

So on November 5, 2003, one of those "only in Boston" moments occurred as Francona—fresh off a marathon interview session with Epstein—met with reporters to discuss what it'd be like to have a job he hadn't even been offered.

Twenty-nine days later, a more traditional press conference was held after the Sox named Francona manager. A manager can't win the World Series on his first official day on the job, but as the likes of Butch Hobson, Jimy Williams, and Kevin Kennedy learned, he can begin to lose the press. Francona elicited plenty of laughs with a self-deprecating attitude that was nonetheless laced with an undercurrent of self-confidence.

"Think about it for a second," Francona told reporters. "I've been released by six teams. I've been fired as a manager. I've got no hair. I've got a nose that's three sizes too big for my face. And I grew up in major league clubhouses.

"My skin's pretty thick. I'll be okay."

The previous quarter-century suggested the thick skin would come in handy. The "Impossible Dream" season of 1967 bought the Sox several seasons of goodwill in which external expectations remained manageable. The Sox advanced to the World Series again in 1975 and again fell in seven games. The *Boston Globe* headline following the Game Seven loss read "Reds win—but what a year we had." The newspaper also produced bumper stickers reading "Wait Til Next Year." And in January 1976, the *Boston Herald-American* published a series of stories titled "Why We'll Win in '76."

The honeymoon came to a screeching halt in 1978. A playoff berth appeared certain when the Sox reached the All-Star Break with a 57–26 record—a 111-win pace—and a nine-game lead in the AL East. But the Yankees, who trailed by as many as 14½ games in mid-July, stormed back and tied the Sox for first place on September 10, when they completed a four-game sweep in which they outscored the Sox 42–9. The trouncing would almost immediately be dubbed the "Boston Massacre."

The Sox fell as many as 3½ games behind the Yankees but won their final eight games and tied the Yankees on the final day of the year to force a one-game playoff for the AL East crown. But light-hitting Bucky Dent deposited a home run into net above the Green Monster—one of only 40 he hit in 4,512 career at-bats—as the Yankees edged the Sox, 5–4.

The 1978 collapse did not immediately cost manager Don Zimmer his job, but it cast a cloud over him that would hover until he was fired with a week remaining in the 1980 season despite owning a .575 winning percentage with the Sox. "I hate to use the phrase 'athletes choke,' but that's what people wrote," Zimmer says.

Zimmer's crusty exterior belied his sensitivity to how he was perceived, and he remained fixated throughout the fateful campaign on a handful of critics in Boston as well as in his locker room. He was the first manager to absorb the fury of talk radio: After the season, one local talk radio station wouldn't allow callers to identify Zimmer by name. Instead, he was referred to as "Chiang Kai-shek," after the Chinese nationalist who lost control of the country to the Communist party.

"I got along tremendously with the [print] media," Zimmer says. "Talk shows never let up on me."

The 1978 Red Sox featured several talkative players such as Bill Lee, Ferguson Jenkins, Bernie Carbo, Dick Pole, and Rick Wise. These players were popular with sportswriters but less so with Zimmer, who was consumed by what they did and didn't say.

"Zim's problem was that he took the newspaper articles to heart," Carl Yastrzemski wrote in his autobiography, *Yaz: Baseball, the Wall and Me.*

"Zim was a very sensitive guy and he's a very fun-loving, good man," says Butch Hobson, who was the third baseman in 1978. "And when your family goes home and reads shit about you that somebody's writing, it hurts. And Zim was very, very protective of his family."

Zimmer had a particularly strained relationship with Lee, who called Zimmer a "gerbil" and accused Zimmer of not starting him during a pivotal late season series against the Yankees because Zimmer didn't like him. Zimmer also reportedly kept a file of stories in which Lee criticized him.

"I don't want to talk about Bill Lee," Zimmer said during a 2005 interview. "I don't want to hear his fucking name."

The relationship between the press and the Red Sox changed following the collapse of '78. The paranoia and/or contempt managers felt towards the press in the first half of the century returned, albeit not with the vengeance exhibited by Cronin, who supposedly chased reporter Huck Finnegan through a train with a butter knife after the Sox lost the 1946 World Series to the St. Louis Cardinals. Cronin was mad at Finnegan because he predicted the Cardinals would win the Series. Finnegan was one of just two writers out of 300 to pick the Cardinals.

Following Zimmer, Sox managers would often display the short temper of Joe McCarthy, who succeeded Cronin in 1948 and chafed at the perceived negativity of reporters who asked him about the club's problems throughout his three-year tenure. According to the book *What's the Matter with the Red Sox?*, he would respond to such inquiries by telling reporters, "You take care of your own business and I'll take care of mine."

Reporters did not care for McCarthy's name-dropping nature, his New York pedigree (he managed the Yankees to seven world championships from 1931–46), or his secretive nature. The night before the one-game playoff for the AL pennant in 1948, he refused to announce his starting pitcher, instead seemingly reveling in keeping reporters guessing. Thirty years earlier, Sox manager Ed Barrow and his Chicago Cubs counterpart, Fred Mitchell, each warmed up two pitchers in order to keep the real starter for Game One of the World Series a mystery.

Players, meanwhile, also felt the coverage of the Sox grew more negative following the 1978 season. "I can remember the days when I would go and do an [interview] and there would be seven or eight writers around and I'd say something," says outfielder Dwight Evans, who played for the Sox from 1972 through 1990. "They would say, 'You sure you want to say that?' [Evans would say] 'What'd I say?' And they said, 'You said this quote unquote.' I would be like, 'That would be great if we could strike that' and they said no problem and it would be stricken. There was a trust.

"And then, I want to say in the late '70s, that changed. And so you had to be on your guard."

Still, prior to the 1986 World Series, neither players nor writers sensed the Red Sox championship drought was a storyline. "Game Six, I remember going over in the press box and the guy I worked with at the *Journal* said to me 'You know, if they win, they haven't won since 1918,'" *Providence Journal* columnist Bill Reynolds remembers. "I guess I knew that. But my point was [there] was never, in '86 any talk of that kind of stuff. All that happened post-Buckner—about the 'Curse' and they haven't won since 1918, never going to win again. All that stuff happened post-'86."

The Sox finished within five games of first just twice between 1980 and 1985 as attendance at Fenway Park began to lag once again (the Sox ranked seventh or lower in the AL in attendance from 1983–1985). Another middle-of-the-pack finish was expected in 1986, but the Sox cruised to the AL East title behind Roger Clemens, who went 24–4 in his first full season and won the AL MVP and Cy Young Awards.

The Red Sox were one strike away from elimination in Game Five of the AL Championship Series against the California Angels before Dave Henderson, a late-season acquisition, hit a two-run homer to jumpstart an amazing comeback by the Sox, who won Game Five in extra innings and crushed the Angels in Games Six and Seven at Fenway Park.

In the World Series against the Mets, the Red Sox won the first two games at Shea Stadium and won one of three games at Fenway to return to Shea up three games to two in the best-of-seven series. Game Six went into extra innings, but the Sox scored twice in the top of the 10th to move within three outs of the franchise's first title since 1918. And when the first two Mets went down meekly in the bottom of the frame, the scoreboard at Shea briefly but prematurely flashed the message "Congratulations Boston Red Sox, 1986 World Series Champions."

But the Mets mounted a comeback even more miraculous than the one the Sox had engineered in Anaheim 13 days earlier. Four straight batters reached base for the Mets, who were one strike away from defeat nearly 20 times but tied the game when Kevin Mitchell scored from third base on Bob Stanley's wild pitch.

Mookie Wilson then hit a slow roller up the first base line. Bill Buckner, hobbled by numerous knee and ankle injuries, bent down to field the ball. But it skipped between his legs and into right field as Ray Knight raced home with the winning run. Knight put his hands on his helmet a moment before he reached the plate, as if he couldn't believe what had just happened.

Upstairs in the press box, George Vecsey, a columnist for *The New York Times*, penned the five words that would become baseball's most referenced phrase over the next 18 seasons: "The Curse of the Bambino." And, as former *Globe* writer Ian Thomsen told former co-worker Leigh Montville in the latter's book *Why Not Us?*, his assignment changed from a story about the genius of manager John McNamara to one about his idiocy.

The Sox squandered an early three-run lead in Game Seven two nights later and lost, 8–5. The reputation of the 1986 team was forever altered by the defeat. Had the Red Sox managed to get that elusive third out in Game Six, former general manager Lou Gorman is convinced they would have been viewed as a lovingly quirky bunch, à la the 2004 Red Sox. The '86 Sox had characters such as Clemens, the superstitious Wade Boggs, and emotional pitcher Oil Can Boyd, who left the team for several days after he learned he didn't make the All-Star team.

"Losing, from a media standpoint, the fact we didn't win it, we had to live with it the next couple years," Gorman says. "I think we carried their expectations so high and suddenly we crashed. I think it did affect a lot of things."

It resulted in Buckner being remembered for one error instead of the 2,715 hits he collected in a career that spanned parts of four decades. "I think everybody pretty much agrees that the one play was not the determining factor—there was no guarantee we were going to win that game," Buckner says. "It was the easy thing to do: The Red Sox didn't win, so let's stick one thing out. That was the easy thing."

The loss also caused irreparable damage to the reputation of manager John McNamara, who was lambasted immediately after Game Six—inside and outside the organization—for not lifting Buckner in favor of defensive replacement Dave Stapleton, as he had throughout the playoffs. McNamara said he wanted Buckner to be on the field for the celebration when the Red Sox won.

"I think it ended up costing John McNamara his job," Gorman says. "I thought John did a great job with that ballclub. No one gave us a chance to be in that World Series when we started that spring training. But the fact we lost, it was almost a cross around all of our necks because we had not won it and we carried people to the brink of a tremendous celebration and suddenly it's over.

"Mrs. Yawkey recognized right away he should have put Stapleton in late."

The relationship between McNamara and the press was strained well before 1986. And the manager believed the controversial postseason, as well as the Sox' subsequent struggles in 1987—they finished 78–84—provided further fodder for his critics. "When they got their opportunity, they attacked," McNamara says.

McNamara said he had an "outstanding" relationship with the press in the other cities he managed—Oakland, San Diego, Cincinnati, Cleveland, and the greater Los Angeles area with the California Angels—but felt he was often treated unfairly in Boston and was subjected to erroneous reportage.

"There were certain individuals there that I didn't trust and would write things that were not true and factual," says McNamara, who declined to name those he did not enjoy dealing with. "Old newspapers are today's garbage. Once it's printed, it's supposed to be factual and there's nothing you can do to defend yourself. And by then retracting a story—it's too late."

Red Sox vice president Dick Bresciani, meanwhile, felt McNamara was wary of the press upon his arrival. "John McNamara was, I thought, a great guy, I liked him very much," says Bresciani, who was the club's spokesman during McNamara's tenure. "But John came in [and] I don't know where he got the notion from, but he was kind of chippy with the media his first couple years. And that set a bad tone that carried on after the fact."

During spring training in 1988, McNamara cursed out Shaughnessy for picking the Sox to win the division. "He hated me and I didn't like him," Shaughnessy says. "Two Irish guys who couldn't get along. But boy, he had a chip on his shoulder. In '88, he said 'Some people pick you first to see you get fucking fired.' He [saw] being picked to win as another negative."

1988 proved to be almost unbearably stressful for McNamara: Shortly before he was fired at the All-Star Break, he found red splotches all over his body. But Bresciani recalls McNamara's final season as one in which he struck a peace with the media.

"Funny story from John: It's spring training in 1988—it turned out to be his last year—[and] he was really good with the media," Bresciani says. "And I remember him saying to me near the end of spring training that year 'Gee, these guys have been really good.' And I said 'John, you know what, if you had listened to me four years ago, you wouldn't have this animosity towards you.' But I think people told him to watch out for the media, they're going to get you, so he came in with the wrong opinion."

There would be no such worries about McNamara's successor. Nobody was better prepared to handle the Boston media than Joe Morgan, a blue-collar baseball lifer who grew up in Walpole, a suburb a few miles west of Fenway, and graduated from Boston College.

"I had an advantage over [Francona]," Morgan told the *Globe* in 2005. "I lived here all my life. I knew about a lot of that [media] stuff.

"At least I thought I did."

Morgan played for five teams in a big league career that consisted of 88 games and spanned parts of four seasons. He moved into coaching upon retirement and spent 16 years as a minor league manager, including nine seasons as the manager of the Sox' Triple-A affiliate in Pawtucket, RI.

In order to make ends meet in the winter, he drove a snow plow along the Massachusetts Turnpike. He was so used to living on a budget that he was thrilled to receive a $50 gift certificate from a local clothing store after he appeared on a radio show in 1988.

Morgan did not make his big league coaching debut until 1988, when, at the age of 57, he was named McNamara's third base coach. At that point, even Morgan believed his dreams of managing a big league club had disappeared.

After all that dues paying, his big break was more a matter of happenstance than anything else. McNamara was fired during the 1988 All-Star Break and the man Gorman wanted to manage the Sox, former Mets and Braves manager Joe Torre, was broadcasting California Angels games.

"Lou Gorman told me 'You're the interim manager 'til we get somebody else,'" Morgan later explained to the *Globe*'s Gordon Edes. "I told him, 'Don't worry, you already got somebody.'"

Upon Morgan's hiring, *Globe* writer Kevin Paul Dupont identified him as one of the rare pleasant persons in an increasingly combustible clubhouse. "On a club loaded with players who have traditionally treated media members with the warmth of the Arctic, he has been a delightful maverick," Dupont wrote.

Morgan became one of the most unlikely success stories in franchise history. The summer was dubbed "Morgan Magic" as the Red Sox won a team-record 24 straight home games following his hiring and stormed back from fourth place to win the AL East.

He also endeared himself to reporters on July 21, 1988—six days into his tenure—when he stood up to Jim Rice, the fading Red Sox legend and a longtime foe of the writers. Morgan sent light-hitting shortstop Spike Owen to pinch-hit for Rice, a Hall of Famer, after which Rice and

Morgan nearly came to blows in the tunnel between the dugout and the clubhouse.

"I'm in charge of this nine," Morgan told reporters afterward.

Morgan embraced his sudden celebrity. Before his first game as manager on July 15, he invited photographers to take pictures of him as he filled out the lineup card. He was featured on the dueling morning shows "Today" and "Good Morning America" on the same day later in the summer and said he had to get a "ding ding machine"—an answering machine—to handle all the calls to his house.

He came up with other bizarre—and sometimes incomprehensible—expressions such as "six, two, and even" which he often uttered in 1988. He wowed the media as he told homespun stories of Walpole during the American League Championship Series in October 1988. In 1989, Morgan had his own television show. In 1991, longtime Sox beat writer Nick Cafardo wrote in the *Globe* that Morgan was ". . . the only Red Sox manager in recent history" who was comfortable with second-guessing and discussing his decisions.

"The best, by far, was Joe Morgan, because he was a different person—one of us and one of us in every way," long-time *Globe* columnist Bob Ryan says. "He was folksy and loved to tell stories and liked the press generally. Loved the process."

Morgan also had a disarming ability to immediately ask—or sometimes immediately identify—where a writer was from and give him an anecdote about his hometown. "When they would come in and hit him with tough questions, he would say 'By the way, where are you from?'" Bresciani says. "[The writer would say] Worcester. [Morgan would say] 'You know about that Blackstone Valley League? I saw Joe Blow pitch there in 1935.' He'd have all these great stories which would disarm the media. Joe was very good at it and he was very good with the media."

New York Times reporter Jack Curry learned just how prescient Morgan could be when he interviewed him prior to a game against the Orioles in Baltimore in the late 1980s. "I say 'Excuse me, my name is Jack Curry from *The New York Times*, I was wondering if I could ask you a couple questions,'" Curry says. "He pauses [and asks], 'Did you go to Fordham?'

"I said, 'How did you know that?' He said, 'Ahh, just a good guess.' I have no idea how this guy knew that. Maybe he thought the name Curry was Irish-Catholic and Fordham's a Jesuit school. He kind of broke the ice for me."

In 2005, Morgan asked a New York-based interviewer where he was from. Told "Long Island," Morgan asked "Islip?" The writer was actually calling from Bay Shore, one town west of Islip.

Gorman sensed that Morgan's native-son-made-good-status as well as his organic approach to managing initially spared him the criticism that dogged Morgan's predecessors and successors. But he wasn't immune from it: His decision to travel home from spring training to serve as the guest of honor at Walpole's St. Patrick's Day parade in 1989 was met with general disapproval. In 1990, less than two years after "Morgan Magic," he was named in local papers as the baseball manager most likely to be fired.

Writers believed he was less open and less candid in 1990 and 1991, seasons in which his moves were more scrutinized. "It comes with the territory—the more you go through something [the more] you withdraw, I guess," says Morgan, who signed a contract extension in the middle of the 1991 season but was fired in October after managing 563 games—a mere eight fewer than McNamara.

Patience was not afforded those who followed Morgan. Butch Hobson, who was promoted from Pawtucket to replace Morgan, struggled to be taken seriously after general manager Lou Gorman told reporters the Red Sox felt it was important to promote Hobson, a former Sox third baseman who had never managed above Triple-A, because they didn't want to lose him to another team. Gorman felt his comment was misinterpreted and said several teams had merely called the Red Sox to ask where Hobson fit into their future plans.

In addition, Hobson bore criticism when Roger Clemens, who famously operated by his own rules, didn't return phone calls from management the winter following Hobson's hiring and didn't report to spring training in 1992 until March 1, which was more than a week after the rest of his teammates and the latest a player could arrive in camp and still be on time under the terms of the collective bargaining agreement.

Hobson was subsequently derisively dubbed "Daddy Butch" by some in the press and portrayed as someone who was too easy on his players. His first game as Red Sox manager was at Yankee Stadium, where a crowd of more than three dozen reporters crowded into the tiny visiting manager's office at Yankee Stadium for a postgame press conference.

"Butch, [at] Pawtucket, had three guys covering every game," Gorman says. "We open against the Yankees at Yankee Stadium and when the game was over I went down to the clubhouse and there must have been 40 media [members] in his office—from our media, New York media, television, radio. All kinds of questions and he's dazed. And when they went away, he said, 'God, do I go through this everyday?'"

The Red Sox posted three consecutive losing seasons under Hobson, their first such streak in nearly 30 years, and Hobson was fired by Gorman's replacement, Dan Duquette, after the strike-shortened 1994 season.

Gorman says the ". . . 'Daddy Butch' [comments] began to bother [Hobson] a little bit" by the end of his tenure. "At that point, he withdrew a little bit from the media."

Hobson says he didn't read the newspaper during his time with the Red Sox and avoided talk radio in the car. "I figured what the heck do I need to be reading stuff written about me?" Hobson says. "I didn't allow a newspaper in my house. I know the first home game, I got in my car and WEEI was on. I got out of the car and I went over to [the parking lot attendant and said], 'I don't mind you listening to the game, but when I get in, I want my country station."

Hobson's successor, Kevin Kennedy, was the opposite: He loved the attention—too much, in the minds of some who worked with and covered him. "He's one of the great egomaniacs of the western world," Ryan says. "And [he embraced] anything in which he had a chance to put forth his viewpoints."

Kennedy was fired after the 1996 season and replaced by Jimy Williams, who, according to press accounts, appeared flustered by the large crowd at his introductory press conference. Williams, a folksy Southerner, alternately amused and bemused the audience by revealing a number of unique and sometimes impenetrable analogies.

Williams said oft-injured Red Sox slugger Jose Canseco could do some damage in a full season's worth of at-bats before adding, "I know, if a frog had wings, he wouldn't bump his booty."

He also revealed he helped players such as Otis Nixon learn how to scale the fence during his four seasons as the manager of the Toronto Blue Jays. "You don't learn that in the minors because they use chain link fences," Williams told reporters.

And during his first spring with the Red Sox, Williams said he wasn't sure if an hour-long meeting with disgruntled infielder John Valentin was unusual because ". . . I didn't start my clock."

Such sayings and analogies were dubbed "Jimywocky." Yet while writers lamented how much easier it was for television to convey a quotable person's nature, Williams got along far better with print reporters than television reporters.

He didn't reveal much to either side, choosing to use the wide-ranging phrase "manager's decision" whenever he was asked about something he didn't want to discuss, but in an interview with Ryan in 1997, he said he appreciated the job the media had to do and understood why the coverage was more intense in Boston.

"You're in competition, both with yourselves and with the other papers in our division, just like we are," Williams told Ryan. "I understand that. You've got to express yourselves in an individual manner, and I know that I'm not always going to like it. But, I tell ya, your job isn't easy. First, you've got to get the news, and then you've got to convey it. To me, that's not easy."

Reporters figured they were in for a more revealing experience when Williams was fired in August 2001 and replaced by pitching coach Joe Kerrigan, who had previously been a reliable go-to quote. But Kerrigan's lack of communication skills—during his first day as manager, he didn't tell Derek Lowe he was being lifted as the closer; Lowe learned with the rest of the ballpark when Kerrigan summoned Ugueth Urbina in a save situation—shattered his relationship with the players.

The Red Sox went 17–26 under Kerrigan, who blamed reporters for the Sox' demise because of stories they wrote based on clubhouse conversations, and he was fired shortly after the John Henry group took over in spring 2002.

Kerrigan still harbored resentment over his brief Boston tenure nearly three years later: Approached for an interview at Shea Stadium in September 2004, Kerrigan—then the pitching coach for the Philadelphia Phillies and now the bullpen coach for the Pittsburgh Pirates—said "I haven't talked about the Boston press for three years, and I'm not starting today."

Kerrigan's replacement, Grady Little, was a mix of Williams and Morgan. Little, who was 52 when the Sox offered him his first major league managerial job, regaled reporters with tales of life on his cotton farm in Texas and elicited laughs from the national media hours before Game Seven of the 2003 American League Championship Series, when he was asked if his wife minded he'd joined most of the Sox in shaving his head during the playoffs.

"She doesn't care," Little said. "She cares about me on the first and 15th. She doesn't care what I look like."

But Little's managerial methods did not jibe with those of the front office, which placed a premium on statistical analysis. Little preferred to manage by feel and gut instinct, never more so than in the eighth inning of Game Seven, when Little left Pedro Martinez out to squander a three-run lead even though stats Little had been provided before the game demonstrated that Martinez—who was at 100 pitches through seven innings—was far more effective before his 100th pitch than after.

The Sox went on to lose the pennant in 11 innings and Little's decision to leave Martinez on the mound seemed so obviously wrong to the reporters covering the game that his postgame press conference consisted of just two questions. The loss sealed Little's fate—the Sox officially declined to pick up his options for 2004 and 2005 later in the month—and on his way out he made multiple allusions to how difficult it can be for the Sox to overcome the specter of their own history.

"Hell, I've got people on that field throughout the seventh game thinking about Bill Buckner," Little told reporters on October 18, two days after the Game Seven loss. "That's a tough situation to be in. Everyone knows the environment here in Boston."

Four days later, during an interview with the *Globe*'s Edes, Little seemed resigned to his place in Sox lore. "Just add one more ghost to the list if I'm not there, because there are ghosts—that's certainly evident when you're a player in that uniform," Little said. "If Grady Little is not back with the Red Sox, he'll be somewhere. I'll be another ghost, fully capable of haunting."

Stepping into a potentially haunted house didn't seem to faze Francona. He was more comfortable in the public spotlight than Hobson, more telegenic than Jimy Williams, and less Hollywood than Kennedy. He also realized he could not adopt a falsely combative attitude, a la McNamara, nor take to heart everything written or said about him, which was a mistake Don Zimmer regularly made.

"I think, for the most part, I really enjoy people," Francona says. "So just because somebody has a pen in their hands doesn't mean [the relationship] has to be antagonistic or you're butting heads. I think the nature of the job is sometimes people are going to write things that aren't terribly complimentary. And if that sends me over the edge, I'm the wrong person for this job."

Plus, Francona figured he'd already been exposed to the worst of fandom as well as the height of media lunacy long before he arrived in Boston. As the manager of the Phillies from 1997–2000, he worked in a city even more starved for a championship than Boston, which at least had dynastic runs by the NBA's Celtics in the 1980s and the NFL's Patriots in the early years of the 21st century to lessen the sting of the Sox' championship drought.

The Phillies won a single World Series in their first century (1980) and enjoyed just two winning seasons from 1984–2000. The only Philadelphia team to win a championship in one of the four major sports since then is the NBA's 76ers (1983).

Flyers fans welcomed Francona to Philadelphia by booing as his picture was displayed on the scoreboard above the ice. And someone said goodbye to Francona on his final day with the Phillies in 2000 by slashing the tires of his car.

In between, Francona was lambasted in print and over the airwaves for his managerial acumen and for being too close to his players. "It's a tough place not to have success," Francona says. "It's an eastern city that has an edge to it, and we didn't win when I was there."

In addition, dealing with a massive media corps on a daily basis isn't quite so intimidating after managing America's most famous athlete for several weeks. Francona's third year as a manager in the Chicago White Sox organization coincided with NBA superstar Michael Jordan's dalliance with baseball.

As Francona put it, most minor league managers were used to dealing with ". . . two writers and you're happy to be on the radio." But when Jordan joined the Double-A Birmingham Barons in 1994, every move he and his teammates made was chronicled by an international multimedia press corps.

"Ended up being a great experience," Francona says. "All of a sudden, we have [crews from] "Nightline" and "Hard Copy" and people from all over the world. It helped me to not only deal with the media, but to be organized, because there was more to our day all of a sudden than just the game [and] batting practice. It was people wanting to talk and it was a new experience. It helped me learn."

Francona displayed a relaxed persona during his press conferences, often volunteering information and initiating discussion on any number of topics, from the hits stadium security administered on fans who ran on the field to his own experiences as an emergency fill-in at an unfamiliar position.

The day after Doug Mientkiewicz played at second base against the Blue Jays, Francona recalled a rare game in which he played third base for the Expos. "[Closer] Jeff Reardon had an incentive to get a save and I asked out," Francona says. "I didn't want to fuck up and [cost him] $200,000. I sat out the last two innings."

Francona would also regularly pull out an amusing piece of mail from a fan telling him what a horrible manager he was. Williams approached feedback from demanding fans in much the same way nearly 40 years earlier. As the Red Sox engaged several teams in one of the closest pennant races in history, Williams told reporters his mail was running decidedly negative and that the one supportive letter he'd received was written by his wife and children.

Nor did Francona mind explaining his decisions—a reflection of working with a methodical front office that armed Francona with as much statistical information as possible prior to the first pitch and dissected every game with him almost immediately thereafter.

New York Daily News reporter Roger Rubin, a Boston native who covered the Sox regularly for the tabloid at the height of the Red Sox rivalry with the Yankees, was impressed with Francona's frankness after September 23 decision to save the Sox' most valuable relievers for the weekend series against the Yankees and try to patch together the final four innings of a game against the Orioles with Terry Adams, Ramiro Mendoza, Mike Myers, and Byung-Hyun Kim. But the quartet combined to allow four runs in four innings as the Orioles won, 9–7, to knock the Sox 4½ games behind the Yankees.

"Terry said, 'I tried to get away with some things here, I tried to stretch some things out here,'" Rubin says. "He was trying to have his best pitchers well-rested for the series [against] New York. I had to ask the question directly: 'So you are saying that if you managed this game differently, you guys would have won?' And basically, he threw himself under the bus at that point and conceded that, yeah, maybe they would have won if he had done things differently.

"You don't get that candor all the time."

Francona's composure would come in handy almost immediately. The next night, he seemed to summon the spirit of Little in allowing

Martinez to begin the eighth inning with a one-run lead even though he'd already thrown 101 pitches. Hideki Matsui hit a home run on Martinez' second pitch of the inning and the Yankees went on to win, 6–4.

Afterward, Martinez issued his famous quote about how he should just tip his cap to the Yankees and call them his daddy. The next day, Francona diffused some of the tension during his press conference by asking what "Who's your daddy?" meant while also patiently addressing the questions about his strategy the night before.

"If I take Pedro out and we lose, Red Sox Nation may have been more forgiving to me," Francona says. "I don't think I would be able to look at myself and that's what I have to live with . . . I would never let people's emotions alter my judgment. If that affects what I do, [the Red Sox] got the wrong person. I don't think they do."

"I've got to tell you, my thinking last night was [about] last night— I can't manage any differently because [of history]."

Francona and the Sox were about to make an entirely different kind of history.

Players and managers alike had been reminded annually of the Sox' past failures in the postseason and struggles against the Yankees. In 1989, Dan Shaughnessy wrote the aforementioned book *The Curse of the Bambino*, a historic take on the Red Sox-Yankees rivalry beginning with the trade of Babe Ruth to the Yankees following the 1919 season. Prior to the deal, the Sox had won five World Series and the Yankees none. In the subsequent 84 seasons, the Yankees won 26 titles and the Sox none.

The book was updated three times, the last following the 2003 season, and the idea of "The Curse" became popular headline fodder and subject material for writers and desk editors across the country as well as a natural hook for the networks carrying games. Still, "The Curse" eventually wore on not only Sox fans—who got tired of the nationwide perception they were haunted by the ghost of Babe Ruth—but also writers who thought it was a cheap and lazy story angle.

Players, of course, grew more tired than anyone of "The Curse" as well as continually being asked about and compared to the heartbroken teams of Red Sox past. "They wanted to say 'That's not our history, we're about this year,'" *New York Times* reporter Jack Curry says. "But I don't think the Red Sox could ever escape that. I don't think the teams that were trying to erase that drought could escape the fact that people were going to ask them about 1918."

The franchise's heartbreaking history was referenced so much, Curry believed, that at some point the players had no choice but to allow it to seep into their thinking. "In a season where there's already a lot of obstacles, that's just one more thing that those Red Sox teams had to answer for," Curry says. "And I can't imagine it was easy to have to do it."

Says Zimmer: "It happened [for] so many years, I can understand people saying that or writing it—because, in a sense, they were right. That's the way it went."

It looked like it was going that way again when the 2004 Red Sox, who swept the Angels in the best-of-five AL Division Series, fell behind the Yankees three games to none in the AL Championship Series. No baseball team had ever come back from such a deficit and the Sox appeared especially unlikely to do so after losing Game Three in Boston 19–8.

Wrote Shaughnessy in the next morning's paper: "For the eighty-sixth consecutive autumn, the Red Sox are not going to win the World Series."

The Sox were unusually confident despite the daunting deficit. Before Game Four, the words "We Can Make History! Believe It!" were written on the dry erase board on the back of the clubhouse door. And Kevin Millar walked around telling reporters the Yankees better sweep the Sox because a win by the Sox would get the ball into the hands of Martinez for Game Five and, perhaps, Curt Schilling for Game Six.

The Sox ended up proving history didn't intimidate them by making it. They scored the tying run off the almost impenetrable Mariano Rivera in both Game Four and Game Five and David Ortiz delivered a pair of game-winning hits within a 22-hour span to send the ALCS back to New York.

The Sox didn't trail again until 2005 as they completed the remarkable comeback over their longtime tormentors with wins in Games Six and Seven before they swept the Cardinals in the World Series. The Sox, a franchise synonymous for so long with heartbreak, were the first baseball team to ever win eight straight games in a single postseason.

"I think there were plenty of Red Sox teams during all those years that were capable of winning the World Series," Rubin says. "But I think it takes a special type of person to be able to succeed in an environment where everybody, including the media that covers you, thinks there's a better-than-even chance that you're going to fold your tent and not get it done."

Says Millar: "We knew we were bad dudes. That's the way we lived and that's how we took ourselves every day. We had to keep tricking ourselves that we were the best dudes rolling, you know? True or false, we just had that arrogance and that swagger about us."

There would be no chasing down writers with a butter knife for Francona ("If you're down 3–0 and somebody writes you're down 3–0— I don't think it matters," he said with a laugh a year later). But had he wanted to pursue the skeptics, he wouldn't have had any trouble catching up with an exhausted press corps.

The postseason is a tiring time for writers even under normal circumstances, but the Sox' frenzied comeback—their final eight games were played in an 11-day span—as well as the desire to produce prose appropriate for the moment left even the hardiest scribe completely spent, if not outright ill.

"I know by the final game of the World Series I was just drained," *Globe* beat writer Bob Hohler says. "Everybody said, 'Boy, this must be the greatest feeling of your life, covering the Red Sox in the final game of the World Series, the first time they won in 86 years.' And it was an incredible honor and a privilege.

"But when I got to that point at the end of the marathon—when you're there in St. Louis, in that press box on deadline—the Fox camera zoomed in on Shaughnessy, a *Curse of the Bambino* shot, and people back home said I was just hunched over with my head buried in my laptop. An incredible amount of pressure because I knew I was writing something that could be sort of a memento for generations. And I was really running on fumes at that point. I had some respiratory infection, was on antibiotics, ibuprofen, Sudafed. I was a mess—just trying to get through it all."

Yet everyone was paying attention in the bottom of the ninth inning against the Cardinals October 27. Writers often bolt from the press box before the final out of a World Series clincher in order to beat the rest of the crowd to the winning clubhouse. But nobody budged until after Keith Foulke recorded the final out at 10:40 p.m. CST.

"You're witnessing something that hasn't happened in 86 years," *Boston Herald* beat writer Sean McAdam says. "You don't want your memory of it to be in the hallway watching the TV monitor."

"I remember just thinking, wow, this is an amazing thing that's happening to all of us in our careers right now," says the *Globe*'s Nick Cafardo, who covered both the Sox and Patriots in 2004. "I just wanted to take everything in and make sure I was really understanding how important this was, to be writing about the Patriots and the Red Sox for the *Boston Globe*—the paper of record."

Fans devoured the next day's newspapers—proving that good news can indeed sell better than bad news. Derek Lowe, who won all three series-clinching games in the postseason, was convinced otherwise a mere month earlier.

"You go to the grocery store, you pick up a tabloid or one of those stupid things, they have all positive stuff on the front page, no one's going to buy it," Lowe said during the final series of the regular season in Baltimore. "If someone's doing something bad, people pick it up. The *Boston Herald*'s eight pages of Red Sox stuff. There's not eight pages of positive stuff. You're not going to find it."

It was everywhere on October 28: Both the *Globe* and *Herald* doubled their press runs for the championship edition. The *Globe* distributed more than one million copies, the front page of which read "YES!!!" And the *Herald*, with a front page headline reading "AMEN," produced 600,000 copies. Numerous front pages touting the Sox' championship would be framed and hung along the walls in the hallway leading to the Fenway Park press box.

The title wasn't quite as cathartic for those who had come so close to bringing a championship to Boston, but it provided some relief for the managers and players whose legacies had been defined by their gut-wrenching near-misses.

"Eighty-six years to win a World Series, they were hungry for a winner," Zimmer says. "And unfortunately, we won a lot of games but we weren't lucky enough to have the winners that you would like to have. And they finally got it.

"When the Yankees went up three my first thought was same old story. Then they won a game, and they won another game. Then it got really interesting. I think it was a tremendous thing for baseball that the Red Sox won a World Series. What they did is something people will talk about forever."

Chapter 9
The Evolution of Theo Epstein

Nobody was ever better prepared to be the general manager of the Red Sox—and to deal with the inherent distractions of the job—than Theo Epstein. Raised a mile from Fenway Park in a family of passionate Red Sox fans—his father once said rooting for the Yankees would be like voting Republican—Epstein understood the singular demand placed on the Red Sox every season and how anything other than a drought-busting world championship would be viewed as a disappointment.

As someone who grew up reading coverage of the Red Sox and later flirted with a career in sportswriting, Epstein understood not only the insatiable thirst for information on the Red Sox and the fishbowl existence lived by a Sox general manager but also the jobs of those toting the tape recorders, notebooks, and microphones.

And as the youngest general manager in the history of the game at the time of his appointment, he recognized how the media had evolved into a 24-hour Internet- and talk radio-driven news cycle.

Yet growing up a fan of and consuming all things Red Sox did not fully prepare Epstein for the demands that awaited him. Nor did winning the World Series just two years into his tenure spare him the challenges encountered by his predecessors. And Epstein thought the "noise," as he often and sarcastically referred to some of the more inflammatory coverage of the Sox, grew more unbearable.

As a result, the Epstein who operates the Red Sox today is more cautious, reclusive, and wearied than the one who first occupied the general manager's chair in December 2002.

"My first attempt was to be sort of as open and honest as possible as I could while protecting the interests of the organization," Epstein said in July 2007. "That proved to be: a) extremely difficult; b) extremely time-consuming; and c) as things changed in the media world, not possible. So now I've taken an approach that allows me to do my job."

At least one Epstein contemporary felt he understood where Epstein was coming from as a fan—and how and why he ended up over-whelmed and frustrated once he was the subject of the coverage instead of the consumer.

"I think there's probably two different stories here," says Blue Jays general manager J. P. Ricciardi, a native of Worcester. "When you're not in the game and you're reading as much as you can, it's a great place because there's a lot of information. They cover the team so well. I think we all grew up on Peter Gammons and everybody like that.

"But I think once you get in the game and you start dealing with the media, it's a tough place. It's not an easy place. I can imagine it's not an easy place to play, I can imagine it's not an easy place to work. And it's a double-edged sword because it's a passionate place and they want their baseball covered. But on the other hand, there's no privacy and every-thing is scrutinized."

Long before he was the general manager of the Red Sox—and long before a young sports fan could catch up on what he missed the night before by tuning into one of the endless loops of "SportsCenter" on ESPN—Theo Epstein was just another kid trying to beat his brother to the morning paper.

"Our morning ritual was to race down the hall to see who could grab the sports first from the *Boston Globe*," says Paul Epstein's, Theo's twin brother. "We're old enough to remember Leigh Montville and Peter Gammons and Michael Madden and those guys.

Epstein wasn't the first Red Sox general manager with New England ties, but he was the only one raised within walking distance of Fenway Park. Theo and his brother were born in Manhattan on December 29, 1973 and moved to Brookline, a city of nearly 60,000 located on the Boston border, with their parents Leslie and Ilene in 1978—months before the Yankees beat the Red Sox in a one-game playoff for the AL East title.

The Red Sox weren't the hottest ticket in town in the early-to-mid 1980s, but Fenway Park was a classroom of sorts for Theo Epstein, who regularly attended home games with his family. While Paul would eventually bury his head in a *Highlights* magazine, Theo would keep score for all nine innings even in his pre-teen years.

The reading material was presumably left at home when the Epsteins attended Game Seven of the American League Championship Series on October 15, 1986—a raucous 8–1 victory that allowed the Sox to cap their miraculous comeback from a three-games-to-one deficit to advance to the World Series.

Ten days later, Paul and Theo—alone at home while their parents were at a dinner party—were ready to join the rest of New England in celebrating the Sox' first World Championship since 1918. With the Sox one out away from closing out the Mets in Game Six, the brothers climbed to the top of the family couch and prepared to leap off once the victory was official.

Of course, it never happened.

Baseball was a constant presence during Theo Epstein's high school years. In addition to playing the sport at Brookline High School, he began to analyze it and put his findings into practice as well. Epstein read the works of Bill James, whose sabermetric studies—coming up with new statistical measures by which to evaluate baseball—developed a loyal following in the 1980s.

While many of Epstein's contemporaries were putting their baseball knowledge to use by playing Strat-o-Matic (a board game played with dice and "player cards" that were based on a major leaguer's performance from an earlier season) and fantasy baseball (a burgeoning game in which the fan drafted his own team of major league players), he preferred a computer game called "Micro League Baseball."

"It was cool," Epstein said during an interview in 2004. "It was one of the first games to have a general manager desk [where] you could build a team and things like that."

As interested as he was in constructing his own team, Epstein's collegiate path and familial history suggested he was more likely to write about the game. Epstein's father is an author who has headed the creative writing department at Boston University since 1978. His sister, Anya, is a screenwriter. And the script for the Oscar-winning film *Casablanca* was written by Epstein's grandfather Philip and his twin brother Julius.

Epstein wasn't the first Sox general manager with an appreciation of the written word. Dan Duquette majored in American literature at Williams College and Lou Gorman authored a pair of books long after his stint as Sox general manager.

But Epstein was the only one who appeared headed for a career in journalism. He was the sports editor of the *Yale Daily News* as an undergraduate at the Ivy League school and introduced himself to *Globe* columnist Dan Shaughnessy at a Harvard-Yale football game in 1993, where he told Shaughnessy he wanted to be a sportswriter and gave him a copy of his column in which he wrote it was time for Yale to cut ties with legendary football coach Carm Cozza.

Epstein also worked in the Yale sports information office and took an internship in the media relations department of the Baltimore Orioles in the summer of 1993. After graduation in 1995, Epstein headed west to work for the San Diego Padres, for whom he served a season apiece in the entertainment division and media relations department before Padres general manager Kevin Towers hired him as an assistant in the baseball operations department prior to the 1997 season.

Epstein went to law school at the same time and eventually earned a raise and a promotion to Director of Baseball Operations—i.e., overseeing the minor league department—after he passed the California bar on his first try in 1999. Epstein's work was mostly anonymous, but his brother Paul watched Padres telecasts and scoured the Internet and newspapers in search of any glimpse or mention of his brother.

During the 1998 World Series, Epstein was captured sitting in a box seat behind home plate, operating the radar gun. And his work caught the eye of ESPN's Peter Gammons and the *Providence Journal*'s Sean

McAdam, each of whom would—to the great delight of Paul Epstein—occasionally mention Theo in their columns.

"That was a huge deal," Paul Epstein says. "I would tack it to the bulletin board in my office."

Epstein returned home in early 2002, when Larry Lucchino—the president and CEO of the Orioles and Padres during Epstein's tenure with those two clubs—was named to the same position and lured Epstein from San Diego. He spent 2002 as the Sox' assistant general manager and immediately hit it off with reporters looking to make small talk before a game.

"[I'd] sit in the dugout with him and I talked baseball with him—'What do you think about this guy? What makes him so good? What do you think of this guy from another team? Would you do this trade and that trade?'" CBS4 reporter Dan Roche says. "We'd sit there for half an hour and shoot the breeze about baseball. It was awesome.

"I remember calling him in the offseason before he got the [general manager] job. He says, 'I'm doing the budget now. How much do you think we spend on bats?'"

Epstein appeared primed for a long run as an assistant when Athletics general manager Billy Beane, who had built a perennial contender on a shoestring budget in Oakland, agreed to become the Sox' general manager in November. But Beane backed out of the deal to remain on the west coast, which opened the door for Epstein.

"I grew up second-guessing Red Sox general managers," Epstein said at his introductory press conference on November 25, 2002. "Now, I'll be the target."

Epstein was, by one month, the youngest general manager in baseball history. Yet he was unlike anyone who had ever before run a baseball team.

His predecessor as the youngest general manager ever, Randy Smith, had been groomed for such a position as the son of longtime Astros executive Tal Smith. Brian Cashman was only 30 years old when he was named Yankees general manager in 1998, but seemed much older thanks to his bespectacled and balding appearance and his more than decade-long apprenticeship with the Yankees. Dan Duquette and Dave Dombrowski each became the general manager of the Expos in their early 30s, yet each carried himself with suit-and-tie formality.

Though he appeared comfortable in a suit and tie, Epstein was far more likely to be seen in a polo shirt, jeans, and baseball cap. He was equal parts self-assured and approachable, a marked change from the uptight distance with which general managers tended to carry themselves.

He also had outside interests in a field dominated by men who prided themselves on their insular existences. Steve Phillips was just 34 years old when he was named Mets general manager in 1997 yet admitted he was completely oblivious to pop culture. During the 2002 season, he admitted he hadn't been to a concert since he saw Prince in the mid-'80s and that he'd never heard a song by Pearl Jam, the most notable rock act of the '90s.

Epstein, meanwhile, was not only a Pearl Jam fan—he wore a Pearl Jam hat to his season-ending press conference in 2005—but also played guitar and jammed on stage during an annual benefit concert at Fenway Park.

And unlike so many of his predecessors and contemporaries, Epstein was a celebrity, even if pop culture fame wasn't what he was seeking. Late-night talk shows alternately cracked wise about Epstein's youth—"The Tonight Show"'s Jay Leno said Michael Jackson dangled Epstein from a hotel balcony—and tried to recruit him as a guest.

The New York tabloids reveled in Epstein's image as a young genius: The *Daily News* reported he threw a chair upon learning the Yankees signed Cuban pitcher Jose Contreras, whom the Sox had also been pursuing, in December 2002. The *Daily News'* August 1 back page read "Revenge of the Nerd" after the Sox' successful moves at the trade deadline.

Epstein's family became media darlings, as well, as their passion for the Sox grew even hotter following Theo's ascension. Paul Epstein no longer had to scour the Internet for brief mentions of his brother, but he still immersed himself in coverage of the Sox.

"He tells me and my dad and my mom not to listen to 'EEI, not to read as much as we do," Paul Epstein says. "But good luck getting us to stop."

No other general manager had his family photos in the newspaper or a father providing enthusiastic takes on his son's moves at the trade deadline. "My parents showed pictures of me as a naked baby and others from that awkward phase as a kid, which for me lasted from six to like 20," Epstein told the *Globe* in December 2004.

After the Sox outwitted the Yankees at the 2003 trade deadline for players such as Scott Williamson and Scott Sauerbeck, Leslie Epstein called Yankees owner George Steinbrenner "Darth Vader the Convicted Felon" during an interview with ESPN.com and added ". . . it pleases me to no end" to know Steinbrenner was upset over the Sox' success.

"The fact that my son is part of doing that to him is even better," Epstein said.

Theo, meanwhile, preferred to work in the shadows and was reluctant to utter anything even the slightest bit inflammatory, but during his first two seasons at the helm, he was regularly available to reporters on the field or in the dugout at Fenway Park prior to home games. Reporters who covered him during his first winter meetings said he was candid about the players the Sox were pursuing and why or why not those players would be good fits in Boston.

He also provided behind-the-scenes access to *Lowell Sun* writer Rob Bradford, who was authoring a book called *Chasing Steinbrenner* about the pursuit of the Yankees by the Red Sox and Blue Jays, and was prominently featured in *Still We Believe*, a documentary about Red Sox fans and the 2003 season.

Epstein also reached out to the burgeoning Internet community devoted to dissecting the Red Sox. Whereas Duquette, in his final seasons, would refer beat writers to the Red Sox' official site whenever news broke, Epstein attempted to give fans a taste of the behind-the-scenes machinations of the club by holding online chats at blogs and message boards such as "Boston Dirt Dogs" and Sons of Sam Horn.

"I'm of the mind that no move really needs to be explained," Epstein said in May 2004. "The only thing that matters is the end result: How many games you win, how deep you go in the playoffs, do we win the World Series. That said, there's something to be said for buying in and fans having confidence in our moves. To the extent that [explaining the moves] doesn't betray [a] potential competitive advantage, we'll share some of our thinking."

Epstein said the plethora of media meant he and the Sox had to be careful with how they distributed their information but that he believed he could be open, accessible, and able to discuss most of the club's inner workings. And Epstein showed a knack for keeping the "state secrets" under wraps.

No one outside the organization knew the Sox were close to landing Curt Schilling from the Diamondbacks during Thanksgiving week 2003 until Epstein was in Arizona negotiating a contract extension with Schilling, who appeared headed for the Yankees before the Sox swooped in.

"We wanted negotiations with the Diamondbacks [to proceed] without one person knowing about it," Epstein says. "If [people] had found out that we were going to make a trade with the Diamondbacks for Schilling, there's one other team that probably would have [jumped into the bidding].

"We provide a lot of answers and five percent of the stuff is best not publicized. I think both sides can understand."

At some point, though, the ratio began to tilt. And while his departure as GM in 2005 and his subsequent return would serve as a convenient dividing line between the Epstein eras, his metamorphosis began long before he walked out of Fenway Park that Halloween night he resigned from the Red Sox.

"I'll snap at some point," Epstein said with a laugh during his first interview for this book in September 2004.

There was no snapping by the famously reserved Epstein, just a gradual retreat from public view that was, in fact, under way well before the Sox won the World Series. Shaughnessy wrote in *Reversing the Curse* that Epstein showed up to spring training in 2004 a ". . . less candid executive" than a year earlier.

"It never gets overwhelming," Epstein said in September 2004. "On the bad days, it gets mildly annoying, where we have so much work to do that has nothing to do with the media that I need to get to [and] the one-on-one interviews. It can be difficult at times. Today was one of those days."

It was difficult as well on October 22, 2004, the workout day prior to Game One of the World Series. As a cold drizzle pelted Fenway Park, Epstein held court along the first-base line with national media who asked him to re-tell stories old (the Schilling negotiations 11 months earlier) and new (the Sox' historic comeback from a three-games-to-none deficit against the Yankees in the AL Championship Series) he'd already recounted countless times.

Epstein, who wasn't wearing a coat, stood hunched over with his hands jammed in his pockets and his eyes darting around Fenway Park. It was clear he wanted to find an excuse to make an exit, but he continued to field questions for well over an hour before he finally broke free.

Most general managers can spend the bulk of the offseason holed up in their office building next year's club. But interview requests continued to pour in to Epstein in the aftermath of the Sox' world championship. At the winter meetings in December, reporters covering the Sox said Epstein was reluctant to interrupt marathon negotiating and brainstorming sessions to meet with the media.

The outgoing assistant general manager who used to sit unrecognized behind home plate in San Diego and casually shoot the breeze with reporters in the dugout at Fenway Park couldn't go anywhere—on or off the clock—without being noticed. Epstein now understood what it was like for players who initially welcomed the attention before it became unmanageable. Being the Red Sox general manager was an all-consuming job with no opportunity for privacy or down time.

"He was such a celebrity in this town," Roche says. "He had it tougher than the players, because if Johnny Damon or Kevin Millar or Manny [Ramirez] or [David] Ortiz or whatever is out to dinner, some fans might come up and say 'Hey, take your picture?,' shake your hand, get an autograph.

"Every time Theo has a fan come up to him, it's 'Hey Theo I'm not a crazy person or anything like that, but what do you think about this deal or that deal?' I think he got a lot of that wherever he went and I think it just got really hard on him."

"I can say, without any hesitation, that losing his private life was very important for him and he never really got over that," says Bob Hohler, the former beat writer for the *Globe*. "He's obviously had a girlfriend he's been very involved with the last couple years. I think their privacy may have become more important to him. And he was never really comfortable with that aspect of it." Theo subsequently married and the couple had a child, and the Boston media proved rather respectful of their wish for privacy.

Epstein dramatically cut his media availability once the 2005 season started. Whereas he once regularly ate in the media dining room and watched games—home and away—from a box seat near the field, Epstein now watched most games out of public view. He also grew less revealing about the status of injured players, often saying he could not comment because of national HIPPA (Health Insurance Portability and Accountability Act) regulations that protect a patient's privacy.

The building strains of the job as well as the cumulative effects of the drama taking place behind the scenes as Epstein's contract negotiations with Larry Lucchino grew contentious were clear in the series of photo galleries the *Globe* ran on its website days before his contract was to expire in October 2005.

The *Globe* organized the photos by year to give a visual timeline of Epstein's reign. The first photo in the 2003 gallery was of a fresh-faced Epstein, looking younger than his 28 years as he spoke at his introductory press conference.

The first photo in the 2005 gallery pictured Epstein standing alone at Fenway Park and glancing to the side with a look of weary exhaustion. His forehead and cheeks were creased, bags had formed under his eyes, and his temples were flecked with gray.

The stress finally bubbled over October 31, when Epstein, who had agreed to the terms of a new contract, resigned in the aftermath of the controversial Dan Shaughnessy column. But owner John Henry remained in constant contact with Epstein as he attempted to lure the general manager back to the fold. Epstein didn't do much to discourage the notion he was going to return during a flurry of media appearances promoting the "Hot Stove / Cool Music" concert in early January.

Finally, on January 19, the Sox announced his return. And the Epstein who occupied the general manager's office from then on was far different than the one who first occupied the general manager's office in December 2002.

Indeed, the Epstein who spoke in May 2004 of the challenges in dealing with the Boston media likely had no idea how prescient his words would prove:

"I guess I would say I was surprised initially at how important it is to have the ability to manage every small piece of information, because the smallest piece of information—maybe even a piece that's truly irrelevant—could, in the wrong hands here, become a firestorm publicly [and] distract our attention from the goal of winning that night's ballgame. I'm not a micromanager of information and I don't hoard information and I trust people, and I think now I see how important it is that sometimes the information has to be controlled in a smaller circle—keep it [on] a tighter leash, even truly irrelevant things."

During a day-long press tour on January 25, Epstein admitted the Sox could learn a lot from the New England Patriots in terms of how they managed their information. While many reporters took that to mean the Sox would become as secretive and unrevealing as the Patriots, Epstein said he was referring more to in-house communication and how news would eventually be released.

Epstein wasn't the only executive who believed the drama and news leaks surrounding his departure was the byproduct of too many "insiders." He tightened his circle of advisors in hopes of cutting down on news leaks.

Reporters who covered the team in 2005 and 2006 noticed an immediate change upon Epstein's return. Other front office employees, whom beat reporters could count on for casual off-the-record chatter, were suddenly far less visible and far more careful with their words.

"Internally, we had too many people with access to information—too many people who could share information for their own benefit," Epstein says. "We just kind of tightened up our ship a little bit, made our message a little bit more uniform. It's been helpful."

While Epstein would not be the voice of the Patriots, à la coach Bill Belichick, he would dictate the delivery of the message. Now the secrecy that accompanied the trade for Curt Schilling in November 2003 became the norm, not the exception.

Contract extensions with the likes of Coco Crisp, David Ortiz, and Josh Beckett were quietly executed. The Sox were rarely mentioned as a candidate to land star Japanese pitcher Daisuke Matsuzaka following the 2006 season, yet the Sox far outbid the Yankees and Mets for the right to negotiate with Matsuzaka, who eventually signed a six-year deal.

And manager Terry Francona, who impressed reporters with his candid nature and openness during his rookie season in 2004, would become a bit less forthcoming, even if the Sox' newly cautious approach to the release of information about injuries and personnel moves made for some awkward moments for Francona and the press.

Days before a doubleheader against the Yankees in August 2006, Francona told reporters the Sox would start Jason Johnson and Jon Lester in the twinbill but that he was unsure which games they'd start. After Francona's media session, Lester told reporters he'd been told he was starting the nightcap.

When Doug Mirabelli suffered a hamstring injury in the first game of a doubleheader in August 2007, Francona said during his press conference in between games that the Sox hadn't yet decided who would replace Mirabelli on the roster. As he spoke, NESN's postgame show—which was airing, on mute, on a television on a wall to the right of Francona—displayed a graphic indicating Kevin Cash would be recalled from Triple-A Pawtucket.

"I just think that these days it makes sense just to make sure everyone's on the same page, internally, and to get the information [out] if there's some official means rather than answer a question here or there and letting it trickle out—because, again, [of] the instantaneous nature of some media," Epstein says.

The reluctance to delve too much into injuries, meanwhile, represented quite a transformation for a club that was remarkably forthcoming about Curt Schilling's ankle injury during the 2004 playoffs. Epstein and then-team doctor Bill Morgan held a press conference the day after Schilling struggled in a Game One defeat to the Yankees in the AL Championship Series. *Newsday* columnist Jon Heyman called it ". . . one of the most medically graphic and hideously boring press conferences in ALCS history."

Thomas Gill, who replaced Morgan prior to the 2005 season, was rarely made available to discuss player's injuries. Beginning in 2006, the Sox described injuries in the most general terms possible, and declined to give timetables for a player's return. And in at least four cases, they were able to keep pivotal injuries almost entirely in-house.

Dustin Pedroia played the final three weeks of the 2007 regular season and the entire playoffs with a chipped hamate bone in his right hand that required surgery in November. Similarly, on October 23, 2008, Epstein let it be known that rookie shortstop Jed Lowrie had played most of the season with a sprain and a small non-displaced fracture in his left wrist.

It wasn't revealed until early 2008 that Curt Schilling had two cortisone shots in his ailing right shoulder the previous fall.

And the back injury that hampered Tim Wakefield over the final month of the 2007 regular season was actually revealed to be a shoulder injury that eventually limited him to just one postseason start. "Sometimes during a year, I don't feel the need to expound on things that put our guys in not the best position to succeed," Francona said during the AL Division Series. "It's back here [motioning to the back of his shoulder]. You can call it shoulder, you can call it back. We've been calling it back the whole time. I don't know that that's important."

The Sox did not go to the out-of-sight, out-of-mind extremes the

Patriots routinely do regarding injured players, and understood there were times when news of injuries and illnesses could not be minimized. In a five-day span in September 2006, David Ortiz spoke about the irregular heartbeat that sidelined him for nearly a dozen games and Lester held a press conference to discuss his cancer diagnosis.

Epstein made no exceptions, though, when it came to revealing details of his personal life. There was no changing the fact his job was one of the most scrutinized in sports, but he could minimize what the public knew about him away from the park.

He has refused to reveal the terms or length of the contract he signed upon his return to the club. Word of his engagement to long-time girlfriend Marie Whitney trickled out in May 2006, shortly before Epstein appeared at a press conference publicizing his annual benefit concert. Asked by a reporter to confirm the engagement, Epstein said he would be happy to discuss the concert.

During a group interview in August, Epstein grew impatient in declining to address repeated questions from an out-of-town reporter regarding the engagement party Red Sox owner John Henry reportedly hosted for Epstein and Whitney. The only details revealed when Epstein and Whitney were secretly married in January 2007 were of the false variety: Epstein's dad told the *Globe's* Gordon Edes that the two were married at a Nathan's Famous hot dog stand in Brooklyn, NY. Leslie Epstein admitted he was joking after Edes reported the Epsteins were in fact married in Brooklyn. The couple's first child, a son, was born in December 2007 and little about him was revealed other than his name, Jack.

In addition, prior to the 2007 playoffs, Epstein even declined to reveal what was on his iPod during an hour-long interview with Shaughnessy.

Epstein could still rely on his training in public relations when necessary. Epstein was criticized in print for his low profile as the Sox were in the midst of a five-game sweep at the hands of the Yankees in August 2006 that effectively ended the American League East race.

Prior to the Sox-Yankees game August 20, Epstein approached the dozens of reporters—many of whom were from national newspapers or websites—who had gathered on the field at Fenway Park. "I'm here while we're losing," Epstein said. "Fire away."

Epstein spoke for nearly half an hour, assuring—whether it was his intention or not—that early editions of newspapers both locally and around the country (the Sox-Yankees game started after 8 p.m. and, like so many Sox-Yankees prime-time contests, ended well after midnight) would portray him as candid and accessible in a time of crisis.

And in December, as the Sox' 30-day window to negotiate with Daisuke Matsuzaka neared its conclusion with no contract in sight, Matsuzaka's agent, Scott Boras, held a press conference in California in which he said pitchers of Matsuzaka's talent were worth more than $100 million and that the Japanese star would ". . . be known as Fort Knox" in America.

Epstein and the Sox responded by hosting their own overnight conference call with reporters in which Epstein, Lucchino, and owner John Henry all spoke and discussed how Epstein and Lucchino would fly to California to negotiate with Matsuzaka in person. The unusual teleconference occurred less than two weeks after Epstein told reporters the club preferred ". . . not to talk about potential acquisitions until it's done or not done" and that he believed the Matsuzaka negotiations needed to be handled privately and with minimal updates.

The Sox also made it clear that it would be the fault of the obstinate Boras if they failed to sign Matsuzaka. "I think it's also fair to say that we're on Scott Boras' doorstep because he hasn't negotiated with us thus far," Henry said. "So we're taking our fight directly to him—the fight to have a negotiation here."

Generally, though, Epstein continued to keep a low profile around the park and otherwise. All writers had his email address and his assistants were allowed and encouraged to pick up the media responsibilities that once fell on Epstein's shoulders.

"I definitely do that on purpose," Epstein says. "Because, one, it's hard to do my job when I'm available every day to every writer. So I just try to be around less."

Former Mets general manager Steve Phillips would host waves of reporters before every game because he saw newspaper coverage as ". . . millions of dollars in free marketing for your team everyday." But the Sox were a self-sustaining news machine, one that would generate thousands of words of copy per day with or without Epstein's contributions.

"Life goes on—it's not the most important thing in the world to answer the same question 45 times from 45 different writers every day about injury status," Epstein says. "Ultimately, it's not about me, it's not about any one individual, it's about the Red Sox. And there's plenty to write about over the course of nine innings."

While the events of 2005 were a popular explanation for Epstein's transformation, some reporters and observers believed a metamorphosis was inevitable—that Epstein was naturally cautious and preferred to release as little information as possible but that winning the 2004 World Series and returning to the general manager's position on his own terms allowed him to reveal more of his true personality.

"Theo's not giving away the family secrets," Bob Ryan said in early 2005.

"It's pretty gradual," Shaughnessy said in early 2006. "And then [in 2005] not gradual. And now it's dramatically different. It's unfortunate. I think this is more of who he is. It's too bad, because he's extremely smart and anecdotal and funny and we're not getting that.

"This is more how he naturally is. And he's able to flex his muscles now."

And some reporters and observers saw similarities between Epstein and his controversial predecessor, Dan Duquette—in terms of philosophies, if not personalities. Said one beat writer prior to the 2005 season: "He's Dan Duquette with better people skills."

Duquette and Epstein had similar methods of answering questions without revealing a great deal. Asked in November 1995 if the Sox had offered manager Kevin Kennedy a contract extension, Duquette said "We've had discussions over the past week. We're going to bring that issue to closure next week."

In September 2007, one day after top prospect Clay Buchholz threw a no-hitter in his second major league start, Epstein was asked how far the rookie was from his innings limit for the season. "Depends how you define far," Epstein said. "He's still got some pitching left ahead of him."

The new policies of Epstein and the Sox were criticized in the days following his return in January 2006. Shaughnessy, who often compared Duquette to ex-President Richard Nixon, wrote the Sox had ". . . morphed into the Nixon White House" and that fans should ". . . expect managed news from Yawkey Way from this point forward."

"Boston Dirt Dogs," meanwhile, posted a picture of Sergeant Schultz, an intentionally clueless character in the classic sitcom "Hogan's Heroes," underneath a headline that read "I Know Nothing! NOTHING!"

Still, while reporters could not help but notice that the Sox had turned into a less revealing organization, and while some were privately unhappy with the development, there were only occasional references made to Epstein's media philosophies—unlike during the Duquette era, when his contentious relationship with the press threaded much of the coverage of the Sox.

So how did Epstein avoid the negativity that accompanied Duquette for most of his eight-season reign? It surely helped Epstein that it only took the Sox two years under his watch to finally win the World Series. His initial openness and accessibility also provided him a margin for error and the basis for a mutually cordial relationship that Duquette never had working as he typically did through the intermediary of stand-offish media relations executive Kevin Shea.

"It could be so much worse," Shaughnessy says.

"I don't think he's ever been a quote machine," former Sox broadcaster Sean McDonough says of Epstein. "He's pleasant and cordial. Does a good job, too, of deflecting stuff he doesn't want to answer. He does it with a smile on his face. And that's the difference, to me, between the Dan Duquette and Kevin Shea era. I don't think a whole lot more substance has been provided by Theo to the writers and broadcasters over the years than Duquette. The larger difference is in the way it's communicated and body language and the tone and the manner in which it's expressed.

"I think that's why Theo has a lot more fans in the media than Dan Duquette had. He's pleasant about it even when he's not giving very much to you."

In addition, reporters realized the Red Sox were far from alone in terms of trying to search for an edge in the age of instant information by closely guarding and/or releasing misleading information about injuries and other personnel moves. Ricciardi was criticized heavily in Toronto early in the 2007 season after he admitted closer B.J. Ryan's bad back was actually an elbow injury that required season-ending Tommy John surgery

Tensions were raised when Yankees beat writers believed Joe Girardi was misleading them regarding the severity of an injury suffered by pitcher Phil Hughes in May 2008. The Yankees also refused to publicly disclose the timetable to move phenom Joba Chamberlain from the bullpen into the rotation.

"That's the way it's going everywhere," Shaughnessy says.

It took several requests over a year-long span before Epstein agreed in July 2007 to a follow-up interview for this book. He said he was initially reluctant to participate because he didn't want to contribute to the celebrity culture that surrounds some of the city's media members.

Epstein speaks only generally of the events that inspired his more careful and distant approach, blaming no one writer or incident but instead a new media culture that he believes trades accountability for immediacy.

"To me, a few years ago, there was a certain expectation that information would be used a certain way—there'd be a certain level of understanding, decorum," Epstein says. "And I think [that's lacking] with the increased presence of the Internet and the general sort of lack of standards that exist in it.

"More outlets, more blogs, fewer editors, lower standards for accuracy and accountability makes it a little bit more difficult. And it's a shame, because that limits the amount of interaction we have, the information we can put out there with people who still have high standards and still do their jobs very well."

Epstein said it was easier for him and his fellow executives to differentiate between mediums and personalities and judge media members individually instead of collectively than it was for Sox players. But with so many reporters covering the Sox and only so many hours in the day to do a job that consumes most of his waking hours, it was impossible for Epstein to do anything but approach the media far differently than he did four years earlier.

"In a perfect world, yes, there is a way to be open and completely honest and still protect the vital information and allow us to do what's the most important parts of our job—yeah, I guess you could call that ideal," Epstein says. "But the reality is we're in a slightly different age and we're not living in an ideal world. There's a lot of information. There are some people that use information in a way to promote themselves or to promote their media outlets that prove to be sort of obstacles to us achieving our goals—not in any big way, but in a way that adds up over time.

"I think, in a way, it might make me personally less popular. But I couldn't give a shit about that. I care about protecting the interests of the organization, which is to win games."

Chapter 10
Challenges Old and New in the Post-"Curse" Era

Nineteen teams won the World Series during the 86 years in which the Red Sox did not. It took just three more years for the Sox to become the first two-time champion of the new millennium. In the interim, the landscape of the media as well as the composition of the Red Sox—and the dynamic between the Sox and the media—changed greatly, yet a familiar foundation of timeless issues remained.

The Red Sox, long the most chronicled professional sports team in America, vied for worldwide honors as well in 2007 following the signing of Japanese pitching icon Daisuke Matsuzaka.

Japanese reporters covered individual players as passionately as American reporters covered entire teams, yet the coverage of Matsuzaka would be incredible even by the standard of a press corps that was already famous for its exhaustive chronicling of Hideo Nomo, Ichiro Suzuki, and Hideki Matsui.

Nearly 400 reporters attended Matsuzaka's introductory press conference—the largest gathering in Boston since Celtics icon Larry Bird announced his retirement in 1992. More than 100 members of the Japanese press covered Matsuzaka's arrival in Ft. Myers in February 2007 and his first game of catch was captured by more than 20 photographers.

Reporters on both sides of the Pacific wondered how famously cramped Fenway would accommodate the infusion of new journalists, but the Sox created seating by renovating the press box and building an additional work room behind it which also housed the Japanese-language postgame press conferences with Matsuzaka and Hideki Okajima, a reliever whom the Sox signed to far less fanfare shortly before they agreed to terms with Matsuzaka.

The Japanese press had a fascinating relationship with Matsuzaka and Okajima. Most Japanese reporters view superstars such as Matsuzaka as sources of national pride, and as a group, they are far more reverential towards the players they cover than their American counterparts. The Japanese reporters even bought Matsuzaka a birthday cake when he turned 27 in September, leading Josh Beckett—who celebrated his 27th birthday in May—to wonder why no one bought him a cake.

The overwhelming politeness of the Japanese reporters endeared them to the rest of the Sox—just like the Yankees had grown fond of the reporters covering Matsui. Yet Matsuzaka and Okajima tired of the attention and grew less accessible to reporters as the season progressed. Matsuzaka, in particular, frustrated reporters with his curt answers during postseason press conferences.

The rest of the Sox weren't as aloof with the English-speaking media, yet there'd also been an undeniable shift in the player-press relationship. It was by no means toxic, à la 2001, but it was certainly more distant than it had been in 2004.

The 2007 team was molded by Epstein, not inherited, and as a result it reflected Epstein's personality and philosophies. The 2007 Sox were a much more serious club than its championship predecessor. There was little mingling in the locker room: One former beat writer, at Fenway to write a feature story, observed that there was no one holding court at his locker, a la a Johnny Damon, Derek Lowe, Kevin Millar, or Bronson Arroyo in 2004.

When the clubhouse was open to the media, it was not uncommon for most players to disappear into off-limit areas and for reporters to outnumber the players in the room by a 5-to-1 margin. And the red line that ran in front of lockers and signified a player's space was believed to have been placed there at the request of Nomar Garciaparra remained in place until the 2008 season.

Unlike in 2004, there were no 30-something veterans reveling in their sudden fame and notoriety. Designated hitter David Ortiz was the most boisterous of the holdovers, but while he remained an often-hilarious quote—and while his Babe Ruth-ian reputation continued to grow when he hit a home run for a dying child in the summer of 2006—he made a concerted effort to keep a lower profile following the departure of

Millar and Damon. Ortiz also endured his first hiccup with the press late in the 2006 season, when he was unhappy with how his comments regarding Derek Jeter's MVP candidacy were portrayed in the *Boston Globe*.

Beckett, the ace of the staff, conducted interviews only on the day after his starts. Mike Lowell was as unfailingly kind as Damon, from whom he inherited the team spokesman role, yet sans the rock star persona.

The autobiography Damon released in the aftermath of the 2004 title was a bawdy tell-all, Lowell's autobiography *Deep Drive* following the 2007 season was an inspirational, family-friendly tome. And the 2007 Sox would not become pop culture icons—a far cry from 2004, when five players underwent makeovers the following spring training on the popular Bravo fashion show "Queer Eye for the Straight Guy."

Changes to the Collective Bargaining Agreement as well as Terry Francona's schedule further limited the time writers had in the locker room. Per the Collective Bargaining Agreement, clubhouses closed an hour before the first pitch, up from 45 minutes. And with his cramped office no longer a suitable place for his pregame press conferences, Francona spoke in the interview room, which meant reporters could no longer keep one ear on Francona and one eye on the locker room.

The homegrown core Epstein promised in 2005 and 2006, meanwhile, arrived with a fury in 2007. Dustin Pedroia won the Rookie of the Year, Jonathan Papelbon became the first Sox closer ever to record consecutive 30-save seasons, Jon Lester came back from cancer to win the clinching game of the World Series, and 2005 first-round draft picks Jacoby Ellsbury and Clay Buchholz made brilliant late-season cameos.

The younger players and those acquired from outside the organization mirrored Epstein in that they were almost always polite yet rarely revealing in their dealings with the media. It did not seem a coincidence that the new generation of drafted-and-developed Sox had all participated in the "Rookie Program" in which top prospects are brought to Boston for two weeks in January and schooled on what to expect—on and off the field—as a member of the Sox. Past and present Sox players spoke during the program, as did ESPN's Peter Gammons.

"They come up through the system and [are] certainly educated in how to handle the media," WEEI.com editor/writer Rob Bradford says. "And even the guys who come in from other systems—they're briefed on what to expect."

The initial burst of coverage in the bigs was often embraced by the homegrown newcomers, most of whom had already been heavily chronicled by the variety of websites and message boards dedicated to the Sox farm system.

"I don't mind it," rookie Kevin Youkilis said in September 2004. "It's quick, it's pain-free. You've just got to give them something to write [about] . . . I didn't think it was going to be that bad and it's not bad. I don't mind it. You kind of get used to it."

"It's a little overwhelming, but I'm kind of starting to get used to it," Papelbon said in October 2005, two months after his first big league recall. "It's fun and it's exciting and you get to be a part of something special everyday. And that's pretty neat."

But the attention they received in the minor leagues and upon their major league debuts alternately gave players an idea of what was to come and didn't prepare them at all for it. And like so many of their predecessors in the home clubhouse, the novelty of the passionate coverage wore off in a hurry for the likes of Youkilis and Papelbon. There was nowhere near the outward hostility that 1980s-era reporters recalled receiving from players whom they had gotten to know as minor leaguers, but homegrown players soon came to understand that to sit at their locker was an invitation to spend 30 or 45 minutes fielding questions.

As the organization grew farther removed from 2004, the more it realized the expectations—internally as externally—as well as the coverage of the Sox were just as high as prior to the championship. The subsequent three seasons proved the Sox did not need a catchy storyline in order to perpetually generate plenty of news about their on-field performance as well as their off-field drama—everything from who deserved possession of the final ball from the 2004 World Series to Manny Ramirez' quirkiness.

Jason Varitek flashed a tired grin and shook his head when asked in September 2005 if there'd been a change in the coverage of the Sox. "The questions are just different," Varitek said. "But the attention and everything is the same."

Being a part of the title-winning team did not provide a reservoir of goodwill for Keith Foulke, Mark Bellhorn, or Kevin Millar, all of whom were booed throughout a subpar 2005. And there was no patience displayed towards struggling shortstop Edgar Renteria, who signed a four-year deal as a free agent following 2004 but was traded to the Braves after just one disappointing season.

Nor did the 2004 title spare the Sox a barrage of criticism and unhappiness in 2006, when a spate of serious injuries and serious illnesses—as well as Epstein's reluctance to acquire immediate help at the expense of the prospects he'd been cultivating since his first day on the job—derailed the Sox in the second half and led to a third-place finish as well as plenty of empty seats in September at Fenway Park, where the sellout streak was not matched by bodies in the paid-for seats.

The remaining 2004 alumni also realized that as tough as it was to win one title, it was even more difficult to win another one. Nobody knew this better than Francona, whose relaxed demeanor turned wearied—as much by the demands of the job as the market—well before 2007.

Francona was never the picture of health—a series of knee surgeries left him with a painful gait and he suffered a series of near-fatal blood clots following one of those operations in 2002—but the scares he had in 2005 and 2006 served as a reminder of the job's inherent pressures and stresses. He was rushed to a New York hospital in the first week of 2005 with chest pains and missed several games with what he called his "fake heart attack."

And as the 2006 season spiraled downward during a brutal August, Francona spent one postgame interview session spitting up blood. He said he'd overdosed on his blood thinning medication and had also bit the inside of his cheek during the game.

After the 2008 season, Francona said managing in Boston is more taxing on a manager ". . . than any other place I've seen."

The all-encompassing nature of managing the Sox also affected Francona's interaction with the press. He still dealt with the biggest media throng in baseball with far more patience than most managers could have mustered and usually found a way to joke about the only-in-Boston firestorms that inevitably and regularly appeared.

Epstein and Curt Schilling were livid in April 2007, when Baltimore Orioles broadcaster Gary Thorne said on the air that backup catcher Doug Mirabelli told him that the blood on Schilling's sock during the 2004 postseason was fake. The next day, Mirabelli held a press conference at his locker and Thorne said he took Mirabelli seriously when he should have known he was joking ". . . in the context of the sarcasm and the jabbing that goes on in the clubhouse."

But Francona found it entertaining. "We haven't lost a game since it happened," Francona said. "Dougie got to do a press conference. He doesn't usually do [press conferences] except for when [Tim] Wakefield pitches. So good for him. We're fine. I didn't get to finish my puzzle, but other than that, it hasn't been a big distraction. I would have preferred to sleep past 7 [a.m.], but if that's the worst thing that comes of it, we'll be OK."

But Francona no longer had the time to make the type of small talk that dominated his press conferences in 2004. While he always remained composed on the podium, Francona took umbrage with the phrasing of questions more often as well as displayed exasperation with writers who tried to get him to look further ahead than the next ballgame or asked him to reveal personnel moves before it was absolutely necessary. And pity the writer whose cell phone went off during his press conference (though that made Francona no different than most of his brethren).

"I actually think in '04 I was oblivious to a lot of the surroundings and I think it made my job easier," Francona said prior to the 2007 World Series. "After I saw what '04 did for people around here, I think it actually made '05 harder. We came back and won 95 games and it was the hardest 95 games you've ever seen. And I think I started feeling the responsibility of every game a lot more, because I understood more what it meant to people around here. I think it made it tougher."

Along those lines, while the 2004 team refused to ponder the scope of what it was trying to accomplish, the 2007 Sox often seemed consumed by it. The Sox led the AL East for the final 166 days of the season and possessed the best record in baseball for most of that stretch.

Yet even though the Sox were the hunted instead of the hunters, the baseball season remained a unique grind in Boston. Players like to say the season is a marathon, not a sprint. Yet in Boston, even after finally winning the championship in 2004, it often felt as if the Sox were running 162 marathons a year.

The passion often manifests itself in worry amongst the fan base—particularly over the second half of 2007, when the blistering Yankees, who trailed by 14½ games in late May but shaved the gap to 1½ games twice in late September, threatened to topple the Sox—as well as heightened sensitivity by the Sox, who generally believed the press was too negative and paid too much attention to the Yankees.

"Oh the media's always negative, the media will always be the same," Youkilis said in September 2007. "There's always negative talk about something—always negative something somewhere. And that's not going to change. Yeah, we can be 10 games [ahead] and there's always going to be something that's going wrong. It's just the way it is."

After the Yankees lost to the Blue Jays in an afternoon game July 19, Papelbon walked by a television and smirked at the reporters milling about.

"Did the Yankees lose today?" he said. "Can we breathe now? Fuck."

Nearly two years to the day before Papelbon's profane bewilderment, Mirabelli expressed disgust at the exact same issue. The Yankees won three of four games from the Sox immediately after the All-Star Break in 2005 to cut the Sox' AL East lead to a half-game. On July 18, the day after the Yankees left town, Mirabelli saw the media gathered in the middle of the clubhouse and shook his head.

"Here are the sharks, they smell fresh blood," Mirabelli said.

Such scenes were proof that no amount of championships could ever change the composition of a player, who doesn't want to be distracted as he tries to prove wrong the critics—some real, some perceived—that drive him to perform.

These traits were particularly embodied in 2007 by Youkilis and Pedroia. Youkilis had no trouble fitting in with the laid-back Sox as a reserve in 2004, but as the starting first baseman in 2007, his perpetual scowl summarized the intensity of the season as well as made him a modern version of Dwight Evans, who admitted following his retirement that his obsession with the game could have made him seem unapproachable or unhappy.

"I think sometimes you just don't want to talk because you're trying to deal with the game," Youkilis said in September 2007. "I don't take a day for granted. This game, I've seen so much stuff happen—guys that have come and gone. People say, 'You need to relax.' Well, I'm not exactly signed for five years. I've got to play day-to-day and I've got to play year-to-year until I get a contract. I play to get a contract and to win."

Pedroia, meanwhile, had long fed off the doubts of those who took one look at him—he was listed at 5-foot-9 but was believed to be closer to 5-foot-7—and figured he was too small to succeed. He and his teammates sensed the doubters increasing after he hit just .191 in 89 late-season at-bats in 2006 and .182 in 55 at-bats the following April.

"It's tough when you pick up the paper and read 'He can't play, he can't do this,'" Pedroia told reporters in late April. "My family reads this and they get upset. I say you shouldn't listen."

If there was criticism, it was relegated mostly to the message boards and talk radio. The most critical thing to appear in a Boston newspaper was by Bob Ryan, who wrote in the *Globe* in late April that Alex Cora, Pedroia's backup, would have to play more often if he continued his torrid hitting—Cora hit .360 in 25 at-bats in April—and Pedroia continued to bat below .200. And with Pedroia batting .184 on April 27, *Herald* columnist Steve Buckley penned a piece titled "Pedroia's baseball IQ earns favorable grade."

The Sox stuck with Pedroia, who rewarded them with a sizzling final five months. He ended up easily winning the Rookie of the Year by hitting .317—the highest average ever for a rookie second baseman—and committing just six errors at second base.

Pedroia continued to display his defiance both during the postseason, when he said his early struggles gave people a chance to begin ". . . writing that the guy's 5-[foot]-2 and he needs to go" as well as the following spring, when he told reporters the Rookie of the Year was ". . . just something that sportswriters voted on" and that he might use the award as a doorstop.

It sometimes appeared as if the Sox' self-seriousness in 2007 would turn suffocating. But just like in 2004, these Sox proved to have the intestinal fortitude—albeit differently displayed—to handle the marathon-a-day pace of Boston, and exhibited this rare resiliency in the face of imposing postseason odds.

And the catalyst in the comeback from a three-games-to-one deficit over the Indians in the AL Championship Series—as well as a four-game sweep of the Rockies in the World Series—was an unlikely source.

Manny Ramirez' unpredictability was a constant storyline in 2005 and 2006. In addition to once again going silent with the media both seasons, he requested trades both during and following the 2005 campaign and raised eyebrows inside and outside the organization by sitting out most of the final six weeks of 2006 with a right knee injury.

Yet Ramirez turned loquacious again after a game-winning homer against the Angels in the AL Division Series by showing up to a postgame press conference and calling himself a "bad man."

Twelve days later, as the Sox worked out in between Games Four and Five of the ALCS, he told reporters he wasn't worried about his club's daunting deficit. "We're just going to go and play the game, like I've said, and move on," Ramirez said. "If it doesn't happen, who cares? There's always next year. It's not like the end of the world or something. Why should we panic?"

Ramirez' words earned him plenty of criticism—mostly among radio and television talk show hosts—but he helped teammates relax by minimizing the task ahead of the Sox as well as by absorbing the attention.

And when it was over, the Sox responded with exhausted relief instead of a euphoric release. The title-clinching battery of Papelbon and Varitek each wept in the aftermath of the Game Four victory over the Rockies.

Beat writers believed 2007 proved that the Red Sox didn't have to be comprised of self-proclaimed "idiots" in order to win the World Series. But the second title also proved that snapping the World Series drought required a bit of a lightning in a bottle and a serendipitous collection of players.

"I go with the thinking that in order to kind of break the ice and win that first world championship, you almost had to have an aberration of personalities," Bradford says. "In dealing with the media as they get closer [and] you have that kind of deficit that they had—they're going to get more and more pressure from the media. And they certainly had the personality to deal with it."

Executives and players alike had long warned up-and-comers of the potential pitfalls of playing in Boston. But the Red Sox of 2007 had to deal with issues unknown even three years ago—as did the reporters covering the team.

The question posed to Kevin Youkilis in the home locker room at Triple-A Pawtucket in July 2005 seemed innocent enough: What did a veteran of the 2004 world champion Sox have to say to his minor league teammates about what to expect once they reached Boston?

Youkilis' answer, though, sounded surprisingly cynical. "There's a lot of stuff you learn on your own, and in Boston, it's learning how to keep secrets and trying to be quiet," Youkilis said. "People are going to try to get you to do stuff and say stuff in the media the wrong way. Basically, just cover yourself.

"It's just not saying anything that can get you in trouble with the media is the biggest thing."

More than two years later, Youkilis explained he was not bad-mouthing reporters, just merely cautioning his teammates to be careful, every hour of every day, because he believed every move they made in public was for consumption in the media. Athletes had long enjoyed—or endured—a different type of celebrity in Boston, where sports was the city's culture and the Red Sox, Patriots, Celtics, and Bruins were viewed as much as entertainers as athletes.

"No matter who you are in New York, because of the volume of people, there is a community of people—a fairly large one—that doesn't know who you are," says ESPN.com columnist Howard Bryant, who has covered both the Red Sox and Yankees. "In Boston, as an athlete, everybody knows who you are. This is a sports-obsessed city, and it's really not the same in New York. There's so many people there—they go to the operas, they don't go to baseball games. They don't know anything about you."

"In New York, celebrities are real celebrities," *Herald* gossip writer Laura Raposa told *Boston Magazine* in 2005. "Ours are our athletes."

Ted Williams once complained that sportswriters cared too much about his personal life and not his performance. But by a few years into the 21st century, the gossip pages of the *Herald* and the *Globe* were the least of a player's worries. The immediacy and omnipresence of the modern media allowed anyone with a high-speed Internet connection to post news of their interaction with—or observances of—Sox players.

A player could decline an autograph request at dinner and, hours later, read about how he was a jerk. "If you're standoffish and say 'Hey, I'm just talking to my friends, can you please leave me alone,' they write 'So-and-so's an asshole,'" Youkilis says.

Players at a bar were likely to find pictures of them, drinking and mingling, on websites by the next morning. The Sox celebrated their American League East title on the final Friday of the 2007 season by heading to Game On!, a bar adjacent to Fenway Park. Within 24 hours, pictures of the players were posted on numerous websites.

There was no escaping interaction with fans even on the road. With tickets at tiny Fenway Park scarcer than ever—the Red Sox broke the major league record for most consecutive sellouts late in the 2008 season—Boston fans accompanied the Sox and filled up visiting ballparks and hotels from coast to coast.

"You have none," Terry Francona says when asked about the privacy of those in uniform. "You have none. What we have here in Boston is an incredible fan base—incredible. They're over the top. They're maniacs. And I mean that in a good way. So when you go somewhere, on the flip side, you can't just flip the switch and have privacy again. You probably hear some players voice some frustration from time to time, but I think they love the electricity of Boston."

A scene symbolizing the passion of traveling Red Sox fans occurred prior to the second game of the 2004 season in Baltimore, when some of the hundreds of fans gathered behind the visiting dugout started yelling for Kevin Millar—who was jogging around the bases during batting practice—to do his imitation of David Ortiz' home run trot. Millar responded by breaking into an uncannily accurate Ortiz impersonation as the fans roared their approval.

"You go into Anaheim and there are 15, 20,000 Red Sox fans there," former Red Sox spokesman Glenn Geffner says. "You go to play a playoff game in Oakland and there are more Red Sox fans than Oakland fans. Cleveland, Tampa Bay, or Baltimore, the hotels are overrun with Red Sox fans. It's pretty cool . . . you go on the road and the ballpark is full of Red Sox fans."

The Sox were not even immune from prying eyes on their own charter flights—or in their own apartments. Days after the 2007 All-Star Game, BarstoolSports.com obtained and posted pictures of the Sox' All-Stars relaxing on the way to San Francisco. In 2006, pictures of a Sox pitcher sleeping in his apartment were circulated on the Internet.

Message boards crackled with rumors and innuendo regarding the dating lives of Sox players. In 2005, a player's dalliance with a Northeastern coed was the subject of a *Boston Magazine* feature. That story originated when a Northeastern student found the woman's pictures on her Facebook account.

The player was never explicitly identified, but the hints in the story left little doubt it was a married starting pitcher. Yet the woman said the relationship was never sexual and the most damning piece of evidence was a picture of the pitcher—his face obscured by a black dot—with the woman on his lap.

As a result of that teammate's experience, Youkilis no longer poses for pictures with fans in public. "A lot of them go on the Internet—next thing you know, it's on the MySpace [another social networking site]," Youkilis says. "They put so-and-so with this girl, and it's a bad scenario. I don't take pictures just for that reason. And it's sad."

The Sox of the new millennium were far from the first players to believe the media had grown more negative and sensationalistic over the span of a few years. There was no doubt the passion for the Sox, and the frustration with their championship drought continued to increase in the 37 years following the "Impossible Dream" season of 1967. Yet a case could also be made that the perception of the media as a more cynical one was as much about the ever-wearing volume of the coverage as it was about the tone.

This time, though, the Sox could point to a new medium as the reason for the changing coverage. And reporters who wondered around the clock where and when the next big story would develop—and who had to constantly assess the ethics and boundaries of what was right and wrong in the age of instant information, all while trying to differentiate themselves from and beat the competition—understood the skepticism of the players and why they felt they were under the media spotlight 24 hours a day.

"The discussion begins and ends with the Internet," Rob Bradford says. "It changes how people report. It changes the competitiveness of it. You're not just competing against a couple newspapers. You're competing against newspapers and a whole bunch of Internet sites.

"Really, I don't blame the players, in a lot of respects, for being more wary because of the Internet, because writers are getting the instinctual nature to maybe be a little more free-wheeling because they have to get the story."

The popularity and immediacy of the Internet has forced writers and editors to reassess their approaches and priorities. "I think that writers are under pressure that few people sympathize with," former Sox vice president/public affairs Charles Steinberg says. "We're watching a change in how you go about your work.

"Does that mean that the print writers should now get their stories on the Internet right away? If so, do they forego time for crafting? Do they forfeit the literary artistry that really makes them proud of their work?"

Long gone are the uncomplicated days of a writer and a paper sitting on a scoop until it lands on doorsteps at dawn. Newspapermen still love the romanticism of breaking a story in print, but those who are ink-stained sentimentalists run the risk of getting beat.

And while breaking a story on the newspaper's website in the middle of the day leads to several hours of free publicity via the radio and television networks that credit the paper for the news, writers also worry it'll devalue and de-emphasize the print product because the competition can read the story and file its own report for the next morning.

In August 2005, Chris Snow and Gordon Edes learned during the early innings of a game that Red Sox pitcher David Wells had been summoned to New York to meet with Bud Selig regarding negative comments Wells made about the commissioner. The story was posted online shortly thereafter, but their fellow writers saw the story and Wells' meeting was the main topic of postgame conversation with Terry Francona.

"I don't think anybody else would have had that for the next day," Snow says.

Several weeks later, when Red Sox closer Curt Schilling told Snow prior to a game in Chicago against the White Sox that he was returning to the rotation, Snow decided to save the story for the next morning's newspaper. Nobody else had uncovered the story that night and Snow's scoop was still exclusive 12 hours later.

"It's tough, we're sort of always conflicted about if you know something, should you put it on the web?" Snow says. "And often that comes down to will that news come out before the day is over? If it will, it'll go on the web. If not, we won't put it on the web."

The major newspapers also began producing blogs in order to keep up with the 24-hour news cycle. Ideally, it was a place for writers to drop breaking news as well as nuggets of non-essential yet interesting information that might not otherwise have a home in the print edition.

In theory, such practices would make the websites a daily destination for fans as well as preserve the uniqueness of the newspaper. After all, what reason did readers have to plunk down 50 cents for the print product if they could get all the coverage online for free?

Bradford's blog, "The Bradford Files," was named the second-best mainstream sports blog by Boston Sports Media Watch in February 2008, and he was respected by fellow writers and fans as well as the players and executives he covered for his even-handed reporting and entertaining approach to blogging.

Yet he learned how confusing the world of new media could be during spring training in 2007, when he posted a blog item about Brendan Donnelly's dog and how the half pit bull, half German shepherd ate the cell phone belonging to Donnelly's wife. Bradford figured it was an interesting way to introduce a new player to readers.

Unfortunately for Donnelly, his landlord also found the item interesting and told him he could no longer live at the complex because of the dog. Ten years earlier, the story would have existed only in print form and the landlord likely never would have seen it. But Bradford and the rest of the beat writers had a worldwide audience now, which meant that everything—even journalistically sound and seemingly innocuous stories—had to be carefully vetted to make sure it didn't have the potential to create an awkward situation between a reporter and a player.

"On the greater landscape of comparing this generation to years past, you just can't compare it," Bradford says. "I'd like to see what one of the old-time writers—Dave Egan, the Colonel—would do if the Internet was around, you know? It's just apples and oranges."

Nor could Egan and his contemporaries have foreseen the day when Boston, which once featured nine bustling newspapers, would be one of the few in the nation with two. The rivalry between the *Globe* and *Herald* was a classic tale of the establishment versus the upstart: The *Globe* had the erudite reputation, the roster of legendary alumni, and the financial backing of The New York Times Company while the *Herald* was the brassy and independently-owned tabloid whose threadbare staffing was a matter of survival.

The spirited battle grew more intense in 2005, when the *Globe*'s corporate connection to the Sox was not only fodder for online media critics and analysts but also a rallying cry for the *Herald*. The biggest barbs in newspaper wars are typically fired between the competing editors and publishers, but the *Herald*'s accusations of a conflict of interest between the *Globe* and the Sox tested the friendships of writers who vied for stories while they were on the clock but often socialized together afterward.

"I do know for a fact that it's increased tensions between reporters for the paper and guys who do make those kind of accusations," former *Boston Globe* beat writer Bob Hohler says. "Those guys are friends of mine. Professionally, it does cause tension. I know Gordon [Edes] and Tony [Massarotti] had a brief frosty moment on one of those late Sunday night TV shows.

"The *Herald* is a desperate and sinking ship and trying to grab anything they can to stay afloat. [They] try to trip the *Globe* whenever they can. I'm sure that the *Globe*, being a competitor as well, is doing anything it can to get the upper edge. The only places where the *Herald* can compete is in sports and gossip and, once in a while, some crime stuff, investigative stuff. This is what's left. So it's clearly a battleground."

The *Globe* and *Herald* had one thing in common: They were trying to do more with less. With publicly held media companies expected to produce a far higher profit margin than most industries, journalism was well-known as a profession marked by its leanness.

But decreasing profits as well as declining readership and advertising revenue—classified and employment ads were increasingly placed on free sites such as Craigslist—combined to make the opening years of the 21st century particularly bloody for newspapers. The industry's rapid downsizing affected every print outlet covering the Red Sox.

The *Globe* and *Herald* made multiple and sizable staff reductions—most via "voluntary buyouts." Sports section staples such as Jackie Mac-Mullan, Peter May, Ron Borges, Bill Griffith, Michael Gee, George Kimball, and Mike O'Connor were among the writers eliminated.

Gatehouse Media, whose newspapers include dailies in Quincy, Brockton, and Framingham, had begun to "synergize" its coverage of the local pro sports teams long before February 2008, when it didn't send anyone to cover the New England Patriots—who were pursuing the first 19-0 season in NFL history—in the Super Bowl. Gatehouse stock fell by more than 80 percent between June 2007 and June 2008.

The Journal Register Company, which had dozens of newspapers in New England and covered the Red Sox from 2004 through 2006, had its stock delisted from the New York Stock Exchange in 2008 after it failed to average $1 per share over a 30-day period.

Those who remained employed realized no one was immune from the ax and worried about the future—of their jobs as well as the business—and, in many cases, began pondering career changes.

"It's a profession that I don't know that I would recommend to people I like, know, or care about," Chris Snow said late in the 2005 season. "It's a great job—you get to tell the Red Sox story or the team's story every single day. You get to follow them and it's a neat thing to be a part of.

"But the business, you look at it right now—the situation at our paper and *The New York Times:* They're going to offer buyouts to people. And after that, they're going to go based on pure tenure if they have to lay people off. And you're the youngest person getting into the place—there's very little security. So that's scary."

Snow would not be laid off. Nor was he long for the business. Early in the 2006 season, Snow received job offers from Yahoo! Sports as well as *Sports Illustrated.* Uncertain if he should accept a new position or remain at the *Globe*, Snow sought the advice of Minnesota Wild general manager Doug Risebrough, who grew friendly with Snow when Snow covered the National Hockey League team during the 2003–04 season.

In the course of their conversation, Risebrough offered Snow a job with the Wild as the director of hockey operations. Snow accepted and departed for Minnesota at midseason. For those who remained on the beat, Snow's rapid ascent and even quicker departure—he earned one of the destination jobs in sports journalism at age 23 and left the business before he turned 25—served as the starkest reminder yet of the transiency and uncertainty of the profession.

Further confirmations would come in incredibly rapid fashion during the 2008 season. The *Nashua Telegraph* stopped staffing Boston pro sports in the middle of a Red Sox homestand—even though the *Telegraph*'s sports editor and Sox beat writer, Alan Greenwood, was a past president of the Boston chapter of the Baseball Writers Association of America. The *Lowell Sun*, whose beat writer, Charles Scoggins, is the lead scorekeeper at Fenway, also stopped providing regular beat coverage.

The Hartford Courant, which used to have beat writers covering the Red Sox, Patriots, and Celtics as well as a regular columnist presence in Boston, announced it would no longer staff Boston sports following the Red Sox season. The paper's last two Sox beat writers, Jeff Goldberg and David Heuschkel, were both laid off.

While the suburban papers were cutting their presence at Fenway, Sox coverage appeared to be the one thing immune from the ax at the *Globe* and *Herald*, even though both papers endured heavy turnover throughout the summer.

Old media standbys leaped to new media while those who remained in newspapers jumped to longtime rivals. Gordon Edes applied for a buyout at the *Globe*—his request was turned down—and moved to Yahoo! Sports. May and MacMullan landed at Yahoo! and ESPN.com, respectively.

Joining the *Globe* in the aftermath of Edes' departure was the *Herald*'s Tony Massarotti, who was one of the most vocal critics of the *Globe*-Red Sox connection in previous years. Massarotti told media critic David Scott he would serve as a "hybrid" columnist who would pen more pieces for the web than for the printed product as the *Globe* tried to turn its website, boston.com, into a 24-hour destination. The *Globe* also added former intern Adam Kilgore, who had been covering baseball for the *Washington Post*.

Massarotti was one of three baseball writers to leave the *Herald* in the summer. Jeff Horrigan moved to Milwaukee with his family while WEEI, the hugely popular radio station, declared itself ready to challenge the local newspapers as a content provider by re-launching its website and luring Rob Bradford away from the *Herald* to serve as the site editor.

"I think, in their wildest dreams, [WEEI executives] probably see that it could become a local version of ESPN.com, with all these ways to cross-promote and sell," WEEI host John Dennis told media critic David Scott.

Bradford infused the site with writers up-and-coming (Alex Speier, Joe Haggerty, Jessica Camerato) and established alike. Michael Felger, the long-time Patriots beat writer and columnist for the *Herald* who hosted a drive-time show on ESPN Radio for four years, joined WEEI as both a writer and host. Bradford also brought aboard Ron Borges, the controversial football writer who retired from the *Boston Globe* following a plagiarism incident in 2007.

Less than two months later, though, Borges jumped to the *Boston Herald*, where he began writing as a general sports columnist in early October. It was as unexpected a union as the one between the *Globe* and Massarotti: In 2007, *Herald* general columnist Howie Carr lampooned Borges' plagiarism by writing that ". . . if any of my material sounds familiar, take it up with my joke writer, the *Globe*'s Ron Borges."

The *Herald* scored another coup in September, when it hired Sean McAdam away from the *Providence Journal*, where he'd served as the paper's longtime Sox beat writer and baseball columnist. Scott reported that McAdam, one of the biggest multi-media stars in the market, left the *Journal* after newspaper executives ordered him to stop appearing on WEEI and writing for ESPN.com.

In addition, McAdam's fellow beat writer and columnist at the *Journal*, Steve Krasner, accepted a buyout package from the paper.

The wide-spread personnel changes, backroom intrigue, and on-the-fly adaptation process were covered extensively by Scott and Bruce Allen at Boston Sports Media Watch and provided plenty of fodder for the media critique sites and blogs. Such coverage and analysis provided more evidence that Scott was correct when he called watching the media Boston's "fifth major sport" in 2005—and more proof that the mainstream media would have to adapt to the alternative media, not vice versa.

"I'm not saying there aren't alliances everywhere and people aren't in bed at every newspaper and media organization," Scott says. "But certainly, now more than ever—and because, I think, of the Internet—there's this perception of the writers hiding something or that there's dual agendas. And all these suspicions lead to the need for accountability and having people like me point out when there are missteps, [when] there are things that need to be explained.

"It's really caught on for some reason . . . they are realizing that sometimes, all that is written is not all that you're seeing and they're looking for a little more transparency."

2008 contained plenty of intrigue for those as fascinated by the media as by sports. Manny Ramirez, who reportedly told the Red Sox following the 2007 season that he wanted to finish his career in Boston and see his number retired at Fenway Park, continued to fill notebooks during spring training, when he spoke eloquently of his new-found interest in reading and spiritualism. Players and writers alike expected an MVP-caliber season out of Ramirez, who was entering the final guaranteed year of his eight-year contract and had team options the Sox could exercise in 2009 and 2010.

Nobody predicted Ramirez wouldn't even be with the Sox by August 1. But a six-week stretch that was wild and unpredictable even by Ramirez' standards set in motion a blockbuster trade executed just seconds before the deadline July 31 that sent Ramirez to the Los Angeles Dodgers, where he was reunited with Derek Lowe and Nomar Garciaparra.

Ramirez got into a pair of altercations in June with teammate Kevin Youkilis, whom he took a punch at in the dugout after Youkilis threw equipment following an unsuccessful at-bat, and traveling secretary Jack McCormick, whom Ramirez shoved after an argument over the number of complementary tickets Ramirez wanted at the last minute for a game in Houston.

At the All-Star Game in mid-July, Ramirez told the *Boston Herald* he wanted the Sox to let him know if they were going to exercise his options or negotiate a new deal with him and that he didn't want any ". . . more [expletive] where they tell you one thing and behind your back they do another thing." Owner John Henry responded that he was "personally" offended by Ramirez' comments.

Ramirez also began to field familiar criticism for his effort as well as his willingness to play. Against the Angels July 18, he overran the ball while trying to field a base hit, then stumbled after it and fell on top of it before he reached under himself to retrieve it. Ramirez laughed, but television cameras captured the disgusted faces of Theo Epstein and Terry Francona.

Less than a week later, Ramirez told Francona he could not play in consecutive games against the Mariners and Yankees due to soreness in his right knee. The Sox were facing hard-throwing right-handers Felix Hernandez and Joba Chamberlain in those contests and lost the latter game 1-0.

During the game against the Yankees, the Sox announced Ramirez had an MRI performed on both knees and that the tests came back clean—an unusual move for a team that prided itself on keeping even the tamest of team business within the clubhouse. Ramirez returned to the lineup July 26, the same day Theo Epstein told Fox broadcaster Tim McCarver the Sox would try to trade Ramirez if he wanted to waive his no-trade clause.

The day after that, Ramirez told reporters he'd like to be traded. "I'm tired of them, they're tired of me," he said.

Ramirez played his final game for the Red Sox July 30, when the Angels completed a three-game sweep with a 9–2 win. It was the fifth loss in six games for the Sox, and those in attendance at Fenway Park said there was a noticeable pall throughout the three-game series, during which Ramirez was booed for his lackadaisical trots to first base.

The next day, he was traded—and went on to hit .396 with 17 homers and 53 RBIs in leading the Dodgers to the NL West crown while receiving credit for loosening the mood and raising the morale of the entire franchise. Despite all the drama over the final weeks of his Sox tenure, Ramirez was almost as hot prior to the trade: He hit .347 in July and was hitting .487 during an 11-game hitting streak when he asked out of the lineup against the Mariners and Yankees.

Ramirez was not the first Sox superstar to leave in contentious fashion, and the criticism that flowed in his direction prior to and following the trade raised familiar questions about the organization's role in shaping public opinion of an exiled player.

"The Red Sox don't deserve a player like me," Ramirez told ESPN-Deportes.com July 30. "During my years here I've seen how they have mistreated other great players when they didn't want them, to try to turn the fans against them."

The *Providence Journal*'s Sean McAdam reported on August 1 that Epstein traded Ramirez after receiving unanimous approval from a handful of veterans. Exactly two weeks earlier, former television anchor Bob Lobel told WEEI that there was ". . . a strong feeling" within the front office that Ramirez was protesting the fine he received for shoving McCormick when he took three straight strikes during a pinch-hitting appearance against the Yankees' Mariano Rivera on July 6.

The day after the trade, *Boston Herald* columnist Gerry Callahan blasted Ramirez for blowing off cancer-stricken children during a meet-and-greet with the Sox earlier in the season. Listeners to Callahan's show on WEEI were also reminded of the pledge Ramirez made when signing a $160 million deal in 2001 that he would donate $1 million to area programs for Latino youth. By the time he left for the Dodgers, he had still failed to do so.

But nobody was as passionate in criticizing Ramirez as ESPN's Peter Gammons during a blistering three-minute interview on ESPN

Radio 890 hours after the trade. He called Ramirez an "affront, an embarrassment to the game" and said Ramirez had also quit on the Sox in 2006.

"I get sick of people in Boston adoring a guy that didn't play hard and was only interested in the money," Gammons said. "He could have played on a team that had a chance to go to the World Series again. He chose not to. He blackmailed them. He had a sit-down strike.

"What about the integrity of playing the game right and showing up and honoring your contract? When it comes to the Hall of Fame, I think a lot of people will have a lot more questions about Manny Ramirez than Mark McGwire."

Following Gammons' blasting of Ramirez, ESPN Radio co-host Mike Salk said listeners should "consider the source," alluding to Gammons' friendship with Theo Epstein, and added ". . . the spin starts early" after major trades.

The criticism of Ramirez represented a dramatic departure for Gammons, who had praised Ramirez throughout the first several months of the season. When Ramirez got into the scuffle with Youkilis, Gammons told ESPN Radio that he thought ". . . it was good that it was Manny that took it upon himself to say something" to Youkilis, who was famous for his displays of emotion in the dugout.

Earlier in June, Gammons told ESPN Radio there was ". . . no question [Ramirez] cares. He's asked me a couple of times this year about the Hall of Fame and questions like that. There's no question that he cares about his place in the game. As carefree as he pretends to be, he does care about records and his place in history."

On July 30, 2005—when Ramirez appeared to be trying to force his way out of Boston with another spate of oddly timed injuries and lack of hustle—Gammons spoke at the Baseball Hall of Fame, where he was preparing to accept the J.G. Taylor Spink Award for journalistic excellence, and said he thought Ramirez deserved unanimous election into the Hall of Fame.

"The numbers are astounding," Gammons said. "There are myths that we sometimes don't understand, and his latest frustration in Boston over the last two weeks have disappointed me. No matter what's wrong, I think you should always play hard. But there's no question in my mind—Manny Ramirez is a Hall of Fame player."

Ramirez' departure and the coverage of it didn't generate quite as much of an uproar as "Spygate," an eight-month firestorm that began in September 2007, when the New England Patriots were caught videotaping the rival New York Jets' sideline coaches from an unapproved location during the season opener.

Coach Bill Belichick, who claimed he misinterpreted the rule that stipulates teams must not videotape an opponent's signals from a camera on the field, was fined $500,000—the heftiest fine ever for an NFL coach—while the Patriots lost their first-round pick in 2008. Commissioner Roger Goodell also ordered the Patriots to turn over all videotapes, which were quickly destroyed. Goodell said later the league received from the Patriots six tapes from the 2006 regular season and 2007 preseason.

The incident led many national writers and columnists to not only lambaste Belichick but also wonder if the pattern of rule-breaking behavior stained the Patriots' three Super Bowl wins, all of which were decided by four or fewer points.

The Patriots, seemingly inspired by their status as the team everyone outside of the northeast loved to hate, went on a season-long rampage that was as ruthless as it was brilliant as they scored a league-record 589 points on their way to the first 16–0 season in NFL history. The Patriots disposed of the Jacksonville Jaguars and San Diego Chargers in the AFC playoffs before "Spygate" became a headline topic once again February 2, when the *Herald* ran a story in which a source said someone from the Patriots video department taped the St. Louis Rams' walk-through practice the day before Super Bowl XXVI in 2002.

The next night, the Patriots' pursuit of the NFL's second perfect season—and the first since the 16-game schedule was implemented in 1978—came to a shocking halt when the New York Giants mounted a last-minute touchdown drive to beat the Patriots, 17–14, in Super Bowl XLII.

Over the next several months, Pennsylvania senator Arlen Specter—a fan of the Philadelphia Eagles, who lost to the Patriots in Super Bowl XXXIX—continued to push for a meeting with Goodell while *The New York Times* reported that the Patriots had been taping opponent's signals as far back as 2000, Belichick's first year as head coach.

Former Patriots video assistant Matt Walsh, meanwhile, hinted he had more incriminating information about the Patriots' taping practices and eventually agreed to meet with Goodell in exchange for legal indemnification. But Walsh, who gave the NFL eight tapes he produced from 2000 through 2002, admitted during the May 13 meeting with Goodell that he had no knowledge of the Patriots recording the Rams' walkthrough and Goodell announced there would be no more sanctions against the Patriots.

The next day, the *Herald* emblazoned its front page with an apology for the inaccuracy of its story. On May 16, the story's author, Patriots beat writer—and former Sox beat writer—John Tomase penned a 1,454-word apology titled "How It Went Wrong." Tomase wrote he had heard from multiple sources that the walkthrough was taped and that ". . . it only steeled my resolve not to get beat" once he learned his fellow writers were sniffing around the story.

Tomase admitted he ". . . made a devastating leap of logic" in not "confirming . . . explicitly" that a camera was rolling during the Rams' walkthrough. He said the story referred to only one source because while he spoke to numerous people in the writing of the story, he ". . . relied on one more than the others" and that he should have given the Patriots more time to respond to the story before running it.

The apology didn't reduce the venom fired his way on message boards as well as the messages section that appeared underneath his stories on the *Herald*'s website. The coverage of "Spygate"—and the coverage of the coverage—indicated a chasm still existed between writers, who thought fans were provincial and unwilling to read or hear anything negative about their favorite teams, and fans, who thought writers too frequently had agendas that turned their reportage negative.

Fans believed most of the "Spygate" investigation—as well as the scrutiny of his postgame handshakes with Jets coach Eric Mangini as well as with the Colts and Giants following losses in the 2007 AFC Championship Game and Super Bowl XLI, respectively—was nothing more than a rehash of old news and an excuse for local and national reporters alike to finally fire away at Belichick, who was well-known for releasing as little information as possible.

Wrote the *Herald's* Tony Massarotti on May 15: "New England, now the official home of yahoos, hero worshippers and gutless suck-ups. To this entire group, it was all about whether there was a tape; anything else doesn't matter so much."

Said Bruce Allen, the founder of Boston Sports Media Watch: "I think the way 'Spygate' was handled by the media is a direct result of the media's resentment against Belichick for making their jobs more difficult. If you could point out a single thing that really fueled the over-the-top coverage of that episode, I would have to say it is that one . . . the majority of the media show up and expect to be spoon-fed stories and snappy quotes. They resent actually having to put some work into their jobs."

The coverage of "Spygate" coverage further confirmed the celebrity status of writers in Boston yet also provided more evidence that the concept that an old-fashioned insider—whether it be a beat reporter or columnist—as the most powerful and recognizable media person in town may be gone forever, replaced by many voices from new and old media battling for smaller pieces of the pie.

"In Ted Williams' era, there's no conversation, no talk shows—all that stuff is kind of taking away the voice," author and former *Boston Globe* columnist Leigh Montville says. "The newspaper columnist then was everything all wrapped up in one. He was [*Globe* columnist Dan]

Shaughnessy, he was [WEEI] host Glenn Ordway and he was [former WBZ-TV anchor] Bob Lobel. He was the whole ball of wax right there, one guy."

The conversations and talk shows, meanwhile, continued to give players an opportunity to deliver their message in a more direct and un-filtered manner. The Internet revolution still hadn't taken place among major leaguers, but Curt Schilling's blog, 38pitches.com, remained re-quired reading for any beat writer. And his weekly spot on WEEI was still required listening, as Schilling proved again June 20, 2008, when he announced he would undergo season- and potentially career-ending surgery on his right shoulder.

Just because Schilling was likely finished in Boston didn't mean Terry Francona was free of dousing brushfires created by players with their own multi-media appearances. On June 12—a week after a bench-clearing brawl between the Sox and Tampa Bay Rays at Fenway Park—Sox closer Jonathan Papelbon appeared on Comcast SportsNet's "Mohegan Sun Sports Tonight" and hinted the feud wasn't over.

"All I got to say is what comes around goes around," Papelbon said. "Payback is a bitch. In my opinion, and the way I feel right now, this thing isn't all settled and done."

"I'll speak to him . . . we don't need to go there," Francona told reporters June 13, shortly before he pulled Papelbon away from a group interview for a private chat in his office.

The beat reporters who produce the meat and potatoes coverage aren't going anywhere, but for whom will they write? Bradford's com-ments during an interview in May 2008 proved prophetic when he left the *Herald* for WEEI two months later.

"Everyone still talks about the writers like 'woe is us, the newspa-per business is going down the tubes,'" Bradford said during the inter-view. "Well, you know what? If you don't do your best, if you don't excel in what you're doing, when that times comes, you aren't going to have any options anyway.

"I think that everyone knows the end game for aspiring sportswrit-ers is probably the big Internet sites. We're still sportswriters, you know?

I'd rather worry about the job that I'm doing rather than worry about what the job is going to turn into."

The future of the print newspaper—whose coverage provided baseball teams free advertising for decades—remains uncertain, as media companies try to figure out how to make money on the Internet and turn their websites into 24-hour destinations.

"Newspapers in some form will always continue," Allen says. "The role of the company publishing the paper might change into more of a 24-7 news gathering service, with multiple outlets, and to an extent we already see that happening. The paper might not be on paper in the future, but there will always be some sort of daily publication to keep people up-to-speed on what is happening around them."

Further clouding the picture for newspapers is the fact they are no longer the only avenue for teams to promote their product. Every team's television and radio broadcast can be viewed or heard online at Major League Baseball's official website. And those who don't want to subscribe to the service can read and talk about the game—free and instantly—on official team websites as well as the myriad fan-generated message boards.

Will reporters from the traditional newspapers one day be joined in the press box by writers from sites with no connection to the mass media giants? WEEI.com, manned by newspaper veterans, immediately emerged as a viable competitor with and alternative to the *Globe* and *Herald*.

In early 2005, SonsOfSamHorn.net founder Eric Christensen expressed hope that his site would some day get access to the Fenway Park press box. For the first time ever, the Baseball Writers Association of America voted following the 2007 season to grant membership to Internet-only writers, though the first class almost exclusively featured writers from ESPN.com, SI.com, CBSSports.com, Yahoo! Sports, and FoxSports.com who had already earned cards with daily newspapers. ESPN.com writers Rob Neyer and Keith Law, neither of whom has covered a baseball team in the traditional fashion, were the only applicants who were not accepted.

And what kind of access will reporters receive? It has been reduced in increments since the late 1970s, when there were few off-limits areas of the clubhouse and writers were allowed to stay until just before the first pitch. Some writers wonder what will happen when Bud Selig—a steadfast proponent of open access—retires as commissioner, though he'll likely be in office when the next Collective Bargaining Agreement is negotiated. (The CBA expires after the 2011 season and Selig is signed through 2012)

One thing is certain in New England: Whichever medium(s) survive will be anchored by Red Sox-related coverage.

The Patriots are now as popular and as heavily chronicled as the Sox, but as long as the Sox are competitive, it'll be difficult for the Patriots to overcome the generational passion engendered by the Sox as well as the daily narrative of baseball that makes it so enjoyable to chronicle, whether the game is observed from a press box, the bleachers or a living room chair. Even Allen, who began a site called Patriots Daily in 2007, admits that the online passion for the Red Sox means ". . . there are many more blogs dedicated to the Red Sox than to the Patriots."

And while the Red Sox may or may not be the first baseball dynasty of the 21st century, the two world championships in four years proved ownership was accomplishing its dual purpose: to embrace the history of the organization while working as hard as possible to make more of it.

"The seeds were planted long ago and the passion has taken hold," Sox president Larry Lucchino says. "And it will take some concerted mismanagement or mistakes and a good period of time to change the level of passion that exists.

"Winning by itself brings about a continued interest and passion. And I had faith in our abilities as an organization to nurture it and to develop it . . . what we do for the fans, what we do to Fenway Park, what we do to have a competitive team. I knew what our values were and I was optimistic that those would perpetuate the passion.

"That's our goal, right? Perpetuate the passion."

Acknowledgments

Some writers will say every book is a miracle. I don't know about that, but I do know it took several mini-miracles to create the book you are holding in your hands.

I can remember where I was when I got the idea for this book: Covering the 2003 AL Championship Series in the right-field press area at Yankee Stadium. Why, I wondered, were the likes of Nomar Garciaparra, Pedro Martinez, and Manny Ramirez the rule and not the exception in Boston? Why did so many superstars have a strained relationship with the press?

Alas, I was living on Long Island, writing for an alternative weekly, was not nearly well-off enough financially to take a year off to write a book in Boston and had no connections in Boston. I figured I'd have to chalk this up to good idea, bad timing.

Then mini-miracle no. 1 happened: My friend Bryan Hoch—one of the few people with whom I'd shared this idea—called me in February 2004 to tell me Coman Publishing, which published newspapers covering the Mets and Red Sox, was deep into talks about selling the papers to a company in Seattle—a company that wanted to hire a writer to cover each team. Steve Downey, my editor at Coman and somebody else who knew about my idea, recommended me to the new owners. So thanks to Steve for the recommendation as well as to Brian Kosar and Jim Heckman for providing me the opportunity to cover the Red Sox for *Diehard Magazine*.

But it didn't seem as if one mini-miracle would be enough when my book proposal about the Red Sox and the media told through the prism of the 2004 season was pitched to no success. Everyone, it seemed, was writing books about the 2004 Red Sox. Good idea, bad timing.

Then mini-miracle no. 2 happened: I met Bill Nowlin, a writer at *Diehard* who was also the founder of Rounder Books. You could not script such good fortune, even on one of the hokey sitcoms I grew up watching in the 1980s. I cannot thank Bill enough for the opportunity and the leap of faith he took with me, but I'm going to try anyway.

Then mini-miracle no. 3 happened: The Red Sox came back from a three-games-to-none deficit to beat the Yankees in the 2004 AL Championship Series before steamrollering the Cardinals to win the World Series for the first time in 80-something years. This book would not be nearly as interesting if Mariano Rivera had just retired the Sox 1-2-3 in the ninth inning of Game Four.

Then mini-miracle no. 4 happened, albeit over several years. Bill recommended we hold off on publishing *Fighting Words* until the wave of post-'04 Sox books subsided. I am quite sure he did not mean hold off until 2009 and after the wave of post-'07 Sox books subsided. But for various work-related reasons, it was impossible to devote the time necessary to finish the book until my tenure at *Diehard* came to a sudden halt in 2008.

At some point, I began calling this the *Chinese Democracy* of books, always figuring that I'd still beat Guns-n-Roses to the finish line. Well, as I type this in October 2008, *Chinese Democracy* is a few weeks from being released, but I take solace in the fact I, unlike Axl Rose, still have my sanity and my hair (I think).

Yet as frustrated as Bill—an incredibly prolific author—had to be by the delays, he never pulled the plug on the project. To paraphrase Dan Shaughnessy when he was talking about Garciaparra: I can't even imagine what he was saying to himself while he was emailing me. I thank Bill as much for his patience and expert editing (Bill has forgotten more about the Red Sox than most of us will ever know) as for his friendship. Thanks also to Steve Netsky of Rounder Books for his assistance in the editing of this book.

The access provided by the Red Sox media relations department wasn't a miracle, but their cooperation and all-around pleasantness was a wonderful change from what I'd grown used to in a previous life. I thank everyone in the department, particularly former vice president of media relations Glenn Geffner (who pulled some strings and got me into the 2004 LCS and World Series when my original application was turned down), his former assistants Peter Chase and Kerri Moore, current manager of media relations Pam Ganley and John Blake, the latter of whom succeeded Geffner as vice president of media relations and inherited this project but was a huge help in facilitating the final few key interviews. (John announced his departure for a similar position with the Texas Rangers as this book went to press.)

Thanks also to the media relations departments of the New York Yankees and Baltimore Orioles as well as Shannon Forde and Ethan Wilson of the New York Mets.

A list of the people I interviewed for this book is in the bibliography. I thank every one of the writers, executives, players, and fans to whom I spoke, particularly those for whom the subject matter was a sensitive subject. A few people were especially forthright and frank, including Derek Lowe, Pedro Martinez (who gave me 25 wonderful minutes virtually sight unseen during a rather eventful afternoon in Port St. Lucie), Dan Shaughnessy, Charles Steinberg, and Theo Epstein, whose follow-up interview was the Holy Grail of this project. Extra thanks to Kevin Millar for always having a few more minutes to spare and for penning the foreword.

A wonderful byproduct of this book was the friendships I cultivated in Boston. The hunger and passion exhibited by the writers energized and inspired me, as did a press box camaraderie I've never felt before—and one I hope to feel again soon.

Thanks in particular to Alex Speier and Joe Haggerty, who helped make Boston a second home by opening their apartments to me in the summer of '05 and '07, as well as Rob Bradford, Mike Petraglia, Ian Browne, Jessica Camerato, Mike Salk, and fellow Torringtonian David Heuschkel. Thanks too to the staff of the Days Hotel, the best bargain in New England.

As someone whose idea of a good sleep is 7 a.m. to 3 p.m., I relied on the wit, wisdom, and general wackiness of fellow third-shifters—particularly Todd Stumpf, who was a stranger when this project began but is now a valued friend and confidant whose encouragement was a huge help during those doubly dark pre-dawn hours when I was convinced this would never happen. Heaven only knows how much time I wasted riffing on horribly cheesy music videos and *Beverly Hills 90210* minutiae with Todd, but writing the book wouldn't have been as much fun without those diversions.

Thanks also to Todd for allowing me to crash at his place during the 2007 ALCS as well as to Jill Erwin, P.J. Harmer, and Elise Manicke-Russell for the additional late-night laughs.

The best thing about this project was the regular stops in my hometown of Torrington, Connecticut, halfway between Boston and Long Island, and the visits to my wonderful family: My parents Maureen and Jerry, my sister Eileen, my brother-in-law Dave, and my nephew and best little buddy Matthew. I thank them for their love and support and for only occasionally asking if this was ever going to come out.

The same sentiments also apply to my Long Island family—my aunt Gail and the Schoppman cousins on my mom's side as well as my wife's family, including the Leavitts, particularly my mother-in-law Helene and father-in-law Robin, my wife's late grandmother Lillian Mandelbaum, and the Besmanoff and Brown clans.

The computer expertise of Dave and my friend Marcus Amplo saved this book—and, in Marcus' case, saved me the cost of a new computer the night of Game One of the 2007 World Series—multiple times. Thanks, too, to my good friend and groomsman John Guerriero for his free legal advice, especially since he's a Yankee fan who is still convinced the 2004 ALCS was fixed. Extra special thanks go out to Stephen Aita, Christopher Beer and Scott Breneman for their legal counsel during the 2008 season. And thanks to my good friend (and accountant) Lloyd Carroll for his unending support.

Last but certainly not least, I thank my precious wife Michelle, who said it sounded like a great idea to commute between Long Island and Boston for a summer—and then didn't bat an eye when one turned into four. That she loves and believes in me is a miracle greater than any I've ever deserved.

Generally speaking, quotes I collected in one-on-one interviews are denoted with a "says." Sometimes, when I mention the specific time I conducted the interview, I used "said." Quotes I collected in group settings are denoted with a "said." Quotes I collected in my research are credited to the source material. All of the anecdotal information has been culled from the books listed in the bibliography.

Any mistakes and omissions are mine and mine alone.

Bibliography

INTERVIEWS (multiple interviews as noted)

Bruce Allen
Bronson Arroyo
Josh Beckett
Bill Belichick
Mark Bellhorn
Wade Boggs
Rob Bradford
Dick Bresciani
Ian Browne
Howard Bryant
Bill Buckner
Ellis Burks
Nick Cafardo
Eric Christensen
Matt Clement
Jack Curry
Johnny Damon (2)
Dan Duquette
Jim Duquette
Gordon Edes
Alan Embree (2)
Paul Epstein
Theo Epstein (2)
Dwight Evans
Doug Flutie
Casey Fossum
Keith Foulke
Terry Francona (2)
Peter Gammons

Michael Gee
Glenn Geffner
Tom Glavine
Lou Gorman
Steve Grogan
Tommy Harper
Ken Harrelson
Scott Hatteberg
John Henry
David Heuschkel
Butch Hobson
Bob Hohler
Jeff Horrigan
Bobby Howry
Todd Jones
Gabe Kapler
Chris Lang
Curtis Leskanic
Derek Lowe
Larry Lucchino
Pedro Martinez
Tony Massarotti
Sean McAdam
Sean McDonough
John McNamara
Lou Merloni
Kevin Millar (3)
Doug Mirabelli
Leigh Montville

Joe Morgan
Bill Mueller
Mike Myers
Trot Nixon
David Ortiz
Jonathan Papelbon
Jay Payton
Johnny Pesky
Steve Phillips
Bill Reynolds
J.P. Ricciardi
Dan Roche
Roger Rubin
Bob Ryan
Trish Saintelus
Scott Sauerbeck
Curt Schilling

David Scott
Dan Shaughnessy
Steve Silva
Chris Snow
Mike Stanton
Charles Steinberg (2)
Glenn Stout
Mike Timlin
Andre Tippett
Jason Varitek (2)
Tim Wakefield
Dick Williams
Scott Williamson
Carl Yastrzemski
Kevin Youkilis (3)
Don Zimmer

BOOKS

Baldassaro, Lawrence (editor). *Ted Williams Reader*. New York: Fireside/Simon & Schuster, 1991.

Bryant, Howard. *Shut Out: A Story of Race and Baseball In Boston. New York: Routledge, 2002*

Damon, Johnny and Golenbock, Peter. *Idiot: Beating "The Curse" and Enjoying the Game of Life*. New York: Three Rivers Press, 2005.

Gorman, Lou. *One Pitch From Glory: A Decade of Running the Red Sox*. Champaign, IL: Sports Publishing L.L.C., 2005

Hirshberg, Al. *What's the Matter with the Red Sox?* New York: Dodd, Mead & Company, 1973.

Klapisch, Bob and Harper, John. *The Worst Team Money Could Buy: The Collapse of the New York Mets*. New York: Random House, 1993.

Lowell, Mike and Bradford, Rob. *Deep Drive: A Long Journey to Finding the Champion Within*. New York: Celebra Hardcover, 2008.

Massarotti, Tony. *Dynasty: The Inside Story of How the Red Sox Became a Baseball Powerhouse*. New York: St. Martin's Press, 2008.

Massarotti, Tony and Harper, John. *A Tale of Two Cities: The 2004 Yankees-Red Sox Rivalry and the War for the Pennant*. Guilford, CT: The Lyons Press, 2005.

Mnookin, Seth. *Feeding The Monster: How Money, Smarts, and Nerve took a Team to the Top*. New York: Simon & Schuster, 2006.

Montville, Leigh. *Ted Williams: The Biography of an American Hero*. New York: Doubleday, 2004.

Montville, Leigh. *Why Not Us? The 86-Year Journey of the Boston Red Sox Fans from Unparalleled Suffering to the Promised Land of the 2004 World Series*. New York: *Public Affairs*, 2004.

Nowlin, Bill (editor) and Tan, Cecilia (editor). *75: The Red Sox Team that Saved Baseball*. Cambridge, MA: Rounder, 2005.

Nowlin, Bill (editor) and Desrochers, Dan (editor). *The 1967 Impossible Dream Red Sox: Pandemonium on the Field*. Cambridge, MA: Rounder, 2007.

Nowlin, Bill and Prime, Jim. *Blood Feud: The Red Sox, the Yankees, and the Struggle of Good versus Evil*. Cambridge, MA: Rounder, 2005.

Nowlin, Bill. *Fenway Lives: The Team Behind the Team*. Cambridge, MA: Rounder, 2004.

Nowlin, Bill. *Mr. Red Sox: The Johnny Pesky Story*. Cambridge, MA: Rounder, 2004.

Ortiz, David and Massarotti, Tony. *Big Papi: My Story of Big Dreams and Big Hits*. New York: St. Martin's Griffin, 2007.

Reynolds, Bill. *Lost Summer: The '67 Red Sox and the Impossible Dream*. New York: Warner Books, 1992.

Shaughnessy, Dan. *At Fenway: Dispatches From Red Sox Nation*. New York: Three Rivers Press, 1996.

Shaughnessy, Dan. *The Curse of the Bambino*. New York: Penguin Books, 1990, 1991.

Shaughnessy, Dan. *Reversing the Curse: Inside the 2004 Boston Red Sox*. New York: Houghton Mifflin, 2005.

Stout, Glenn (editor). *Impossible Dreams: A Red Sox Collection.* New York: Houghton Mifflin, 2003.

Stout, Glenn and Johnson, Richard A. *Red Sox Century: The Definitive History of Baseball's Most Storied Franchise.* New York: Houghton Mifflin, 2000, 2004.

Williams, Ted and Underwood, John. *My Turn at Bat: The Story of My Life.* New York: Fireside / Simon & Schuster, 1969, 1988.

Williams, Dick and Plaschke, Bill. *No More Mr. Nice Guy: A Life of Hardball.* San Diego: Harcourt Brace Jovanovich, 1990.

Yastrzemski, Carl and Eskenazi, Gerald. *Yaz: Baseball, The Wall, and Me.* New York: Doubleday, 1990.

NEWSPAPERS/PERIODICALS/WEBSITES

baseball-reference.com

Boston Baseball

BostonDirtDogs.com

The *Boston Globe*

Boston Herald

BostonSportsMediaWatch.com

cbssports.com

ESPN.com

The Hartford Courant

Newsday

New York Daily News

New York Post

New York Times

Providence Journal

redsox.com

si.com

SonsOfSamHorn.net

Sports Illustrated

The Sporting News